MEI STRUCTURED MATHEMATICS

THIRD EDITION

AS Further Pure Mathematics

Catherine Berry
Terry Heard
David Martin

Series Editor: Roger Porkess

Hodder & Stoughton
A MEMBER OF THE HODDER HEADLINE GROUP

Acknowledgements

We are grateful to the following companies, institutions and individuals who have given permission to reproduce photographs in this book. Every effort has been made to trace and acknowledge ownership of copyright. The publishers will be glad to make suitable arrangements with any copyright holders whom it has not been possible to contact.

OCR, AQA and Edexcel accept no responsibility whatsoever for the accuracy or method of working in the answers given.

Papers used in this book are natural, renewable and recyclable products. They are made from wood grown in sustainable forests. The logging and manufacturing processes conform to the environmental regulations of the country of origin.

Photo page 115 © Craig Lovell / CORBIS

Figure page 128 by Jeff Edwards

Orders: please contact Bookpoint Ltd, 130 Milton Park, Abingdon, Oxon OX14 4SB.
Telephone: (44) 01235 827720, Fax: (44) 01235 400454. Lines are open from 9 am to 6 pm, Monday to Saturday, with a 24-hour message-answering service.
You can also order through our website at www.hodderheadline.co.uk.

British Library Cataloguing in Publication Data
A catalogue record for this title is available from the The British Library.

ISBN 0 340 814608

First Edition Published 1995
Second Edition Published 2001
Third Edition Published 2004
Impression number 10 9 8 7 6 5 4 3
Year 2010 2009 2008 2007 2006 2005 2004

Typeset by Pantek Arts Ltd, Maidstone, Kent.
Printed in Great Britain for Hodder & Stoughton Educational, a division of Hodder Headline, 338 Euston Road, London NW1 3BH by J. W. Arrowsmith, Bristol.

MEI Structured Mathematics

Mathematics is not only a beautiful and exciting subject in its own right but also one that underpins many other branches of learning. It is consequently fundamental to the success of a modern economy.

MEI Structured Mathematics is designed to increase substantially the number of people taking the subject post-GCSE, by making it accessible, interesting and relevant to a wide range of students.

It is a credit accumulation scheme based on 45 hour units which may be taken individually or aggregated to give Advanced Subsidiary (AS) and Advanced GCE (A Level) qualifications in Mathematics and Further Mathematics. The units may also be used to obtain credit towards other types of qualification.

The course is examined by OCR (previously the Oxford and Cambridge Schools Examination Board) with examinations held in January and June each year.

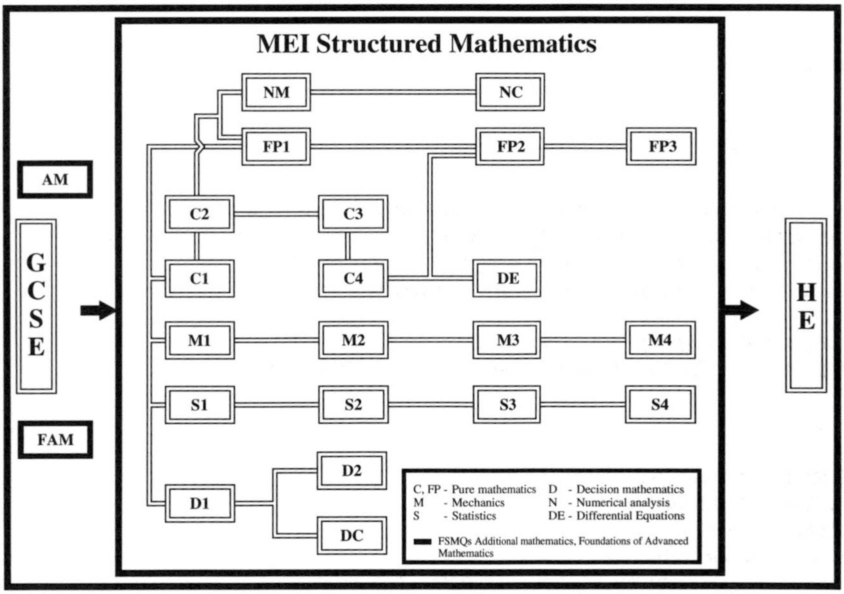

This is one of the series of books written to support the course. Its position within the whole scheme can be seen in the diagram above.

Mathematics in Education and Industry is a curriculum development body which aims to promote the links between Education and Industry in Mathematics at secondary school level, and to produce relevant examination and teaching syllabuses and support material. Since its foundation in the 1960s, MEI has provided syllabuses for GCSE (or O Level), Additional Mathematics and A Level.

For more information about MEI Structured Mathematics or other syllabuses and materials, write to MEI Office, Albion House, Market Place, Westbury, Wiltshire, BA13 3DE or visit www.mei.org.uk.

Introduction

This book covers the MEI Structured Mathematics AS unit (or module) FP1 *Further Concepts for Advanced Mathematics.* This unit is a requirement for AS and A Levels in Further Mathematics in this specification. It provides an introductory course for important areas of pure mathematics that are not covered by the A Level Subject Criteria (and so do not feature in the units C1 to C4).

The material in this book is also relevant to other AS Further Mathematics specifications and so it will be found useful by all students at this level.

Throughout the series the emphasis is on understanding rather than mere routine calculations, but the various exercises do nonetheless provide plenty of scope for practising basic techniques. Extensive on-line support is available via the MEI wesite, www.mei.org.uk.

This book is designed to be accessible to those who have just taken Higher Tier GCSE Mathematics. Alternatively it is equally suitable for those who have just taken AS Mathematics. The main prerequisite is a reasonable level of fluency and accuracy in basic algebra.

This is the third edition of this series. Much of the content in this book was previously covered in *Pure Mathematics 4* but it has now been substantially rewritten to make it suitable as an AS unit, and in addition it has been reorganised to meet the requirements of the new specification being first taught in September 2004.

Catherine Berry
Terry Heard
David Martin

Key to symbols in this book

This symbol means that you may want to discuss a point with your teacher. If you are working on your own there are answers in the back of the book. It is important, however, that you have a go at answering the questions before looking up the answers if you are to understand the mathematics fully.

This is a warning sign. It is used where a common mistake, misunderstanding or tricky point is being described.

This is the ICT icon. It indicates where you should use a graphic calculator or a computer.

This symbol and a dotted line down the right-hand side of the page indicates material which is beyond the criteria for the unit but which is included for completeness.

Harder questions are indicated with stars. Many of these go beyond the usual examination standard.

Contents

1 Matrices

As for everything else, so for a mathematical theory – beauty can be perceived but not explained.

Arthur Cayley, 1883

Figure 1.1 shows a pack of cards. Initially the cards are piled up neatly forming a cuboid, but two other arrangements are shown.

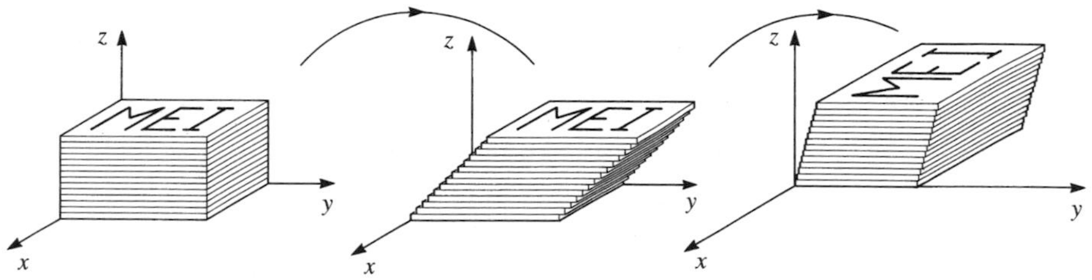

Figure 1.1

? Describe what has happened in words. Can you suggest ways of representing this symbolically?

In this chapter you will learn about matrices, and how they give you the ability to use algebraic techniques in geometrical and other situations. Matrices are often used when creating effects on TV – particularly when the picture is rotated, flipped, enlarged or reduced.

Matrices

Figure 1.2 shows the number of ferry crossings per hour offered by a certain ferry company from English to Continental ports during peak times.

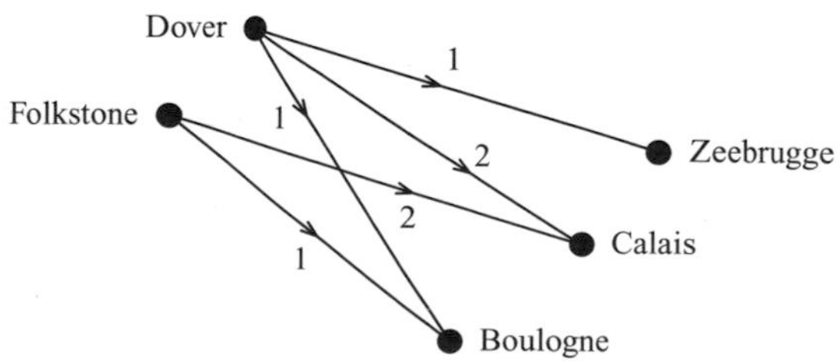

Figure 1.2

This information can be represented as an array of numbers, called a *matrix* (plural *matrices*).

$$\text{From}\quad \begin{matrix} & \text{To} \\ & \begin{matrix} Z & C & B \end{matrix} \\ \begin{matrix} D \\ F \end{matrix} & \begin{pmatrix} 1 & 2 & 1 \\ 0 & 2 & 1 \end{pmatrix} \end{matrix}$$

❓ What information does the zero in the matrix give?

Any rectangular array of numbers is known as a matrix. It is usual to represent matrices by capital letters, often in bold print. (In handwriting, use a capital letter with a wavy line under it.)

A matrix consists of rows and columns, and the entries in the various cells are known as *elements.* The matrix $\mathbf{M} = \begin{pmatrix} 1 & 2 & 1 \\ 0 & 2 & 1 \end{pmatrix}$ representing the ferry crossings has six elements, arranged in two rows and three columns. We describe **M** as a 2×3 matrix, and this is known as the *order* of the matrix. It is important to note that you state the number of rows first, then the number of columns.

Matrices such as $\begin{pmatrix} 1 & 3 & -2 \\ -7 & 5 & 4 \\ 9 & 0 & 6 \end{pmatrix}$ and $\begin{pmatrix} 3 & 2 \\ 5 & 3 \end{pmatrix}$ which have the same number of rows as columns are known as *square matrices.*

The matrix $\mathbf{O} = \begin{pmatrix} 0 & 0 \\ 0 & 0 \end{pmatrix}$ is known as the 2×2 *zero matrix.*

Working with matrices

The number of crossings offered per hour by the ferry company is the same for every hour in the ten-hour period from 9 am until 7 pm.

❓ What matrix represents the total number of ferry crossings offered by this company between the hours of 9 am and 7 pm?

The number of ferry crossings per hour offered by a second ferry company between the same ports is shown by the following matrix.

$$\begin{pmatrix} 3 & 1 & 1 \\ 2 & 1 & 0 \end{pmatrix}$$

What matrix represents the total number of ferry crossings per hour offered by the two companies?

This example shows that matrices can be multiplied by a number or added together.

To multiply a matrix by a number, multiply each element by that number.

$$3 \times \begin{pmatrix} 1 & 3 \\ 2 & 4 \end{pmatrix} = \begin{pmatrix} 3 & 9 \\ 6 & 12 \end{pmatrix}$$

You can add or subtract matrices *of the same order* element by element:

$$\begin{pmatrix} 1 & 3 \\ 2 & 4 \end{pmatrix} + \begin{pmatrix} 5 & 0 \\ -2 & 7 \end{pmatrix} = \begin{pmatrix} 6 & 3 \\ 0 & 11 \end{pmatrix}$$

$$\begin{pmatrix} 1 & 4 \\ 2 & 5 \\ 3 & 6 \end{pmatrix} - \begin{pmatrix} 4 & -2 \\ -3 & 7 \\ 5 & 6 \end{pmatrix} = \begin{pmatrix} -3 & 6 \\ 5 & -2 \\ -2 & 0 \end{pmatrix}$$

But $\begin{pmatrix} 1 & 3 \\ 2 & 4 \end{pmatrix} + \begin{pmatrix} 1 \\ 0 \end{pmatrix}$ cannot be evaluated because the matrices are not of the same order. They are incompatible, or do not *conform*.

Explain why matrix addition is:

(i) commutative, i.e. $\mathbf{A} + \mathbf{B} = \mathbf{B} + \mathbf{A}$

(ii) associative, i.e. $\mathbf{A} + (\mathbf{B} + \mathbf{C}) = (\mathbf{A} + \mathbf{B}) + \mathbf{C}$.

Equality of matrices

Two matrices are equal if and only if they have the same order and each element in one matrix is equal to the corresponding element in the other matrix. If, for example,

$$\mathbf{A} = \begin{pmatrix} 1 & 3 \\ 2 & 4 \end{pmatrix} \qquad \mathbf{B} = \begin{pmatrix} 1 & 2 \\ 3 & 4 \end{pmatrix} \qquad \mathbf{C} = \begin{pmatrix} 1 & 3 & 0 \\ 2 & 4 & 0 \end{pmatrix} \qquad \mathbf{D} = \begin{pmatrix} 1 & 3 \\ 2 & 4 \end{pmatrix}$$

then **A** and **D** are equal but no other pair of matrices from **A**, **B**, **C** and **D** is equal.

EXERCISE 1A

For Questions 1 *and* 2 *use:*

$$\mathbf{A} = \begin{pmatrix} 1 & 2 \\ 3 & -1 \end{pmatrix} \qquad \mathbf{B} = \begin{pmatrix} -2 & 3 \\ 1 & -4 \end{pmatrix} \qquad \mathbf{C} = \begin{pmatrix} 2 & 1 & 5 \\ 3 & 0 & 1 \end{pmatrix}$$

$$\mathbf{D} = \begin{pmatrix} -3 & 6 & 0 \\ 1 & 2 & -1 \end{pmatrix} \qquad \mathbf{E} = \begin{pmatrix} 5 & 2 \\ 0 & -1 \\ -2 & 4 \end{pmatrix} \qquad \mathbf{F} = \begin{pmatrix} -1 & 6 \\ 3 & 2 \\ 8 & -4 \end{pmatrix}$$

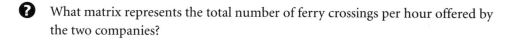

1 Write down the order of these matrices.

(i) A **(ii)** C **(iii)** E

2 Calculate, if possible, the following.

(i) $A + B$ **(ii)** $C - D$ **(iii)** $A + F$

(iv) $3B$ **(v)** $3E - 2F$ **(vi)** $2D - A$

3 The diagram below shows the number of direct flights on one day offered by an airline between cities P, Q, R and S.
The same information is also given in the partly-completed matrix **X**.

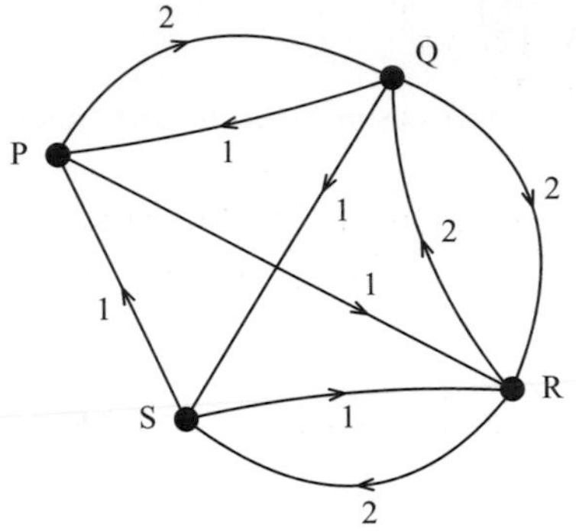

$$\mathbf{X} = \begin{array}{c} \\ \text{From} \end{array} \begin{array}{c} \\ P \\ Q \\ R \\ S \end{array} \overset{\text{To}}{\begin{array}{cccc} P & Q & R & S \end{array}} \begin{pmatrix} 0 & 2 & 1 & 0 \\ 1 & & & \\ & & & \\ & & & \end{pmatrix}$$

(i) Copy and complete the matrix **X**.

A second airline also offers flights between these four cities. The following matrix represents the total number of direct flights offered by the two airlines.

$$\begin{pmatrix} 0 & 2 & 3 & 2 \\ 2 & 0 & 2 & 1 \\ 2 & 2 & 0 & 3 \\ 1 & 0 & 3 & 0 \end{pmatrix}$$

(ii) Find the matrix **Y** representing the flights offered by the second airline.

(iii) Draw a diagram similar to the one above, showing the flights offered by the second airline.

4 Four local football teams took part in a competition in which they each played each other twice, once at home and once away.
Here is the results matrix after half of the games had been played.

	Win	Draw	Lose	Goals for	Goals against
City	2	1	0	6	3
Rangers	0	0	3	2	8
Town	2	0	1	4	3
United	1	1	1	5	3

(i) The results of the next three matches are as follows.

City	2	Rangers	0
Town	3	United	3
City	2	Town	4

Find the results matrix for these three matches and hence find the complete results matrix for all the matches so far.

(ii) Here is the complete results matrix for the whole competition.

$$\begin{pmatrix} 4 & 1 & 1 & 12 & 8 \\ 1 & 1 & 4 & 5 & 12 \\ 3 & 1 & 2 & 12 & 10 \\ 1 & 3 & 2 & 10 & 9 \end{pmatrix}$$

Find the results matrix for the last three matches (City v United, Rangers v Town and Rangers v United) and deduce the result of each of these three matches.

5 A mail-order clothing company stocks a jacket in three different sizes and four different colours.

The matrix $\mathbf{P} = \begin{pmatrix} 17 & 8 & 10 & 15 \\ 6 & 12 & 19 & 3 \\ 24 & 10 & 11 & 6 \end{pmatrix}$ represents the number of jackets in stock at the start of one week.

The matrix $\mathbf{Q} = \begin{pmatrix} 2 & 5 & 3 & 0 \\ 1 & 3 & 4 & 6 \\ 5 & 0 & 2 & 3 \end{pmatrix}$ represents the number of orders for jackets received during the week.

(i) Find the matrix $\mathbf{P} - \mathbf{Q}$.
What does this matrix represent?
What does the negative element in the matrix mean?

A delivery of jackets is received from the manufacturers during the week.

The matrix $\mathbf{R} = \begin{pmatrix} 5 & 10 & 10 & 5 \\ 10 & 10 & 5 & 15 \\ 0 & 0 & 5 & 5 \end{pmatrix}$ shows the number of jackets received.

(ii) Find the matrix which represents the number of jackets in stock at the end of the week after all the orders have been dispatched.

(iii) Assuming that this week is typical, find the matrix which represents sales of jackets over a six-week period.
How realistic is this assumption?

Transformations

You are probably already familiar with several different types of transformation, including reflections, rotations and enlargements. The original shape or point is sometimes called the *object* and the new shape or point, after the transformation, is called the *image*.

Some examples of transformations are illustrated in figure 1.3.

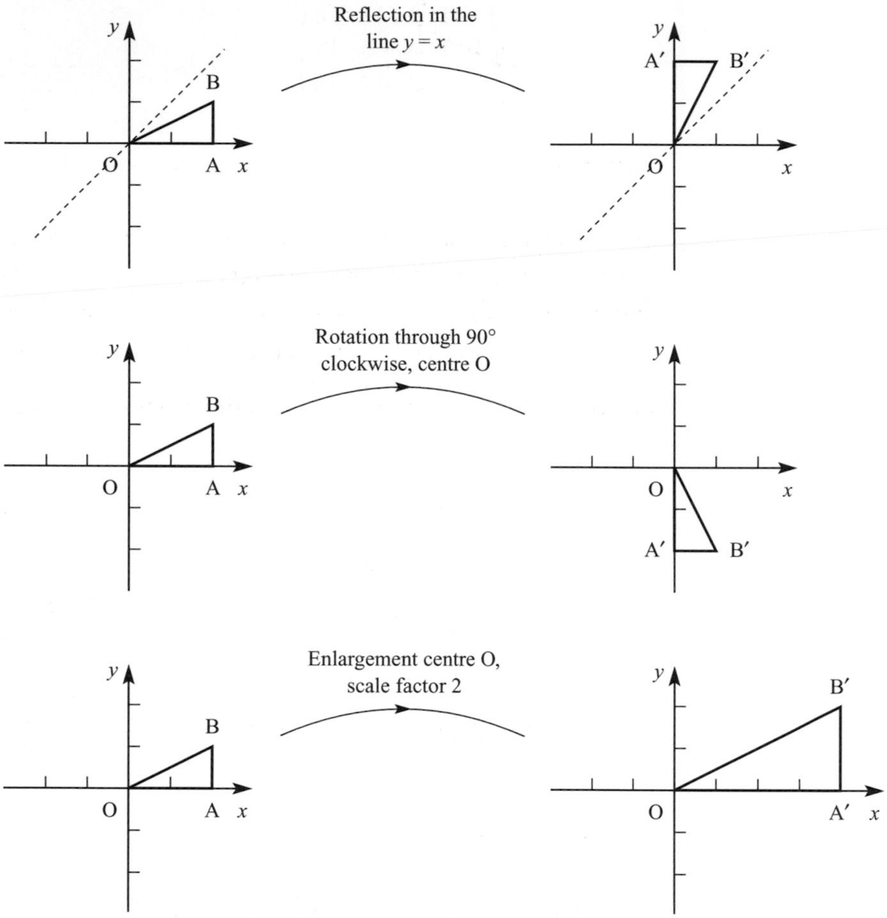

Figure 1.3

In this section you will also meet two other types of transformation which may be new to you: the *two-way stretch* and the *shear*. Examples of these are illustrated in figure 1.4.

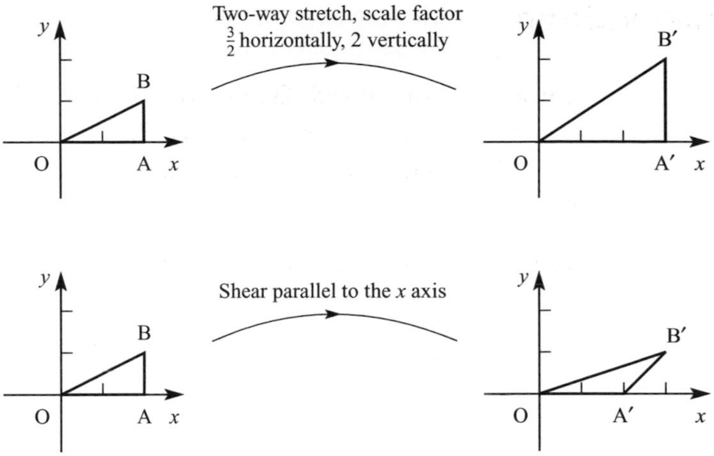

Figure 1.4

So far you have described transformations using words. You have to include information about mirror lines for reflections, information about centre, angle and direction for rotations, and so on. For some transformations, all the information about the transformation can be given in the form of a matrix.

Figure 1.5 shows a flag rotated 90° anticlockwise about the origin.

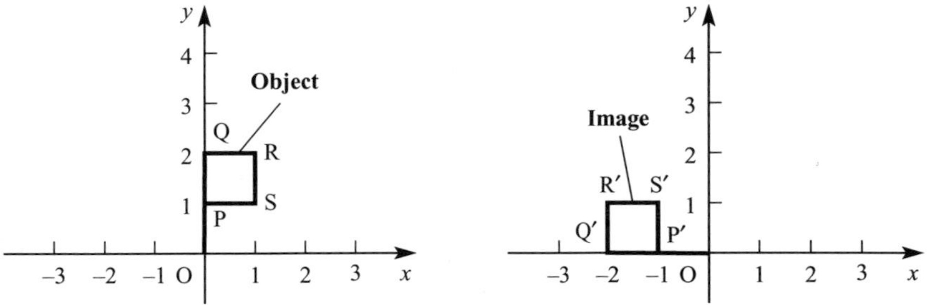

Figure 1.5

This table shows the effect of the rotation on the co-ordinates of each point on the flag.

Point	Co-ordinates	Image point	Co-ordinates
O	(0, 0)	O	(0, 0)
P	(0, 1)	P′	(–1, 0)
Q	(0, 2)	Q′	(–2, 0)
R	(1, 2)	R′	(–2, 1)
S	(1, 1)	S′	(–1, 1)

You can describe the effect of this rotation by saying that the x and y co-ordinates have been exchanged and the sign of the original y co-ordinate has been changed. You can express this algebraically as

$$\begin{cases} x' = -y \\ y' = x. \end{cases}$$

Many other transformations, such as reflections and enlargements, can be expressed as a pair of equations of the form

$$\begin{cases} x' = ax + cy \\ y' = bx + dy \end{cases}$$

A transformation of this type is called a *linear transformation.*

where a, b, c and d are constants.

You can summarise a pair of equations like this by writing just the coefficients in the form of a matrix: $\begin{pmatrix} a & c \\ b & d \end{pmatrix}$.

? What are the values of a, b, c and d for the transformation shown in figure 1.5?

ACTIVITY 1.1

Figure 1.6 shows the effect of two other transformations on the flag OPQRS, shown in figure 1.5.

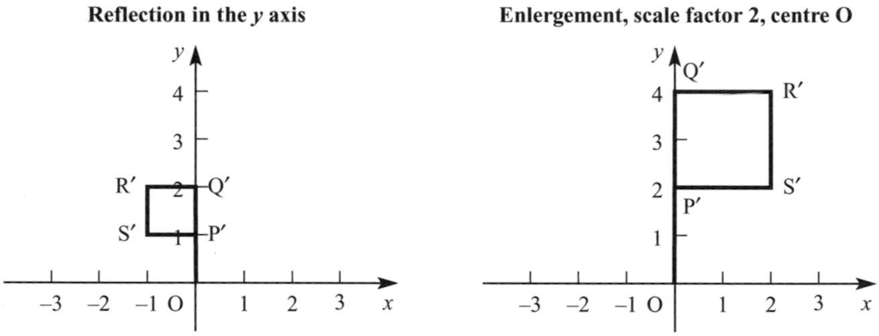

Figure 1.6

In each case, find the co-ordinates of the points P′, Q′, R′ and S′ and express the transformation in the form $\begin{cases} x' = ax + cy \\ y' = bx + dy \end{cases}$.

Hence find the matrix of each transformation.

Straight lines

The diagrams in this chapter so far have shown the images of straight lines as straight lines. You should assume that this is the case for any transformation which can be represented by a matrix. So the image of a line through the points A and B is the line through the image points A′ and B′.

EXAMPLE 1.1

A transformation (an example of a shear) maps points as follows:

- each point is moved parallel to the x axis
- each point is moved twice its distance from the x axis
- points above the x axis are moved to the right
- points below the x axis are moved to the left.

Figure 1.7 shows a flag, and points P and Q and their images P′ and Q′.

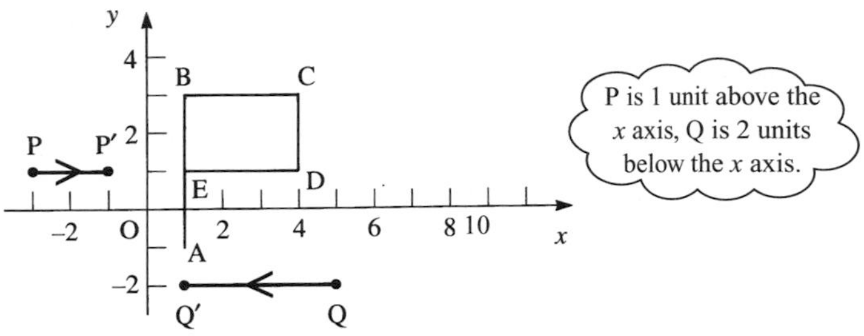
y
4
B
C
P
P′
2
E
D
–2
O
2
4
6
8 10
x
A
–2
Q′
Q
P is 1 unit above the x axis, Q is 2 units below the x axis.

Figure 1.7

(i) Copy the diagram and draw the image of the flag.

(ii) Show that the image of (x, y) is the point $(x + 2y, y)$ and find the matrix which represents this transformation.

SOLUTION

(i)

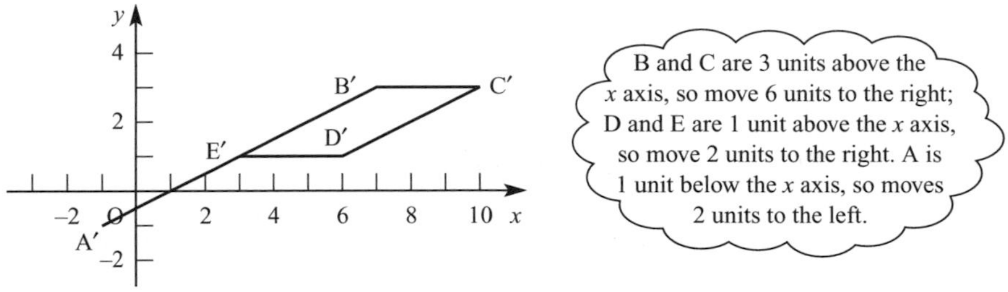
y
4
B′
C′
2
D′
E′
–2
O
2
4
6
8
10 x
A′
–2
B and C are 3 units above the x axis, so move 6 units to the right; D and E are 1 unit above the x axis, so move 2 units to the right. A is 1 unit below the x axis, so moves 2 units to the left.

Figure 1.8

(ii) The distance of the point (x, y) from the x axis is y units.
The point (x, y) moves $2y$ units parallel to the x axis so its new position is $(x + 2y, y)$.
(Notice that if y is negative, then this means moving to the left.)
The transformation can be written as

$$\begin{cases} x' = 1x + 2y \\ y' = 0x + 1y \end{cases}$$

so the matrix which represents this transformation is $\begin{pmatrix} 1 & 2 \\ 0 & 1 \end{pmatrix}$.

EXAMPLE 1.2

Draw the triangle ABC, where A is the point (1, 0), B is the point (3, 0) and C is the point (3, 1).

Draw the image A′B′C′ of the triangle under the transformation represented by the matrix $\begin{pmatrix} 0 & 1 \\ 1 & 0 \end{pmatrix}$ and describe the effect of the transformation.

SOLUTION

The matrix $\begin{pmatrix} 0 & 1 \\ 1 & 0 \end{pmatrix}$ represents the transformation $\begin{cases} x' = y \\ y' = x \end{cases}$.

The co-ordinates of A′ are therefore (0, 1), the co-ordinates of B′ are (0, 3) and the co-ordinates of C′ are (1, 3).

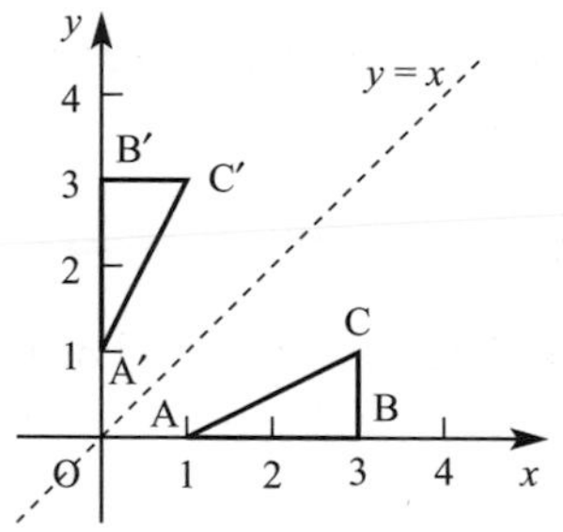

Figure 1.9

The effect of the transformation is a reflection in the line $y = x$.

ACTIVITY 1.2

Investigate the effects of the transformation matrices $\begin{pmatrix} 1 & 0 \\ 0 & 0 \end{pmatrix}$ and $\begin{pmatrix} 0 & 0 \\ 0 & 1 \end{pmatrix}$.

Notice that substituting $x = 0$ and $y = 0$ into $\begin{cases} x' = ax + cy \\ y' = bx + dy \end{cases}$ gives $\begin{cases} x' = 0 \\ y' = 0 \end{cases}$.

This means that whenever you can represent a transformation by a matrix in the way described above, the image of the origin O is O. Thus you can only use this method of representing a transformation if the origin is a point which does not move.

- Rotations can only be represented in this way if the centre of rotation is at O.
- Reflections can only be represented in this way if the mirror line passes through O.
- Enlargements can only be represented in this way if the centre of enlargement is at O.

? Explain why it is not possible to represent translations by matrices in this way.

The columns of a matrix

It is useful to look at the effect of the transformation represented by the matrix $\mathbf{M} = \begin{pmatrix} a & c \\ b & d \end{pmatrix}$ on the points I and J with co-ordinates (1, 0) and (0, 1).

Substituting $x = 1$, $y = 0$ in the defining equations $\begin{cases} x' = ax + cy \\ y' = bx + dy \end{cases}$ you find that I′, the image of I, has co-ordinates (a, b), which is the first column of matrix **M**.

Similarly J′, the image of J, has co-ordinates (c, d), the second column of **M**. The connection between the co-ordinates of I′ and J′ and the matrix representing a transformation provides you with a quick and usually easy way of finding the matrix.

EXAMPLE 1.3

Find the matrix which represents a rotation through angle θ anticlockwise about the origin.

SOLUTION

Figure 1.10 shows the points I(1, 0) and J(0, 1) and their images I′ and J′ after rotation through angle θ anticlockwise about the origin.

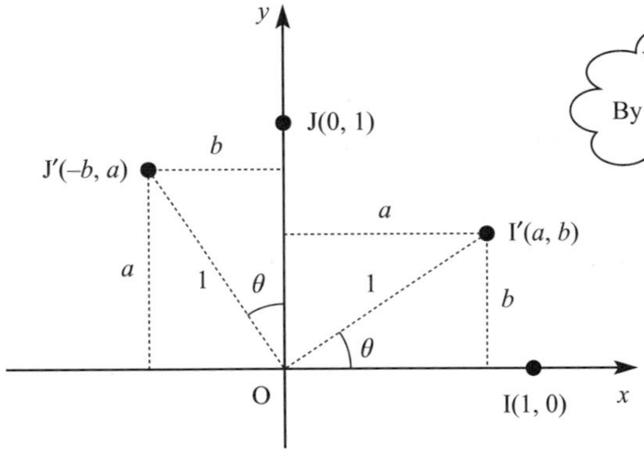

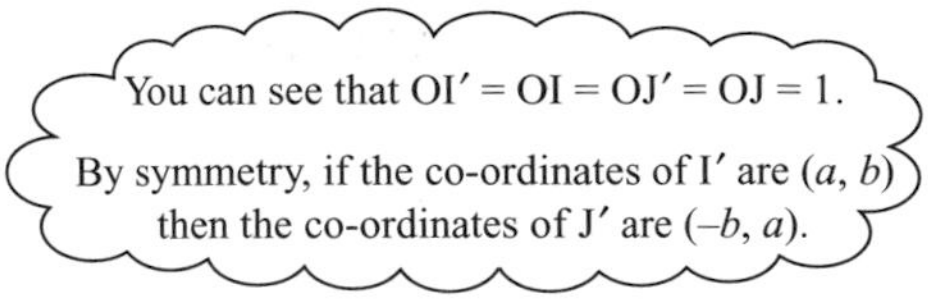
You can see that OI′ = OI = OJ′ = OJ = 1.
By symmetry, if the co-ordinates of I′ are (a, b) then the co-ordinates of J′ are (–b, a).

Figure 1.10

From Figure 1.10, $\cos\theta = \frac{a}{1} \Rightarrow a = \cos\theta$

$\sin\theta = \frac{b}{1} \Rightarrow b = \sin\theta.$

Therefore I′ is $(\cos\theta, \sin\theta)$ and J′ is $(-\sin\theta, \cos\theta)$.

The transformation matrix is $\begin{pmatrix} \cos\theta & -\sin\theta \\ \sin\theta & \cos\theta \end{pmatrix}$.

? What matrix represents a rotation through angle θ clockwise about the origin?

Make sure that you are able to spot a rotation matrix. Remember that either or both of $\cos\theta$ and $\sin\theta$ may be negative for values of θ between 90° and 360°.

ACTIVITY 1.3 Investigate rotation matrices for

(i) angles between 90° and 180°
(ii) angles between 180° and 270°
(iii) angles between 270° and 360°.

e Transformations in three dimensions

So far your work has applied to transformations of sets of points from a plane (i.e. two dimensions) to the same plane. Similar procedures apply when you transform a set of points within three-dimensional space.

The shear illustrated in figure 1.11 is defined by the equations $\begin{cases} x' = x \\ y' = y + z \\ z' = z \end{cases}$

so you can represent this transformation by the matrix $\begin{pmatrix} 1 & 0 & 0 \\ 0 & 1 & 1 \\ 0 & 0 & 1 \end{pmatrix}$.

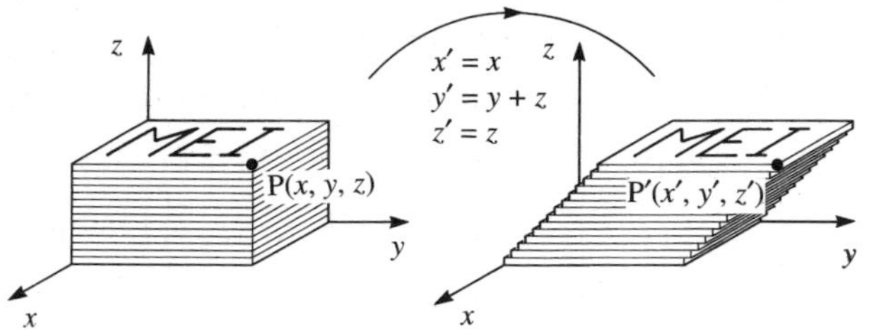

Figure 1.11

Figure 1.12 illustrates a reflection in the plane $y = 0$ (i.e. the plane containing the x and z axes).

This transformation is represented by the matrix $\begin{pmatrix} 1 & 0 & 0 \\ 0 & -1 & 0 \\ 0 & 0 & 1 \end{pmatrix}$.

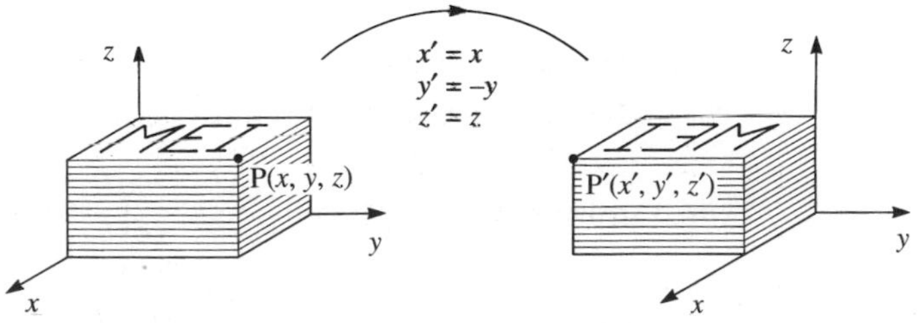

Figure 1.12

EXERCISE 1B

1 The diagram shows a triangle with vertices at O, A(1, 2) and B(0, 2).

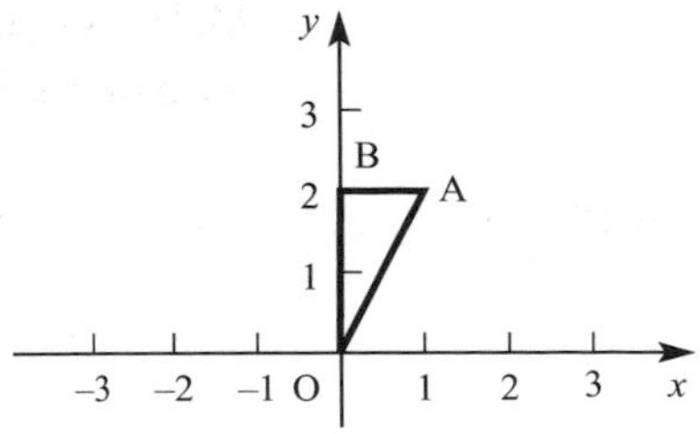

For each of the transformations below

(a) draw a diagram to show the effect of the transformation on triangle OAB

(b) give the co-ordinates of A′ and B′, the images of points A and B

(c) find expressions for x' and y', the co-ordinates of P′, the image of a general point P(x, y)

(d) find the matrix of the transformation.

(i) Enlargement, centre the origin, scale factor 3

(ii) Reflection in the x axis

(iii) Reflection in the line $x + y = 0$

(iv) Rotation 90° clockwise about O

(v) Two-way stretch, scale factor 3 horizontally and scale factor $\frac{1}{2}$ vertically

2 The triangle OAB in question 1 is rotated through 20° anticlockwise about the origin.
Use the transformation matrix $\begin{pmatrix} \cos\theta & -\sin\theta \\ \sin\theta & \cos\theta \end{pmatrix}$ to find the co-ordinates of A′ and B′, the images of A and B under this transformation.
Give your answers to 3 decimal places.

3 Each of the following matrices represents a rotation about the origin.
Find the angle and direction of rotation in each case.

(i) $\begin{pmatrix} \frac{1}{2} & -\frac{\sqrt{3}}{2} \\ \frac{\sqrt{3}}{2} & \frac{1}{2} \end{pmatrix}$ **(ii)** $\begin{pmatrix} 0.574 & -0.819 \\ 0.819 & 0.574 \end{pmatrix}$

(iii) $\begin{pmatrix} -\frac{1}{\sqrt{2}} & \frac{1}{\sqrt{2}} \\ -\frac{1}{\sqrt{2}} & -\frac{1}{\sqrt{2}} \end{pmatrix}$ **(iv)** $\begin{pmatrix} -\frac{\sqrt{3}}{2} & -\frac{1}{2} \\ \frac{1}{2} & -\frac{\sqrt{3}}{2} \end{pmatrix}$

4 For each of the matrices below

(a) draw a diagram to show the effect of the transformation it represents on the triangle OAB in question 1

(b) give the co-ordinates of A′ and B′

(c) give a full description of the transformation.

(i) $\begin{pmatrix} -1 & 0 \\ 0 & 1 \end{pmatrix}$ **(ii)** $\begin{pmatrix} 2 & 0 \\ 0 & 3 \end{pmatrix}$ **(iii)** $\begin{pmatrix} \frac{1}{2} & 0 \\ 0 & \frac{1}{2} \end{pmatrix}$

(iv) $\begin{pmatrix} 1 & 3 \\ 0 & 1 \end{pmatrix}$ **(v)** $\begin{pmatrix} -1 & 0 \\ 0 & -1 \end{pmatrix}$ **(vi)** $\begin{pmatrix} 0.6 & -0.8 \\ 0.8 & 0.6 \end{pmatrix}$

5 The unit square OABC has its vertices at (0, 0), (1, 0), (1, 1) and (0, 1). OABC is mapped to OA′B′C′ by the transformation defined by the matrix $\begin{pmatrix} 4 & 3 \\ 5 & 4 \end{pmatrix}$.

Find the co-ordinates of A′, B′ and C′ and show that the area of the shape has not been changed by the transformation.

6 A transformation maps P to P′ as follows:

- each point is mapped on to the line $y = x$
- the line joining a point to its image is parallel to the y axis.

Find the co-ordinates of the image of the point (x, y) and hence show that this transformation can be represented by means of a matrix.
What is that matrix?

e *The remaining questions relate to enrichment material.*

7 Find the matrices which represent the following transformations of three-dimensional space.

(i) Enlargement, centre O, scale factor 3

(ii) Rotation 180° about the z axis

(iii) Reflection in the plane $x = 0$

8 Describe the transformations represented by these matrices.

(i) $\begin{pmatrix} 1 & 0 & 0 \\ 0 & 0 & 1 \\ 0 & -1 & 0 \end{pmatrix}$ **(ii)** $\begin{pmatrix} 1 & 0 & 0 \\ 0 & 1 & 0 \\ 0 & 0 & -1 \end{pmatrix}$ **(iii)** $\begin{pmatrix} 2 & 0 & 0 \\ 0 & 3 & 0 \\ 0 & 0 & \frac{1}{2} \end{pmatrix}$

Multiplying matrices

The co-ordinates (x, y) of a point P in two dimensions can be written as the *column vector* $\begin{pmatrix} x \\ y \end{pmatrix}$. This is called the *position vector* of the point P. A column vector is a 2×1 matrix and is sometimes called a column matrix. Column vectors are often represented by lower case bold letters such as **p** or **v**. In handwriting, a lower case letter with a wavy line underneath is used.

Using this notation allows you to write the effect of a transformation as a matrix product. The transformation defined by the matrix $\mathbf{M} = \begin{pmatrix} 2 & 5 \\ 4 & 3 \end{pmatrix}$ maps the point P with position vector $\mathbf{p} = \begin{pmatrix} x \\ y \end{pmatrix}$ to the point P′ with position vector $\mathbf{p}' = \begin{pmatrix} x' \\ y' \end{pmatrix}$.

You can write $\mathbf{p}' = \begin{pmatrix} 2x + 5y \\ 4x + 3y \end{pmatrix}$.

The 2×1 matrix $\mathbf{p}'$ is the product of the 2×2 matrix **M** with the 2×1 matrix **p**, *in that order.*

$$\begin{pmatrix} 2 & 5 \\ 4 & 3 \end{pmatrix} \begin{pmatrix} x \\ y \end{pmatrix} = \begin{pmatrix} 2x + 5y \\ 4x + 3y \end{pmatrix}$$

EXAMPLE 1.4

Calculate $\begin{pmatrix} 1 & 6 \\ 3 & 4 \end{pmatrix}\begin{pmatrix} 5 \\ 8 \end{pmatrix}$.

SOLUTION

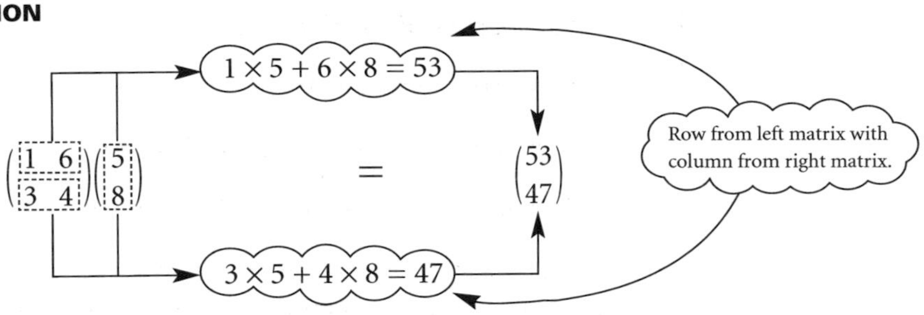

Figure 1.13

A similar technique applies to all matrix multiplications. You use each row of the first (i.e. left) matrix with each column, in turn, of the second matrix. Figure 1.14 shows the steps used when multiplying a 2×2 matrix by a 2×3 matrix. The product is another 2×3 matrix.

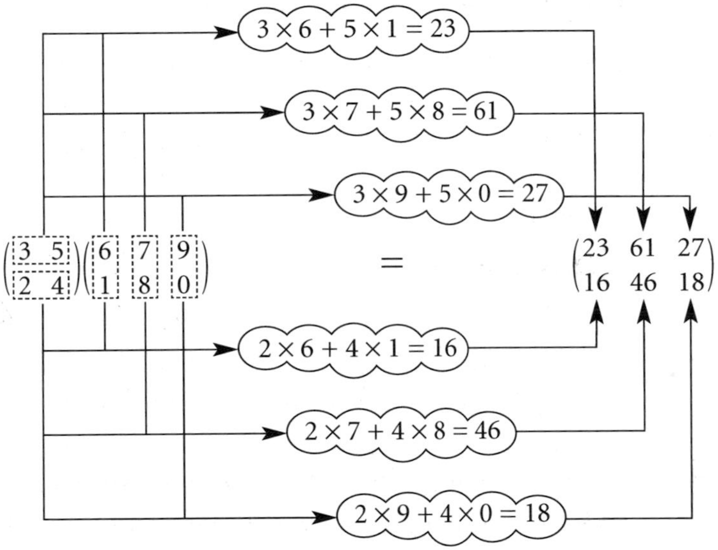

Figure 1.14

If you multiply a 3×4 matrix (on the left) by a 4×2 matrix (on the right) similar rules apply: the product is a 3×2 matrix. For example:

$$\begin{pmatrix} 1 & 2 & 4 & 7 \\ -3 & 5 & 0 & 1 \\ 4 & 2 & 3 & 5 \end{pmatrix}\begin{pmatrix} 5 & 1 \\ -6 & 4 \\ 8 & 9 \\ 2 & 2 \end{pmatrix} = \begin{pmatrix} 39 & 59 \\ -43 & 19 \\ 42 & 49 \end{pmatrix}.$$

Matrix products and transformations

Figure 1.15 shows the flag ABCD and its image A′B′C′D′ after applying the rotation matrix $\begin{pmatrix} 0.8 & -0.6 \\ 0.6 & 0.8 \end{pmatrix}$.

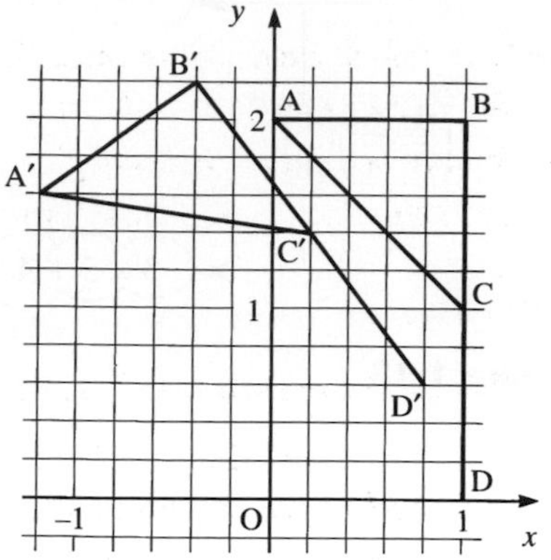

Figure 1.15

You can write the co-ordinates of A, B, C and D as the single 2 × 4 matrix $\begin{pmatrix} 0 & 1 & 1 & 1 \\ 2 & 2 & 1 & 0 \end{pmatrix}$. This provides a quick method of finding the co-ordinates of A′, B′, C′ and D′.

ACTIVITY 1.4

By calculating the product $\begin{pmatrix} 0.8 & -0.6 \\ 0.6 & 0.8 \end{pmatrix}\begin{pmatrix} 0 & 1 & 1 & 1 \\ 2 & 2 & 1 & 0 \end{pmatrix}$, check that the points A′, B′, C′ and D′ in figure 1.15 have been plotted correctly.

Other applications of matrix multiplication

The use of matrices to describe transformations is just one of the many applications of matrices. You saw some other uses of matrices at the start of this chapter and others are explored in Exercise 1C.

EXAMPLE 1.5

A pizza company wants to set up a computer program to keep track of orders. Pizzas are available in three sizes: Regular, Large and Family, and four combinations of toppings: Hawaiian, Seafood, Meat Feast and Vegetarian. The number of pizzas of each type is entered in the form of a 4 × 3 matrix **P**.

One day the matrix **P**, representing the orders, is as follows.

$$\begin{array}{cc} & \text{Toppings} \\ & \begin{array}{cccc} \text{H} & \text{S} & \text{M} & \text{V} \end{array} \\ \text{Sizes} \begin{array}{c} \text{R} \\ \text{L} \\ \text{F} \end{array} & \begin{pmatrix} 2 & 3 & 0 & 1 \\ 5 & 7 & 8 & 4 \\ 6 & 4 & 3 & 3 \end{pmatrix} \end{array}$$

(i) Find a matrix **A** so that the product **PA** gives the number of each size of base required, and hence find the matrix representing the number of each size of base required on this day.

(ii) A regular pizza requires 1 quantity of topping, a large pizza requires 1.5 quantities of topping and a family-size pizza requires 2 quantities of topping. Find a matrix **B** so that the product **BP** gives the quantities of each type of topping required, and hence find the matrix representing the quantities of each type of topping required on this day.

(iii) The cost of each size of pizza, in pounds, whatever the topping, is given by the matrix $\mathbf{C} = (2.5 \quad 3.5 \quad 4)$.
What matrix product will give the total cost of the pizzas?
Find the total cost of this day's pizzas.

SOLUTION

(i) You need to find a matrix **A** so that

$$\begin{pmatrix} 2 & 3 & 0 & 1 \\ 5 & 7 & 8 & 4 \\ 6 & 4 & 3 & 3 \end{pmatrix} \mathbf{A} = \begin{pmatrix} 2+3+0+1 \\ 5+7+8+4 \\ 6+4+3+3 \end{pmatrix}.$$

The matrix **A** is therefore $\begin{pmatrix} 1 \\ 1 \\ 1 \\ 1 \end{pmatrix}$.

$$\begin{pmatrix} 2 & 3 & 0 & 1 \\ 5 & 7 & 8 & 4 \\ 6 & 4 & 3 & 3 \end{pmatrix} \begin{pmatrix} 1 \\ 1 \\ 1 \\ 1 \end{pmatrix} = \begin{pmatrix} 6 \\ 24 \\ 16 \end{pmatrix}$$

(ii) You need to find a matrix **B** so that

$$\mathbf{B}\begin{pmatrix} 2 & 3 & 0 & 1 \\ 5 & 7 & 8 & 4 \\ 6 & 4 & 3 & 3 \end{pmatrix} = (1 \times 2 + 1.5 \times 5 + 2 \times 6 \qquad \ldots \qquad \ldots \qquad \ldots).$$

The matrix **B** is therefore $(1 \quad 1.5 \quad 2)$.

$$(1 \quad 1.5 \quad 2)\begin{pmatrix} 2 & 3 & 0 & 1 \\ 5 & 7 & 8 & 4 \\ 6 & 4 & 3 & 3 \end{pmatrix} = (21.5 \quad 21.5 \quad 18 \quad 13)$$

(iii) You already know that the matrix product **PA** gives the total number of each size of pizza in the form of a 3×1 matrix. To find the total cost, you need to pre-multiply this product by **C**.

The total cost is given by the product **CPA**.

$$\begin{aligned} \mathbf{CPA} &= (2.5 \quad 3.5 \quad 4)\begin{pmatrix} 2 & 3 & 0 & 1 \\ 5 & 7 & 8 & 4 \\ 6 & 4 & 3 & 3 \end{pmatrix}\begin{pmatrix} 1 \\ 1 \\ 1 \\ 1 \end{pmatrix} \\ &= (2.5 \quad 3.5 \quad 4)\begin{pmatrix} 6 \\ 24 \\ 16 \end{pmatrix} \\ &= (163) \end{aligned}$$

The total cost is £163.

Properties of matrix multiplication

Matrices must be conformable for multiplication

To be able to multiply two matrices together, the number of columns in the first (left) matrix must equal the number of rows in the second matrix. For example, if the first matrix is 3×4, the second must be $4 \times$ something. You say that the matrices need to *conform.*

Generally, if $\mathbf{M}$ is of order $p \times q$, and $\mathbf{N}$ is of order $q \times r$, the product $\mathbf{MN}$ exists and is of order $p \times r$. It may be helpful to think of the rules for joining dominoes end to end.

p	q		q	r	gives	p	r

Matrix multiplication is not commutative

You have already seen that matrix addition is commutative, i.e. $\mathbf{A} + \mathbf{B} = \mathbf{B} + \mathbf{A}$.

However, matrix multiplication is *not* commutative.

If $\mathbf{A} = \begin{pmatrix} 3 & 1 \\ 2 & 7 \end{pmatrix}$ and $\mathbf{B} = \begin{pmatrix} 4 & -2 \\ 1 & 5 \end{pmatrix}$, the product $\mathbf{AB}$ is given by

$$\mathbf{AB} = \begin{pmatrix} 3 & 1 \\ 2 & 7 \end{pmatrix}\begin{pmatrix} 4 & -2 \\ 1 & 5 \end{pmatrix} = \begin{pmatrix} 13 & -1 \\ 15 & 31 \end{pmatrix}$$

and the product $\mathbf{BA}$ is given by

$$\mathbf{BA} = \begin{pmatrix} 4 & -2 \\ 1 & 5 \end{pmatrix}\begin{pmatrix} 3 & 1 \\ 2 & 7 \end{pmatrix} = \begin{pmatrix} 8 & -10 \\ 13 & 36 \end{pmatrix}.$$

So $\mathbf{AB} \neq \mathbf{BA}$. It matters which way round you write your matrices.

Sometimes the product $\mathbf{MN}$ exists but the product $\mathbf{NM}$ does not exist, because the number of columns in $\mathbf{N}$ does not match the number of rows in $\mathbf{M}$.

? If $\mathbf{A} = \begin{pmatrix} a & c \\ b & d \end{pmatrix}$, $\mathbf{B} = \begin{pmatrix} e & h \\ f & i \\ g & j \end{pmatrix}$ and $\mathbf{C} = \begin{pmatrix} k & m & o \\ l & n & p \end{pmatrix}$, which of the products $\mathbf{AB}$, $\mathbf{BA}$, $\mathbf{AC}$, $\mathbf{CA}$, $\mathbf{BC}$ and $\mathbf{CB}$ exist?

Matrix multiplication is associative

Whenever matrices $\mathbf{P}$, $\mathbf{Q}$, $\mathbf{R}$ are conformable for multiplication, $(\mathbf{PQ})\mathbf{R} = \mathbf{P}(\mathbf{QR})$. This is the associative property of matrix multiplication.

ACTIVITY 1.5 Using $\mathbf{P} = \begin{pmatrix} a & c \\ b & d \end{pmatrix}$, $\mathbf{Q} = \begin{pmatrix} e & g \\ f & h \end{pmatrix}$ and $\mathbf{R} = \begin{pmatrix} i & k \\ j & l \end{pmatrix}$, find

(i) $\mathbf{PQ}$ **(ii)** $(\mathbf{PQ})\mathbf{R}$ **(iii)** $\mathbf{QR}$ **(iv)** $\mathbf{P}(\mathbf{QR})$

and so demonstrate that matrix multiplication is associative.

Note

Since $(\mathbf{PQ})\mathbf{R} = \mathbf{P}(\mathbf{QR})$, the brackets are not needed and the product can be written simply as $\mathbf{PQR}$.

You will see how transformations justify the associativity of matrix multiplication on page 25.

(e) Matrix multiplication is distributive over matrix addition

Provided the matrices **P**, **Q** and **R** conform so that the sums and products exist,

$$\mathbf{P}(\mathbf{Q} + \mathbf{R}) = \mathbf{PQ} + \mathbf{PR}$$

and

$$(\mathbf{P} + \mathbf{Q})\mathbf{R} = \mathbf{PR} + \mathbf{QR}.$$

These two properties are what we mean when we say that matrix multiplication is distributive over matrix addition.

ACTIVITY 1.6 Using $\mathbf{P} = \begin{pmatrix} a & c \\ b & d \end{pmatrix}$, $\mathbf{Q} = \begin{pmatrix} e & g \\ f & h \end{pmatrix}$ and $\mathbf{R} = \begin{pmatrix} i & k \\ j & l \end{pmatrix}$, find

(i) $\mathbf{P}(\mathbf{Q} + \mathbf{R})$ **(ii)** $\mathbf{PQ} + \mathbf{PR}$

(iii) $(\mathbf{P} + \mathbf{Q})\mathbf{R}$ **(iv)** $\mathbf{PR} + \mathbf{QR}$

and so demonstrate the distributive property of matrix multiplication over matrix addition.

The identity matrix

Whenever you multiply a 2×2 matrix **M** by $\mathbf{I} = \begin{pmatrix} 1 & 0 \\ 0 & 1 \end{pmatrix}$ the product is **M**.

It makes no difference whether you pre-multiply by **I**, as in

$$\begin{pmatrix} 1 & 0 \\ 0 & 1 \end{pmatrix}\begin{pmatrix} 3 & 5 \\ 7 & -2 \end{pmatrix} = \begin{pmatrix} 3 & 5 \\ 7 & -2 \end{pmatrix}$$

or post-multiply by **I**, as in

$$\begin{pmatrix} a & c \\ b & d \end{pmatrix}\begin{pmatrix} 1 & 0 \\ 0 & 1 \end{pmatrix} = \begin{pmatrix} a & c \\ b & d \end{pmatrix}.$$

For multiplication of 2×2 matrices, **I** behaves in the same way as the number 1 when dealing with the multiplication of real numbers. **I** is known as the 2×2 identity matrix.

The 3×3 identity matrix, $\mathbf{I}_3$, is $\begin{pmatrix} 1 & 0 & 0 \\ 0 & 1 & 0 \\ 0 & 0 & 1 \end{pmatrix}$.

ACTIVITY 1.7 Show that $\mathbf{I}_3\mathbf{M} = \mathbf{M}\mathbf{I}_3 = \mathbf{M}$ for a 3×3 matrix of your choice.

? Why is there no such thing as a 2×3 identity matrix?

ACTIVITY 1.8 Find out how to input matrices into your calculator. Particularly notice whether the calculator encourages you to input by rows or columns.
Find out how to add and multiply matrices on your calculator.

Historical note

The multiplication of matrices was first fully defined by Arthur Cayley (1821–95) in 1858. Cayley's mathematical talent was noticed while he was at school (in London), and his first mathematical paper was published in 1841, while he was an undergraduate at Cambridge. He worked as a lawyer for some 14 years, refusing more cases than he accepted as he only wanted to earn sufficient to enable him to get on with 'his work'; during this period he published nearly 200 mathematical papers. In 1863 he returned to Cambridge as a professor. As well as his work on matrices, he developed the geometry of *n*-dimensional spaces and is known for his work on the theory of invariants, much of this in collaboration with his life-long friend, James Joseph Sylvester (1814–97). It was Sylvester who, in 1850, coined the word 'matrix', Latin for 'womb'; in geology a matrix is a mass of rock enclosing gems, so in mathematics a matrix is a container of (valuable) information. It was at about this time that Florence Nightingale was one of Sylvester's students.

EXERCISE 1C

In questions 1–3 *use:*

$\mathbf{A} = \begin{pmatrix} 3 & 1 \\ 2 & 4 \end{pmatrix}$ $\quad \mathbf{B} = \begin{pmatrix} -3 & 7 \\ 2 & 5 \end{pmatrix}$ $\quad \mathbf{C} = \begin{pmatrix} 2 & 3 & 4 \\ 5 & 7 & 1 \end{pmatrix}$

$\mathbf{D} = \begin{pmatrix} 3 & 4 \\ 7 & 0 \\ 1 & -2 \end{pmatrix}$ $\quad \mathbf{E} = \begin{pmatrix} 4 & 7 \\ 3 & -2 \\ 1 & 5 \end{pmatrix}$ $\quad \mathbf{F} = \begin{pmatrix} 3 & 7 & -5 \\ 2 & 6 & 0 \\ -1 & 4 & 8 \end{pmatrix}$

1 Calculate, if possible, the following.

(i) AB **(ii)** CA **(iii)** BC
(iv) CD **(v)** DC **(vi)** AF
(vii) BE **(viii)** 4F + EC **(ix)** EA
(x) FE **(xi)** EF **(xii)** $\mathbf{A}^2$

2 By calculating, if possible, **AB**, **BA**, **AD** and **DA** demonstrate that matrix multiplication is not commutative.

3 Demonstrate the associative property of matrix multiplication by calculating both (**AC**)**F** and **A**(**CF**).

4 The diagram shows a flag.

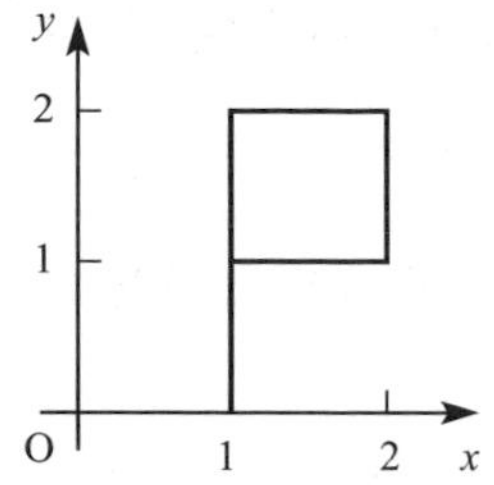

(i) Write down the co-ordinates of the five points of the flag. Hence write down a 2×5 matrix to describe the flag.

(ii) The flag is to be transformed using the matrix $\begin{pmatrix} -0.6 & 0.8 \\ 0.8 & 0.6 \end{pmatrix}$.
Use matrix multiplication to find a 2×5 matrix to describe the image of the flag.

(iii) Draw the original flag and its image on one diagram, and describe the transformation in words.

5 The diagram shows a rectangle.

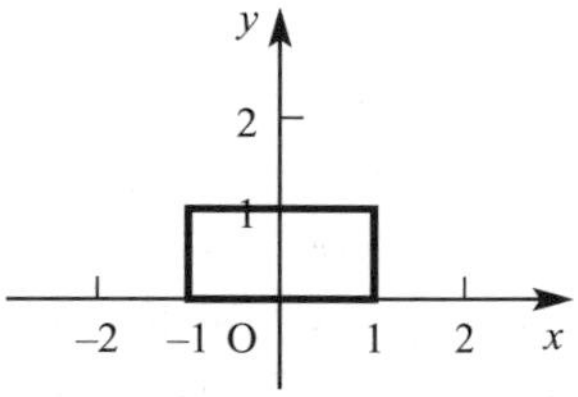

(i) Write down the co-ordinates of the four points of the rectangle. Hence write down a 2×4 matrix to describe the flag.

(ii) The rectangle is to be transformed using the matrix $\begin{pmatrix} 1 & 0 \\ 2 & 1 \end{pmatrix}$.
Use matrix multiplication to find a 2×4 matrix to describe the image of the rectangle.

(iii) Draw the original rectangle and its image on one diagram, and describe the transformation in words.

6 **(i)** Choose a shape of your own. Call it S. Write down a matrix to describe S.

(ii) Transform S using the matrix $\mathbf{M} = \begin{pmatrix} 2 & 1 \\ 1 & -2 \end{pmatrix}$ to form the image S′. Draw a diagram to show S and S′.

(iii) Calculate $\mathbf{M}^2$.

(iv) Describe as simply as you can the single transformation represented by $\mathbf{M}^2$.

7 The matrix $\mathbf{S} = \begin{pmatrix} 5 & 0 & 1 & 6 & 2 \\ 7 & 8 & 4 & 3 & 9 \end{pmatrix}$ contains the numbers of first and second class stamps used in an office each day last week. (Top row denotes first class.)

(i) Find a matrix **D** such that **DS** gives the total number of stamps used each day.

(ii) Find a matrix **N** such that **SN** gives the total number of each type of stamp used in the week.

(iii) First class stamps cost 28 pence and second class stamps cost 21 pence. Find a way of calculating the total cost of last week's stamps using only matrix multiplication.

8 The stylised map below shows the bus routes in a holiday area. Lines represent routes that run each way between the resorts. Arrows indicate one-way scenic routes.
M is the partly completed 4×4 matrix which shows the number of direct routes between the various resorts.

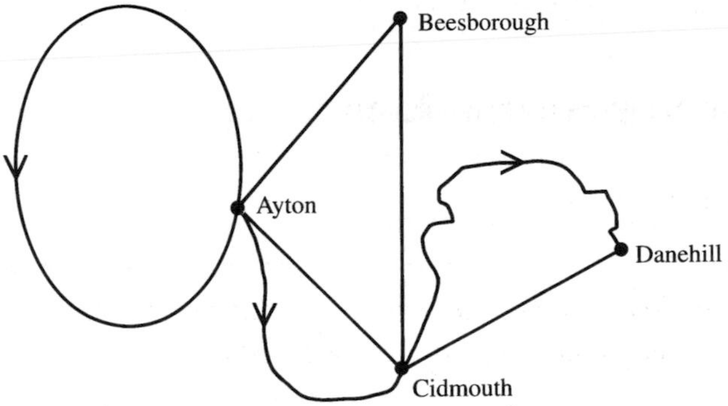

$$\mathbf{M} = \begin{array}{c c} & \text{To} \\ & \begin{array}{cccc} A & B & C & D \end{array} \\ \text{From} \begin{array}{c} A \\ B \\ C \\ D \end{array} & \begin{pmatrix} 1 & 1 & 2 & 0 \\ & & & \\ & & & \\ & & & \end{pmatrix} \end{array}$$

(i) Copy and complete **M**.

(ii) Calculate $\mathbf{M}^2$ and explain what information it contains.

(iii) What information would $\mathbf{M}^3$ contain?

9 ☆ The diagram shows the start of the plaiting process, using three strands *a*, *b* and *c*.

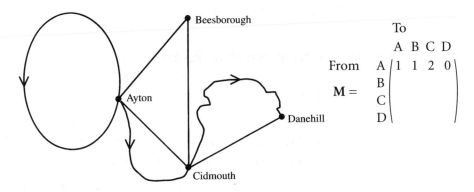

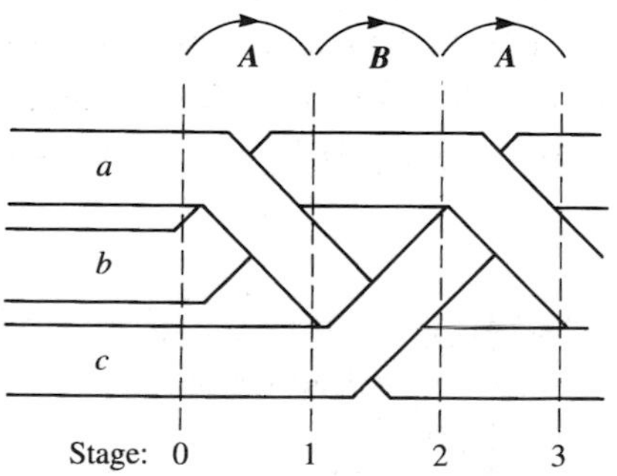

The process has only two steps, repeated alternately:

A: cross the top strand over the middle strand
B: cross the middle strand under the bottom strand.

At Stage 0 the order of the strands is given by $\mathbf{s}_0 = \begin{pmatrix} a \\ b \\ c \end{pmatrix}$.

(i) Show that pre-multiplying $\mathbf{s}_0$ by the matrix $\mathbf{A} = \begin{pmatrix} 0 & 1 & 0 \\ 1 & 0 & 0 \\ 0 & 0 & 1 \end{pmatrix}$ gives $\mathbf{s}_1$, the matrix which represents the order of the strands at Stage 1.

(ii) Find the 3×3 matrix **B** which represents the transition from Stage 1 to Stage 2.

(iii) Find matrix $\mathbf{M} = \mathbf{BA}$ and show that $\mathbf{Ms}_0$ gives $\mathbf{s}_2$, the matrix which represents the order of the strands at Stage 2.

(iv) Find $\mathbf{M}^2$ and hence find the order of the strands at Stage 4.

(v) Calculate $\mathbf{M}^3$. What does this tell you?

Composition of transformations

Notation

A single letter, such as *T*, is often used to represent a transformation. The matrix **T** represents the transformation ***T***. (Notice that bold italic ***T*** is used for the transformation and bold upright **T** for the matrix).

The point P has position vector **p**. The image of the point P can be denoted by ***T***(P) or by P′. The image ***T***(P) has position vector **p**′ = ***T***(**p**). We find ***T***(**p**) by evaluating the matrix product **Tp**.

Two or more successive transformations

Figure 1.16 shows the effect of two successive transformations on a triangle. The transformation ***X*** represents a reflection in the *x* axis. ***X*** maps the point P to the point ***X***(P). The transformation ***Q*** represents a rotation of 90° anticlockwise about O. When you apply ***Q*** to the image formed by ***X***, the point ***X***(P) is mapped to the point ***Q***(***X***(P)). This is abbreviated to ***QX***(P).

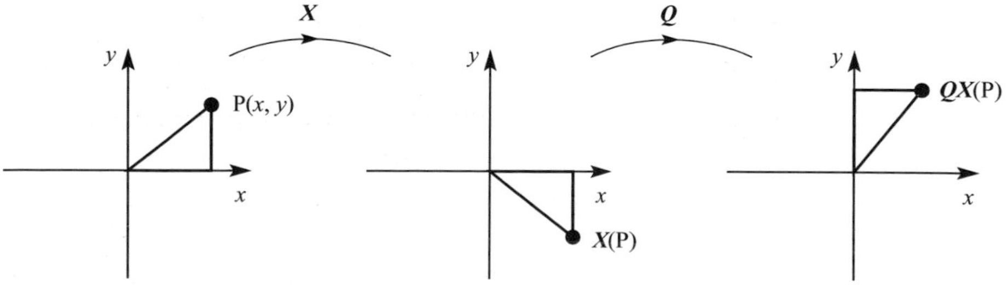

Figure 1.16

The composite transformation 'reflection in the x axis followed by rotation of 90° anticlockwise about O' is represented by ***QX***. Notice the order: ***QX*** means 'carry out ***X***, then carry out ***Q***'.

? Look at figure 1.16 and compare the original triangle with the final image after both transformations.
What single transformation is represented by ***QX***?

The transformation ***X*** is represented by the matrix $\mathbf{X} = \begin{pmatrix} 1 & 0 \\ 0 & -1 \end{pmatrix}$.

The transformation ***Q*** is represented by the matrix $\mathbf{Q} = \begin{pmatrix} 0 & -1 \\ 1 & 0 \end{pmatrix}$.

The product $\mathbf{QX} = \begin{pmatrix} 0 & -1 \\ 1 & 0 \end{pmatrix}\begin{pmatrix} 1 & 0 \\ 0 & -1 \end{pmatrix} = \begin{pmatrix} 0 & 1 \\ 1 & 0 \end{pmatrix}$.
This is the matrix which represents reflection in the line $y = x$.

Notice the order in which the matrices were arranged for the multiplication: the matrix representing the first transformation is on the right and the matrix for the second transformation is on the left.

In general, the matrix of a composite transformation is found by multiplying the matrices of the component transformations, in the correct order.

Activity 1.9 shows how this is proved.

ACTIVITY 1.9 The transformations T and S are represented by the matrices $\mathbf{T} = \begin{pmatrix} a & c \\ b & d \end{pmatrix}$ and $\mathbf{S} = \begin{pmatrix} p & r \\ q & s \end{pmatrix}$.

T is applied to the point P with position vector $\mathbf{p} = \begin{pmatrix} x \\ y \end{pmatrix}$. The image of P is P′ with position vector $\mathbf{p}'$. S is then applied to the point P′. The image of P′ is P″ with position vector $\mathbf{p}''$.

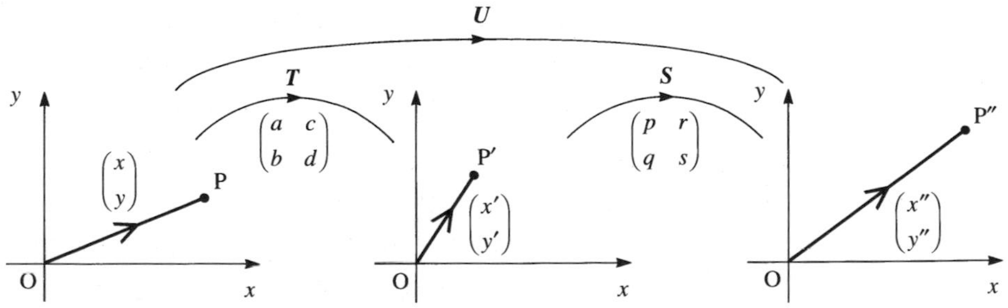

Figure 1.17

(i) Find $\mathbf{p}'$ by finding the matrix product $\mathbf{Tp}$.
(ii) Find $\mathbf{p}''$ by finding the matrix product $\mathbf{Sp}'$.
(iii) Find the matrix product $\mathbf{U} = \mathbf{ST}$ and show that $U(\mathbf{p})$ is the same as $\mathbf{p}''$.

? How can you use the idea of successive transformations to justify the associativity of matrix multiplication: (**PQ**)**R** = **P**(**QR**)?

e Proving results in trigonometry

Using successive transformations allows us to prove some useful results in trigonometry.

If you carry out a rotation about the origin through angle α, followed by a rotation about the origin through angle β, then this is equivalent to a single rotation through the origin through angle $\alpha + \beta$.

ACTIVITY 1.10

(i) Write down the matrix **A** representing a rotation about the origin through angle α, and the matrix **B** representing a rotation about the origin through angle β.

(ii) Find the matrix **BA**, representing a rotation about the origin through angle α, followed by a rotation about the origin through angle β.

(iii) Write down the matrix **C** representing a rotation through the origin through angle $\alpha + \beta$.

(iv) By equating **C** to **BA**, write down expressions for $\sin(\alpha + \beta)$ and $\cos(\alpha + \beta)$.

(v) Explain why **BA** = **AB** in this case.

(vi) Write down the matrix **D** representing a rotation about the origin through angle $-\beta$.
Use the matrix product **AD** to find expressions for $\sin(\alpha - \beta)$ and $\cos(\alpha - \beta)$.

EXERCISE 1D

Use the following matrix transformations in questions 1 *to* 4.

The matrix **X** represents reflection in the x axis.
The matrix **Y** represents reflection in the y axis.
The matrix **Q** represents rotation of 90° anticlockwise about the origin.
The matrix **R** represents rotation of 90° clockwise about the origin.
The matrix **S** represents rotation of 180° about the origin.
The matrix **T** represents reflection in the line $y = x$.
The matrix **U** represents reflection in the line $y = -x$.

1 **(i)** Write down the matrices **Y** and **Q**.

(ii) Find the matrix **QY** and describe the transformation ***QY*** as simply as you can.

(iii) Draw diagrams to show the effect of applying ***Y*** followed by **Q**, and check that the result agrees with your answer to part **(ii)**.

(iv) Find the matrix **YQ** and describe the transformation ***YQ*** as simply as you can.

(v) Draw diagrams to show the effect of applying **Q** followed by **Y**, and check that the result agrees with your answer to part **(iv)**.

2 **(i)** Write down the matrices **R** and **T**.

(ii) Find the matrix **RT** and describe the transformation *RT* as simply as you can.

(iii) Draw diagrams to show the effect of applying *T* followed by *R*, and check that the result agrees with your answer to part **(ii)**.

(iv) Find the matrix **TR** and describe the transformation *TR* as simply as you can.

(v) Draw diagrams to show the effect of applying *R* followed by *T*, and check that the result agrees with your answer to part **(iv)**.

3 **(i)** Write down the matrices **X** and **Y**.

(ii) Find the matrix **XY** and describe the transformation *XY* as simply as you can.

(iii) Find the matrix **YX**.

(iv) Explain why **XY** = **YX** in this case.

4 **(i)** Write down the matrices **S** and **U**.

(ii) Find the matrix **SU** and describe the transformation *SU* as simply as you can.

(iii) Find the matrix **US**.

(iv) Explain why **SU** = **US** in this case.

5 The transformations *R* and *S* are represented by the matrices $\mathbf{R} = \begin{pmatrix} 2 & -1 \\ 1 & 3 \end{pmatrix}$ and $\mathbf{S} = \begin{pmatrix} 3 & 0 \\ -2 & 4 \end{pmatrix}$.

(i) Find the matrix which represents the transformation *RS*.

(ii) Find the image of the point (2, –1) under the transformation *RS*.

6 R_1 and R_2 are rotations of the plane anticlockwise about the origin through angles 25° and 40° respectively. The corresponding matrices are $\mathbf{R}_1$ and $\mathbf{R}_2$.

(i) By considering the effects of the rotations, explain why $R_1R_2 = R_2R_1$.

(ii) Write down $\mathbf{R}_1$ and $\mathbf{R}_2$ and calculate $\mathbf{R}_1\mathbf{R}_2$.

(iii) What single transformation is represented by $\mathbf{R}_1\mathbf{R}_2$?

7 There are two basic types of four-terminal electrical network, as shown in the diagram.

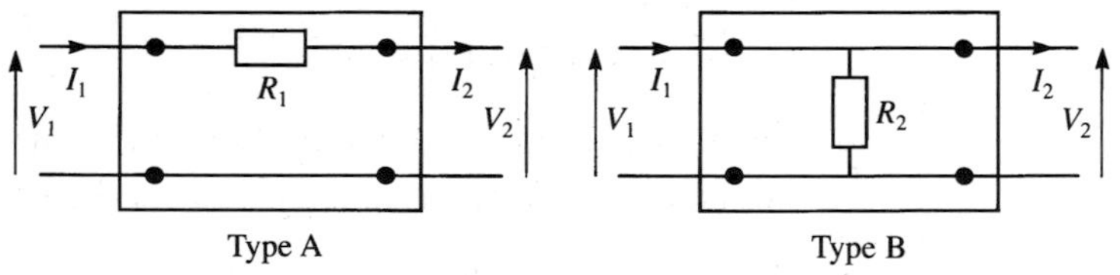

(i) In Type A the output voltage V_2 and current I_2 are related to the input voltage V_1 and current I_1 by the simultaneous equations

$$V_2 = V_1 - I_1R_1$$
$$I_2 = I_1.$$

You can write $\begin{pmatrix} V_2 \\ I_2 \end{pmatrix} = \mathbf{A}\begin{pmatrix} V_1 \\ I_1 \end{pmatrix}$.

Write down matrix **A**.

(ii) In Type B the corresponding simultaneous equations are

$$V_2 = V_1$$
$$I_2 = I_1 - \frac{V_1}{R_2}.$$

Write down the matrix **B** which represents the effect of a Type B network.

(iii) Find the matrix which represents the effect of Type A followed by Type B.

(iv) Is the effect of Type B followed by Type A the same as the effect of Type A followed by Type B?

In questions 8 *to* 10 *you will need to use the matrix which represents reflection in the line* $y = mx$. *This can be written as* $\frac{1}{1+m^2}\begin{pmatrix} 1-m^2 & 2m \\ 2m & m^2-1 \end{pmatrix}$.

8 **(i)** Find the matrix **P** which represents reflection in the line $y = \frac{1}{\sqrt{3}}x$, and the matrix **Q** which represents reflection in the line $y = \sqrt{3}x$.

(ii) Use matrix multiplication to find the single transformation equivalent to reflection in the line $y = \frac{1}{\sqrt{3}}x$ followed by reflection in the line $y = \sqrt{3}x$. Describe this transformation fully.

(iii) Use matrix multiplication to find the single transformation equivalent to reflection in the line $y = \sqrt{3}x$ followed by reflection in the line $y = \frac{1}{\sqrt{3}}x$. Describe this transformation fully.

9 **(i)** Find the matrix **R** which represents rotation through 30° anticlockwise about the origin. (Use exact values. You may find the diagram helpful.)

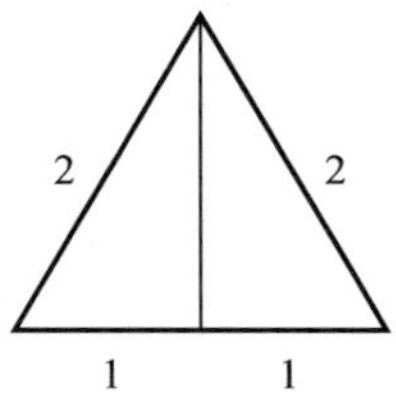

(ii) Find the matrix **M** which represents reflection in the line $y = \sqrt{3}x$.

(iii) Calculate **MR**.
What single transformation does this matrix represent?

10 ☆☆ The matrix **T** represents a reflection in the line $y = mx$.
Show that $\mathbf{T}^2 = \mathbf{I}$, and explain geometrically why this is the case.

11 ☆☆☆☆☆☆☆☆☆☆☆☆ The one-way stretch *S*, ×5 parallel to the line $y = \frac{1}{2}x$, can be accomplished by

A rotating the plane clockwise about O through the angle a, where $\tan a = \frac{1}{2}$, and then

B doing a one-way stretch, ×5 parallel to the x axis, and then

C rotating the plane anticlockwise about O through the angle a.

(i) Find the matrix for each of transformations *A*, *B* and *C*,

(ii) Hence find the matrix which represents *S*.

(iii) Transformation *S* maps figure F to figure F′.
Describe the transformation which maps F′ to F, and find its matrix.

Inverse matrices

The transformation **Q** represents a rotation of 90° anticlockwise about the origin. The corresponding matrix $\mathbf{Q} = \begin{pmatrix} 0 & -1 \\ 1 & 0 \end{pmatrix}$.

To undo the effect of **Q**, you need to carry out a rotation of 90° clockwise about the origin. This is known as the inverse of **Q**, and is denoted by $\mathbf{Q}^{-1}$. The matrix $\mathbf{Q}^{-1}$ which represents this inverse transformation is $\begin{pmatrix} 0 & 1 \\ -1 & 0 \end{pmatrix}$.

? Find the matrix product $\mathbf{QQ}^{-1}$.
Is $\mathbf{Q}^{-1}\mathbf{Q}$ equal to $\mathbf{QQ}^{-1}$?
Explain your answers.

ACTIVITY 1.11 Find several pairs of transformations and their inverses, together with the matrices that represent the transformations.

Find the product of each matrix with its inverse.
What do you notice?

If the product of two square matrices, **M** and **N**, is the identity matrix $\mathbf{I} = \begin{pmatrix} 1 & 0 \\ 0 & 1 \end{pmatrix}$, then **N** is the inverse of **M**. We write $\mathbf{N} = \mathbf{M}^{-1}$.

For simple transformation matrices such as the ones you looked at above, it is easy to find the inverse matrix by considering the inverse transformation. However, a method is needed to find the inverse of any 2 × 2 matrix.

ACTIVITY 1.12 The matrix $\mathbf{M} = \begin{pmatrix} 4 & 2 \\ 5 & 3 \end{pmatrix}$. Let $\mathbf{M}^{-1} = \begin{pmatrix} w & y \\ x & z \end{pmatrix}$.

$$\mathbf{MM}^{-1} = \begin{pmatrix} 4 & 2 \\ 5 & 3 \end{pmatrix}\begin{pmatrix} w & y \\ x & z \end{pmatrix} = \begin{pmatrix} 1 & 0 \\ 0 & 1 \end{pmatrix}.$$

Show that $4w + 2x = 1$
and $5w + 3x = 0$

Solve these equations to find w and x.

Now form and solve two equations in y and z.

Hence find $\mathbf{M}^{-1}$.

Now generalise this method to find the inverse of the matrix $\mathbf{N} = \begin{pmatrix} a & c \\ b & d \end{pmatrix}$.

Let $\mathbf{N}^{-1} = \begin{pmatrix} w & y \\ x & z \end{pmatrix}$, and again find two equations in w and x, and two equations in y and z.

Solve these to find the values of w, x, y and z in terms of a, b, c and d.

Hence show that $\mathbf{N}^{-1} = \frac{1}{\Delta}\begin{pmatrix} d & -c \\ -b & a \end{pmatrix}$,

where $\Delta = ad - bc$, provided $\Delta \neq 0$.

Notice that the elements on the leading diagonal (from the top left to bottom right) are interchanged, and the signs of the other two elements are changed.

The number $ad - bc$ is known as the *determinant* of the 2×2 matrix. If the determinant is zero, the matrix $\begin{pmatrix} a & c \\ b & d \end{pmatrix}$ does not have an inverse and is described as *singular*. If the determinant is not zero, then the inverse of the matrix exists, and the matrix is described as *non-singular*.

EXAMPLE 1.6

Find the inverses of these matrices, if they exist.

(i) $\begin{pmatrix} 7 & 8 \\ 3 & 4 \end{pmatrix}$ **(ii)** $\begin{pmatrix} 2 & 8 \\ 1 & 4 \end{pmatrix}$

SOLUTION

(i) The determinant of $\begin{pmatrix} 7 & 8 \\ 3 & 4 \end{pmatrix} = 7 \times 4 - 8 \times 3 = 28 - 24 = 4.$

The inverse of $\begin{pmatrix} 7 & 8 \\ 3 & 4 \end{pmatrix}$ is $\frac{1}{4}\begin{pmatrix} 4 & -8 \\ -3 & 7 \end{pmatrix}$ which may be written as $\begin{pmatrix} 1 & -2 \\ -\frac{3}{4} & \frac{7}{4} \end{pmatrix}$.

Interchange the elements on the leading diagonal and change the sign of the other two elements.

(ii) The determinant of $\begin{pmatrix} 2 & 8 \\ 1 & 4 \end{pmatrix}$ is $2 \times 4 - 8 \times 1 = 8 - 8 = 0$.

So $\begin{pmatrix} 2 & 8 \\ 1 & 4 \end{pmatrix}$ has no inverse.

As matrix multiplication is not commutative, you may have been wondering if it matters in which order you multiply the two matrices in Activity 1.12. The next activity investigates this.

ACTIVITY 1.13

(i) Example 1.6 showed that the inverse of the matrix $\begin{pmatrix} 7 & 8 \\ 3 & 4 \end{pmatrix}$ is $\begin{pmatrix} 1 & -2 \\ -\frac{3}{4} & \frac{7}{4} \end{pmatrix}$.

Show that $\begin{pmatrix} 7 & 8 \\ 3 & 4 \end{pmatrix}\begin{pmatrix} 1 & -2 \\ -\frac{3}{4} & \frac{7}{4} \end{pmatrix} = \mathbf{I}$ and $\begin{pmatrix} 1 & -2 \\ -\frac{3}{4} & \frac{7}{4} \end{pmatrix}\begin{pmatrix} 7 & 8 \\ 3 & 4 \end{pmatrix} = \mathbf{I}$.

(ii) The matrix $\mathbf{M} = \begin{pmatrix} a & c \\ b & d \end{pmatrix}$.

Write down the inverse matrix $\mathbf{M}^{-1}$, and show that $\mathbf{MM}^{-1} = \mathbf{M}^{-1}\mathbf{M} = \mathbf{I}$.

This is an important result: it means that the inverse of a matrix, if it exists, is unique. This applies to all square matrices, not just 2×2 matrices.

The inverse of a product

? How would you undo the effect of a rotation followed by a reflection?

How would you write down the inverse of a matrix product **MN** in terms of $\mathbf{M}^{-1}$ and $\mathbf{N}^{-1}$?

Suppose you want to find the inverse of the product **AB**, where **A** and **B** are non-singular matrices. This means that you need to find a matrix **X** such that $\mathbf{X}(\mathbf{AB}) = \mathbf{I}$.

$$\begin{aligned}
\mathbf{X}(\mathbf{AB}) = \mathbf{I} \Rightarrow \mathbf{XABB}^{-1} &= \mathbf{IB}^{-1} \quad \leftarrow \text{Post-multiply by } \mathbf{B}^{-1}. \\
\Rightarrow \quad \mathbf{XA} &= \mathbf{B}^{-1} \\
\Rightarrow \quad \mathbf{XAA}^{-1} &= \mathbf{B}^{-1}\mathbf{A}^{-1} \quad \leftarrow \text{Post-multiply by } \mathbf{A}^{-1}. \\
\Rightarrow \quad \mathbf{X} &= \mathbf{B}^{-1}\mathbf{A}^{-1}
\end{aligned}$$

Thus $(\mathbf{AB})^{-1} = \mathbf{B}^{-1}\mathbf{A}^{-1}$, where **A** and **B** are non-singular matrices of the same order. To undo two transformations, you must undo the second transformation before undoing the first. You put your socks on before your shoes, but presumably you take your shoes off before your socks!

ACTIVITY 1.14

As often happens, it is easier to prove a result when you know the answer! Use the associative property of matrix multiplication to show that $(\mathbf{AB})(\mathbf{B}^{-1}\mathbf{A}^{-1})$ simplifies to **I** and so provide an alternative proof that $(\mathbf{AB})^{-1} = \mathbf{B}^{-1}\mathbf{A}^{-1}$.

EXERCISE 1E

1 Where possible, find the inverses of the following matrices.

(i) $\begin{pmatrix} 4 & 3 \\ 6 & 5 \end{pmatrix}$ **(ii)** $\begin{pmatrix} 6 & -3 \\ -4 & -2 \end{pmatrix}$ **(iii)** $\begin{pmatrix} 4 & 2 \\ -6 & -3 \end{pmatrix}$

(iv) $\begin{pmatrix} 5 & 6 \\ 2 & 3 \end{pmatrix}$ **(v)** $\begin{pmatrix} 3 & 1 \\ 2 & -1 \end{pmatrix}$ **(vi)** $\begin{pmatrix} 3 & 4 \\ 5 & 7 \end{pmatrix}$

(vii) $\begin{pmatrix} 3 & -9 \\ -2 & 6 \end{pmatrix}$ **(viii)** $\begin{pmatrix} \frac{1}{3} & \frac{3}{4} \\ \frac{2}{3} & 2 \end{pmatrix}$ **(ix)** $\begin{pmatrix} e & f \\ g & h \end{pmatrix}$

2 The matrix $\begin{pmatrix} 1-k & 2 \\ -1 & 4-k \end{pmatrix}$ is singular.

Find the possible values of k.

3 $\mathbf{A} = \begin{pmatrix} 5 & 3 \\ 6 & 4 \end{pmatrix}$ and $\mathbf{B} = \begin{pmatrix} 4 & 3 \\ 1 & 2 \end{pmatrix}$.

Calculate the following.

(i) $\mathbf{A}^{-1}$ **(ii)** $\mathbf{B}^{-1}$ **(iii)** $\mathbf{A}^{-1}\mathbf{B}^{-1}$

(iv) $\mathbf{B}^{-1}\mathbf{A}^{-1}$ **(v)** $(\mathbf{BA})^{-1}$ **(vi)** $(\mathbf{AB})^{-1}$

Comment on your results.

4 Triangle T has its vertices at (1, 0), (0, 1) and (–2, 0).
It is transformed to triangle T′ by means of the matrix $\mathbf{M} = \begin{pmatrix} 3 & 1 \\ 1 & 1 \end{pmatrix}$.

(i) Find the co-ordinates of the vertices of T′, and show T and T′ on one diagram.

(ii) Find the ratio of the area of T′ to the area of T, and the value of the determinant of **M**.

(ii) Find $\mathbf{M}^{-1}$, and verify that this matrix maps the vertices of T′ to the vertices of T.

5 A 2 × 2 singular matrix **M** is given as $\begin{pmatrix} a & c \\ b & d \end{pmatrix}$.

Find $\mathbf{M}^2$ and give your answer as a multiple of **M**.
Hence find a formula which gives $\mathbf{M}^n$ in terms of **M**.

6 **(i)** Two square matrices **M** and **N** (of the same size) have inverses $\mathbf{M}^{-1}$ and $\mathbf{N}^{-1}$ respectively. Show that the inverse of **MN** is $\mathbf{N}^{-1}\mathbf{M}^{-1}$.

(ii) $\mathbf{A} = \begin{pmatrix} 1 & 7 & 4 \\ 0 & 1 & 2 \\ 0 & 0 & 1 \end{pmatrix}$, $\mathbf{B} = \begin{pmatrix} 1 & 0 & 0 \\ 3 & 1 & 0 \\ -1 & -4 & 1 \end{pmatrix}$ and $\mathbf{C} = \mathbf{AB}$.

(a) Evaluate the matrix **C**.

(b) Work out the matrix product $\mathbf{A}\begin{pmatrix} 1 & a & b \\ 0 & 1 & c \\ 0 & 0 & 1 \end{pmatrix}$.

(c) By equating the product in part **(b)** to $\begin{pmatrix} 1 & 0 & 0 \\ 0 & 1 & 0 \\ 0 & 0 & 1 \end{pmatrix}$, find $\mathbf{A}^{-1}$.

(d) Using a similar method, or otherwise, find $\mathbf{B}^{-1}$.

(e) Using your results from parts **(c)** and **(d)**, find $\mathbf{C}^{-1}$.

[MEI]

Using the determinant of a 2 × 2 matrix

On page 29 the determinant of the 2 × 2 matrix $\mathbf{M} = \begin{pmatrix} a & c \\ b & d \end{pmatrix}$ was defined as the number $ad - bc$. It is denoted in several ways: det **M**, |**M**|, or $\begin{vmatrix} a & c \\ b & d \end{vmatrix}$.

The following activity shows the geometrical significance of determinants.

ACTIVITY 1.15 **(i)** Figure 1.18 shows the unit square OIPJ and its image OI′P′J′ under a transformation *T*, defined by the matrix $\mathbf{T} = \begin{pmatrix} 3 & 1 \\ 1 & 2 \end{pmatrix}$.

Find the area of the image and evaluate det **T**.

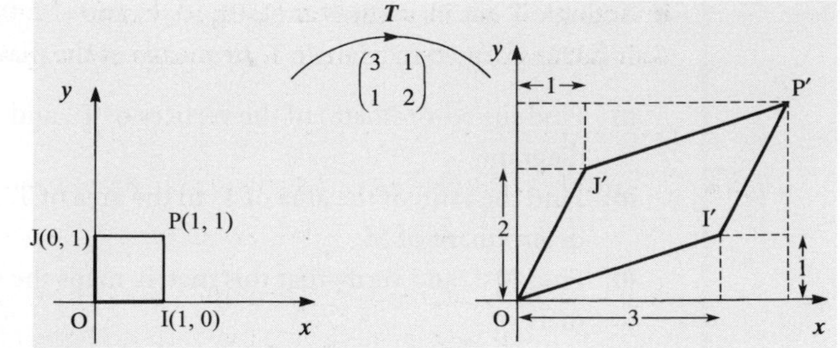

Figure 1.18

(ii) Transformation $\boldsymbol{R}$ is defined by the matrix $\mathbf{R} = \begin{pmatrix} 3 & 5 \\ 1 & 1 \end{pmatrix}$.

Apply **R** to the unit square.
Find the area of the image and evaluate det **R**.

(iii) What do you notice?

Ignoring for the moment the sign of the determinant, you will have found that the determinant is the area scale factor of the transformation.

The sign of the determinant also has significance. If you move anticlockwise around the original shape, the unit square, you come to the vertices O, I, P, J, in that order. Moving anticlockwise around the image in figure 1.18 you come to the vertices in the same order. However, when you apply $\boldsymbol{R}$ to the unit square, the order of the vertices is reversed. It is this reversal of sense that is indicated by the negative sign of det **R**.

In the next activity you will prove that when a general matrix $\mathbf{M} = \begin{pmatrix} a & c \\ b & d \end{pmatrix}$ is applied to the unit square, then the area of its image is equal to det **M**.

ACTIVITY 1.16 Figure 1.19 shows the unit square OIPJ and its image OI′P′J′ under the transformation $\boldsymbol{M}$ defined by the matrix $\mathbf{M} = \begin{pmatrix} a & c \\ b & d \end{pmatrix}$.

You may assume that det **M** is positive.

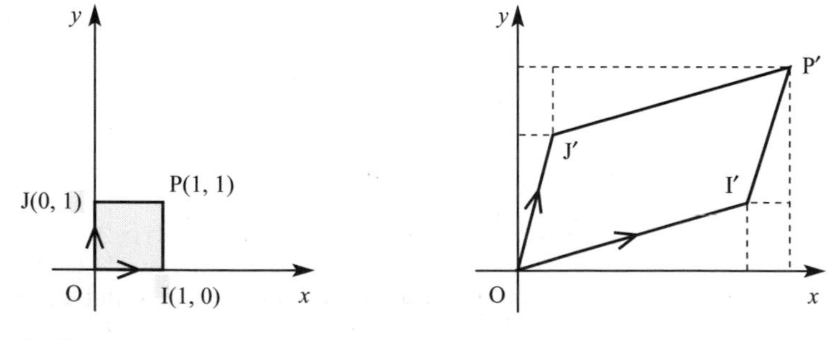

Figure 1.19

Find the co-ordinates of the image points I′, P′ and J′.
Hence show that the area of OI′P′J′ is equal to det **M**.

In Activity 1.16 you should have proved that the determinant gives you the area scale factor of the area of any transformation of a square using a 2×2 matrix.

? Explain how this result can be extended to any plane shape.

So $ad - bc$ is the area scale factor of the transformation. Strictly you should say that $\det \mathbf{T} = ad - bc$ is the *signed* scale factor, as it can be negative, signifying that the sense (clockwise or anticlockwise) has been reversed.

ACTIVITY 1.17 Show that the matrices which represent reflections in the x axis, the y axis, the line $y = x$ and the line $y = -x$ all have a determinant of -1.
In each case, draw diagrams to demonstrate that vertices labelled clockwise around a shape are transformed to vertices labelled anticlockwise around the image.

Matrices with determinant zero

ACTIVITY 1.18

(i) The transformation T is defined by $\mathbf{T} = \begin{pmatrix} 6 & 4 \\ 3 & 2 \end{pmatrix}$.
Find det **T**.

(ii) Draw the rectangle with vertices (0, 0), (4, 0), (4, 3), (0, 3).
Draw the image of this rectangle under T.

(iii) Find some more 2×2 matrices with determinant zero.
Find the image of the rectangle in part **(ii)** under the transformations defined by your matrices.

(iv) What do you notice?

If $\det \mathbf{T} = 0$ the matrix **T** is said to be *singular*, and the transformation represented by **T** maps every point in the plane on to a single line which passes through the origin, as shown in figure 1.20. This is called *transforming the plane.*

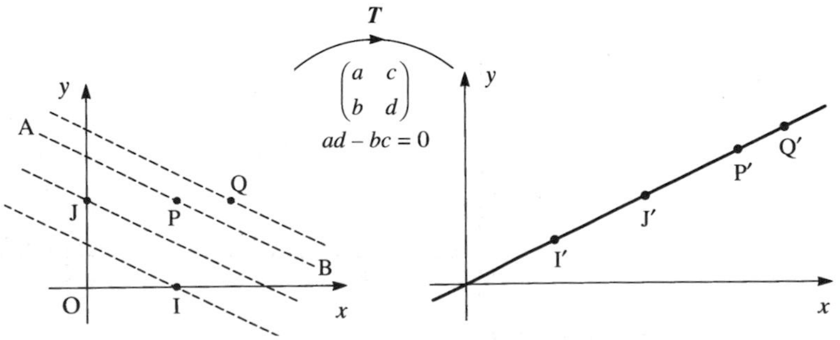

Figure 1.20

Each point on the image line P′Q′ is the image of infinitely many points. All the points which map to P′ fall on a straight line, labelled AB in figure 1.20, and every point on AB maps to P′. Similarly, I′ is the image of all points on a line through I parallel to AB and each point on a line through Q parallel to AB maps to Q′.

? What happens when you map any shape using the zero matrix $\begin{pmatrix} 0 & 0 \\ 0 & 0 \end{pmatrix}$?

How is the plane transformed?

EXAMPLE 1.7

The plane is transformed by means of the matrix $\mathbf{M} = \begin{pmatrix} 4 & -6 \\ 2 & -3 \end{pmatrix}$.

(i) Show that det $\mathbf{M} = 0$.

(ii) Show that the whole plane is mapped to a straight line, and find the equation of this line.

(iii) Find the equation of the line of points that map to (6, 3).

SOLUTION

(i) det $\mathbf{M} = (4 \times -3) - (-6 \times 2) = -12 + 12 = 0$

(ii) $\begin{pmatrix} 4 & -6 \\ 2 & -3 \end{pmatrix}\begin{pmatrix} x \\ y \end{pmatrix} = \begin{pmatrix} x' \\ y' \end{pmatrix}$

$$\begin{cases} 4x - 6y = x' \\ 2x - 3y = y' \end{cases}$$

$x' = 2(2x - 3y) = 2y'$

The plane is mapped to the line $x = 2y$.

(iii) $\begin{pmatrix} 4 & -6 \\ 2 & -3 \end{pmatrix}\begin{pmatrix} x \\ y \end{pmatrix} = \begin{pmatrix} 6 \\ 3 \end{pmatrix}$

$$\begin{cases} 4x - 6y = 6 \\ 2x - 3y = 3 \end{cases}$$

These two statements give the same information.

Points on the line $2x - 3y = 3$ map to the point (6, 3).

ACTIVITY 1.19

The plane is transformed using the matrix $\begin{pmatrix} a & c \\ b & d \end{pmatrix}$, where $ad - bc = 0$.

Prove that the general point P(x, y) maps to P′ on the line $bx - ay = 0$.

EXERCISE 1F

1 Find the value of the determinant of each of the following matrices and decide whether each matrix is singular or non-singular.

(i) $\begin{pmatrix} 6 & 4 \\ 2 & 3 \end{pmatrix}$ (ii) $\begin{pmatrix} 4 & 8 \\ -1 & -2 \end{pmatrix}$ (iii) $\begin{pmatrix} 5 & 3 \\ 1 & \frac{3}{5} \end{pmatrix}$ (iv) $\begin{pmatrix} 1 & -2 \\ 2 & 3 \end{pmatrix}$

2 $\mathbf{M} = \begin{pmatrix} 5 & 3 \\ 4 & 2 \end{pmatrix}$ and $\mathbf{N} = \begin{pmatrix} 3 & 2 \\ -2 & 1 \end{pmatrix}$.

(i) Find the determinants of **M** and **N**.

(ii) Find **MN** and det (**MN**). What do you notice?

(iii) By considering the geometrical significance of the determinant, explain why det (**MN**) = det **M** × det **N**.

3 The two-way stretch with matrix $\begin{pmatrix} a & 0 \\ 0 & d \end{pmatrix}$ preserves area (i.e. the area of the image is equal to the area of the original shape).
What is the relationship connecting a and d?

4 A shear moves each point parallel to the x axis by a distance k times its distance from the x axis.
Find the matrix for this transformation and hence show that whatever the value of k, the shear preserves area.

5 The matrix $\mathbf{M} = \begin{pmatrix} 7 & -3 \\ -4 & 6 \end{pmatrix}$ defines a transformation in the (x, y) plane.

A triangle S, with area 5 square units, is transformed by **M** into triangle T.

(i) Find the area of triangle T.

(ii) Find the matrix which transforms triangle T into triangle S.

Triangle U is obtained by rotating triangle S through 135° anticlockwise about the origin.

(iii) Find the matrix which transforms triangle S into triangle U.

(iv) Find the matrix which transforms triangle T into triangle U.

[MEI, *part*]

6 The plane is transformed by means of the matrix $\mathbf{M} = \begin{pmatrix} 2 & 4 \\ 1 & 2 \end{pmatrix}$.

(i) Show that det **M** = 0, and that the whole plane is mapped on to the line $x - 2y = 0$.

(ii) The point P(x, y) is mapped to P′(4, 2).
Use the equation **p′** = **Mp** to show that P could be anywhere on the line $x + 2y = 2$.

(iii) Find the equation of the line of points that map to (10, 5).

7 A matrix **T** maps all points on the line $x + 2y = 1$ to the point (1, 3).

(i) Find the matrix **T** and show that its determinant is zero.

(ii) Show that **T** maps all points on the plane on to the line $y = 3x$.

(iii) Find the co-ordinates of the point that all points on the line $x + 2y = 3$ are mapped to.

8 The point P is mapped to P′ on the line $3y = x$, so that PP′ is parallel to $y = 3x$.

(i) Find the equation of the line parallel to $y = 3x$ passing through the point P with co-ordinates (s, t).

(ii) Find the co-ordinates of P′, the point where this line meets the line $3y = x$.

(iii) Find the matrix of the transformation which maps P to P′, and show that the determinant of this matrix is zero.

9 ☆ A shear moves each point parallel to the line $y = mx$.
Each point is moved k times its distance from the line $y = mx$.
(Points to the right of the line are moved upwards, points to the left of the line are moved downwards).

(i) Find the images of the points I(1, 0) and J(0, 1).

(ii) Hence write down the matrix which represents the shear.

(iii) Show that whatever the value of m, the shear preserves area.

Matrices and simultaneous equations

You are already able to solve a pair of simultaneous linear equations such as

$$\begin{cases} 3x + 2y = 9 \\ 4x + 5y = 5 \end{cases}$$

by the method of elimination.

An alternative method, which can be used to solve any number of simultaneous linear equations, involves the use of matrices.

The equations above can be written as a single matrix equation

$$\begin{pmatrix} 3 & 2 \\ 4 & 5 \end{pmatrix}\begin{pmatrix} x \\ y \end{pmatrix} = \begin{pmatrix} 9 \\ 5 \end{pmatrix}.$$

The inverse of the matrix $\begin{pmatrix} 3 & 2 \\ 4 & 5 \end{pmatrix}$ is $\frac{1}{7}\begin{pmatrix} 5 & -2 \\ -4 & 3 \end{pmatrix}$.

$$\frac{1}{7}\begin{pmatrix} 5 & -2 \\ -4 & 3 \end{pmatrix}\begin{pmatrix} 3 & 2 \\ 4 & 5 \end{pmatrix}\begin{pmatrix} x \\ y \end{pmatrix} = \frac{1}{7}\begin{pmatrix} 5 & -2 \\ -4 & 3 \end{pmatrix}\begin{pmatrix} 9 \\ 5 \end{pmatrix}$$

Pre-multiply both sides of the matrix equation by $\frac{1}{7}\begin{pmatrix} 5 & -2 \\ -4 & 3 \end{pmatrix}$.

$$\begin{pmatrix} x \\ y \end{pmatrix} = \frac{1}{7}\begin{pmatrix} 35 \\ -21 \end{pmatrix} = \begin{pmatrix} 5 \\ -3 \end{pmatrix}$$

As $\mathbf{M}^{-1}\mathbf{Mp} = \mathbf{p}$, the left-hand side simplifies to $\begin{pmatrix} x \\ y \end{pmatrix}$.

The solution is $x = 5$, $y = -3$.

The equation

$$\begin{pmatrix} 3 & 2 \\ 4 & 5 \end{pmatrix}\begin{pmatrix} x \\ y \end{pmatrix} = \begin{pmatrix} 9 \\ 5 \end{pmatrix}$$

has the form $\mathbf{Mp} = \mathbf{p}'$, where $\mathbf{M}$ and $\mathbf{p}'$ are known and you are trying to find $\mathbf{p}$. This is equivalent to finding the co-ordinates of the unknown point P which is transformed on to the known point P′ by the given matrix $\mathbf{M}$.

An alternative geometrical interpretation of solving a pair of simultaneous equations, which may already be familiar to you, is to think of the two equations as the equations of two lines in a plane. You are looking for any points which lie on both lines.

Whichever geometrical interpretation you use, there are three possible alternatives.

Case 1

The lines cross at a single point, as shown in figure 1.21. This is the case when det $\mathbf{M} \neq 0$, so the inverse matrix $\mathbf{M}^{-1}$ exists and there is a unique position for P, as shown in figure 1.22.

Both interpretations show that there is a unique solution to the equations.

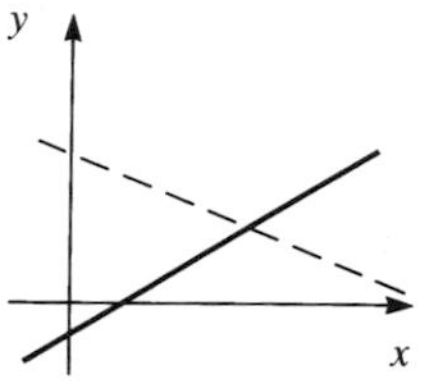

Figure 1.21

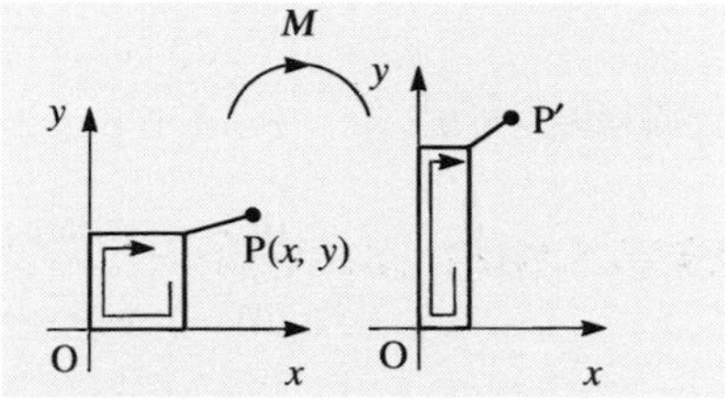

Figure 1.22

Case 2

The lines are distinct parallel lines, as shown in figure 1.23. In this case det $\mathbf{M} = 0$, so the inverse matrix $\mathbf{M}^{-1}$ does not exist, and the transformation maps all points on to a single line l through the origin. In this case P′ is not on l, so P′ is not the image of any point (see figure 1.24).

Both interpretations show that the equations have no solution. We say that the equations are inconsistent.

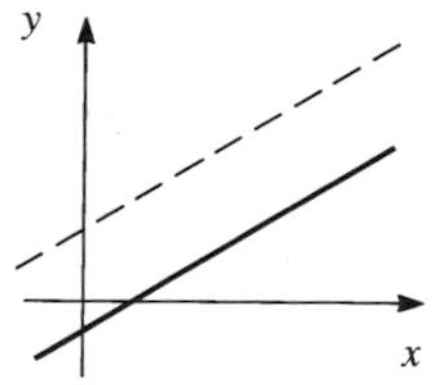

Figure 1.23

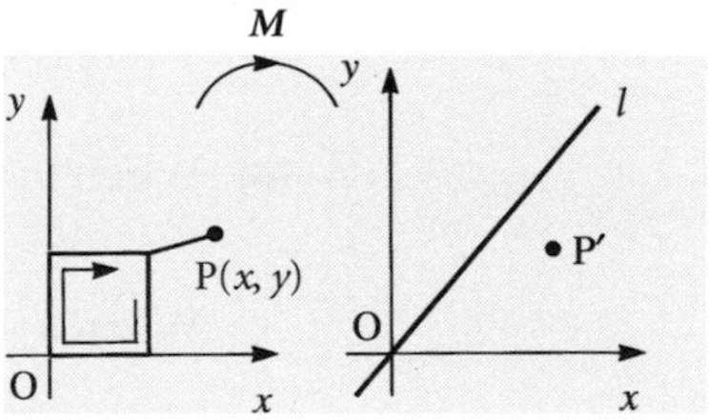

Figure 1.24

Case 3

The lines are coincident lines, i.e. they are the same line, as shown in figure 1.25. In this case det $\mathbf{M} = 0$ again, so the inverse matrix $\mathbf{M}^{-1}$ does not exist and the transformation maps all points on to a single line l through the origin. In this case, P′ is on l, so there are infinitely many positions for P, all the points on a particular line (see figure 1.26).

Both interpretations show that the equations have infinitely many solutions, which may be expressed in terms of a single parameter (see Example 1.8 part **(iii)**).

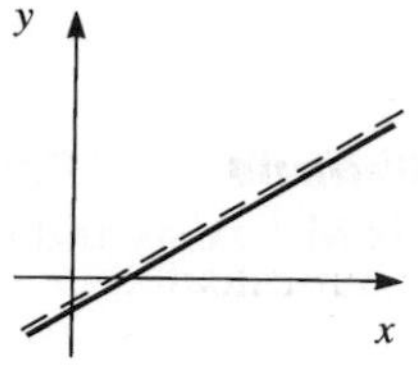

Figure 1.25

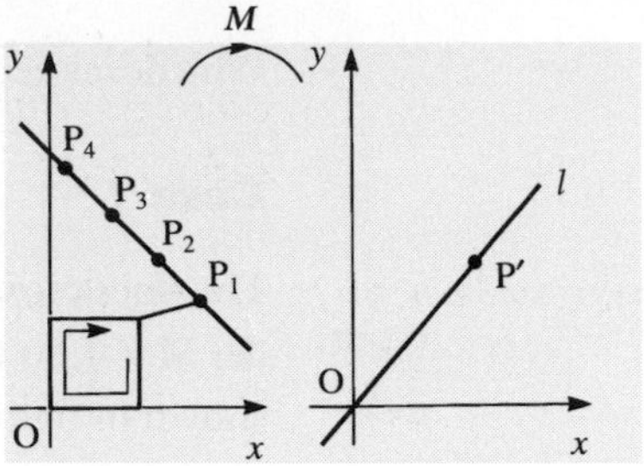

Figure 1.26

EXAMPLE 1.8

Find, if possible, the solution of the equations $\begin{cases} 2x - 3y = 4 \\ 4x + my = k \end{cases}$

(i) when $m = 1$ and $k = 1$

(ii) when $m = -6$ and $k = 3$

(iii) when $m = -6$ and $k = 8$.

SOLUTION

The simultaneous equations may be written as the following matrix equation.

$$\begin{pmatrix} 2 & -3 \\ 4 & m \end{pmatrix}\begin{pmatrix} x \\ y \end{pmatrix} = \begin{pmatrix} 4 \\ k \end{pmatrix}$$

(i) When $m = 1$, $\begin{vmatrix} 2 & -3 \\ 4 & 1 \end{vmatrix} = 14$, so the inverse matrix exists and is equal to $\frac{1}{14}\begin{pmatrix} 1 & 3 \\ -4 & 2 \end{pmatrix}$.

$$\begin{pmatrix} x \\ y \end{pmatrix} = \frac{1}{14}\begin{pmatrix} 1 & 3 \\ -4 & 2 \end{pmatrix}\begin{pmatrix} 4 \\ 1 \end{pmatrix} = \frac{1}{14}\begin{pmatrix} 7 \\ -14 \end{pmatrix} = \begin{pmatrix} \frac{1}{2} \\ -1 \end{pmatrix}$$

There is a unique solution: $x = \frac{1}{2}$, $y = -1$.

(ii) When $m = -6$, $\begin{vmatrix} 2 & -3 \\ 4 & -6 \end{vmatrix} = 0$, so the inverse matrix does not exist.

When $k = 3$, the equations are $\begin{cases} 2x - 3y = 4 \\ 4x - 6y = 3 \end{cases}$.

These equations are inconsistent as $2x - 3y$ cannot be both 4 and $\frac{3}{2}$.
There are no solutions.

(iii) As for part **(ii)**, the inverse matrix does not exist.

When $k = 8$, the equations are $\begin{cases} 2x - 3y = 4 \\ 4x - 6y = 8 \end{cases}$.

Both equations reduce to $2x - 3y = 4$.
There are infinitely many solutions, which can be given in terms of a parameter λ as $x = \lambda$, $y = \dfrac{2\lambda}{3} - \dfrac{4}{3}$.

The strength of the matrix method for solving simultaneous equations is that it can be used for any number of equations. Of course, to solve a set of n simultaneous equations in n unknowns, you do need to be able to find the inverse of an $n \times n$ matrix. At this stage you will only be dealing with the case where $n = 2$ unless you are given help with finding the inverse of a larger matrix, such as 3×3.

ACTIVITY 1.20 ***Three simultaneous equations***

(i) Use the matrix facility on your calculator to find the inverse of the matrix $\begin{pmatrix} 3 & 2 & 1 \\ 1 & 4 & -2 \\ 2 & 1 & 1 \end{pmatrix}$.

Hence find the solution of the equations $\begin{cases} 3x + 2y + z = 5 \\ x + 4y - 2z = 3 \\ 2x + y + z = 3 \end{cases}$.

(ii) What happens if you try to solve the equations $\begin{cases} x + 3y - 2z = 7 \\ 2x - 2y + z = 3 \\ 3x + y - z = 10 \end{cases}$ using the matrix facility on your calculator?

Why do you think this is?
Try to solve the equations algebraically. What happens?

(iii) Repeat part **(ii)** for the equations $\begin{cases} x + 3y - 2z = 7 \\ 2x - 2y + z = 3 \\ 3x + y - z = 12 \end{cases}$.

? e ***Geometrical interpretation of three simultaneous equations***

What is the geometrical interpretation of each of the three situations in Activity 1.20?

EXERCISE 1G

1 (i) Find the inverse of the matrix $\begin{pmatrix} 2 & 3 \\ -1 & 1 \end{pmatrix}$.

(ii) Hence solve the equation $\begin{pmatrix} 2 & 3 \\ -1 & 1 \end{pmatrix}\begin{pmatrix} x \\ y \end{pmatrix} = \begin{pmatrix} 1 \\ -3 \end{pmatrix}$.

2 Use matrices to solve the following pairs of simultaneous equations.

(i) $\begin{cases} 3x - y = 2 \\ 2x + 3y = 5 \end{cases}$

(ii) $\begin{cases} 3x + 2y = 4 \\ x - 2y = 4 \end{cases}$

(iii) $\begin{cases} x + 3y = 11 \\ 2x - y = 1 \end{cases}$

(iv) $\begin{cases} 3x - 2y = 9 \\ x - 4y = -2 \end{cases}$

3 For each of the following pairs of equations, decide whether the equations are consistent or inconsistent.
If they are consistent, solve them, in terms of a parameter if necessary.
In each case, describe the configuration of the corresponding pair of lines.

(i) $\begin{cases} 3x + 5y = 17 \\ 2x + 4y = 11 \end{cases}$ **(ii)** $\begin{cases} 3x + 6y = 12 \\ 2x + 4y = 15 \end{cases}$

(iii) $\begin{cases} 6x - 3y = 12 \\ 2x - y = 4 \end{cases}$ **(iv)** $\begin{cases} 8x - 4y = 11 \\ y = 2x - 4 \end{cases}$

4 Find the two values of k for which the equations $\begin{cases} 2x + ky = 3 \\ kx + 8y = 6 \end{cases}$ do not have a unique solution. Where possible, find the solution set for the equations.

5 (i) Find **AB**, where $\mathbf{A} = \begin{pmatrix} 5 & -2 & k \\ 3 & -4 & -5 \\ -2 & 3 & 4 \end{pmatrix}$ and $\mathbf{B} = \begin{pmatrix} -1 & 3k+8 & 4k+10 \\ -2 & 2k+20 & 3k+25 \\ 1 & -11 & -14 \end{pmatrix}$.

Hence write down the inverse matrix $\mathbf{A}^{-1}$, stating a necessary condition on k for this inverse to exist.

(ii) Using the result from part **(i)**, or otherwise, solve the equation

$$\begin{pmatrix} 5 & -2 & k \\ 3 & -4 & -5 \\ -2 & 3 & 4 \end{pmatrix}\begin{pmatrix} x \\ y \\ z \end{pmatrix} = \begin{pmatrix} 28 \\ 0 \\ m \end{pmatrix}$$

in each of these cases.

(a) $k = 8$, giving x, y and z in terms of m
(b) $k = 1$ and $m = 4$
(c) $k = 1$ and $m = 2$

[MEI, *part, adapted*]

6 Matrices **A** and **B** are given by

$$\mathbf{A} = \begin{pmatrix} 1 & -2 & 0 \\ 0 & 2 & -2 \\ a & 0 & 3 \end{pmatrix}, \mathbf{B} = \begin{pmatrix} 6 & 6 & 4 \\ k & 3 & 2 \\ k & k & 2 \end{pmatrix} (\text{where } a \neq -\tfrac{3}{2} \text{ and } k \neq 3).$$

(i) Find the matrix **AB**.
(ii) Show that there is a relationship between a and k for which **AB** is a scalar multiple of the identity matrix **I**.
(iii) Deduce that $\mathbf{A}^{-1} = \dfrac{1}{6 + 4a}\begin{pmatrix} 6 & 6 & 4 \\ -2a & 3 & 2 \\ -2a & -2a & 2 \end{pmatrix}$ and find $\mathbf{B}^{-1}$ in terms of k.
(iv) Given that $\begin{pmatrix} 1 & -2 & 0 \\ 0 & 2 & -2 \\ a & 0 & 3 \end{pmatrix}\begin{pmatrix} x \\ y \\ z \end{pmatrix} = \begin{pmatrix} 2 \\ -2 \\ 3 \end{pmatrix}$, express each of x, y and z in terms of a.
(v) Find $(\mathbf{AB})^{-1}$ in terms of a and k.

[MEI]

7 You are given the matrices

$$\mathbf{P} = \begin{pmatrix} -2 & 26 & -16 \\ 1 & -11 & 7 \\ -1 & 21 & -13 \end{pmatrix} \text{ and } \mathbf{Q} = \begin{pmatrix} -2 & 1 & k \\ 3 & 5 & -1 \\ 5 & 8 & -2 \end{pmatrix}.$$

(i) Calculate the matrix product **PQ**.

(ii) For the case $k = 3$, write down the inverse matrix $\mathbf{Q}^{-1}$ and hence solve the following equation.

$$\mathbf{Q}\begin{pmatrix} x \\ y \\ z \end{pmatrix} = \begin{pmatrix} 19 \\ 4 \\ 5 \end{pmatrix}$$

(iii) For the case $k = 5$, you are given that **Q** has no inverse. Solve the equation

$$\mathbf{Q}\begin{pmatrix} x \\ y \\ z \end{pmatrix} = \begin{pmatrix} 19 \\ 4 \\ 5 \end{pmatrix},$$

giving x, y and z in terms of a parameter t.

[MEI, *part*]

Invariant points

? In a reflection, which points map to themselves?

In a rotation, are there any points which map to themselves?

Points which map to themselves under a transformation are called *invariant points.*

The product $\begin{pmatrix} 6 & 5 \\ 2 & 3 \end{pmatrix}\begin{pmatrix} 2 \\ -2 \end{pmatrix} = \begin{pmatrix} 2 \\ -2 \end{pmatrix}$. This means that the transformation $\begin{pmatrix} 6 & 5 \\ 2 & 3 \end{pmatrix}$ maps the point $(2, -2)$ to itself. This is an example of an invariant point.

? Explain why the origin is always an invariant point in any transformation that can be represented by a matrix.

EXAMPLE 1.9

Find the invariant points under the transformation given by the matrix $\begin{pmatrix} 2 & -1 \\ 1 & 0 \end{pmatrix}$.

SOLUTION

Suppose $\begin{pmatrix} x \\ y \end{pmatrix}$ maps to itself. Then

$$\begin{pmatrix} 2 & -1 \\ 1 & 0 \end{pmatrix}\begin{pmatrix} x \\ y \end{pmatrix} = \begin{pmatrix} x \\ y \end{pmatrix} \Leftrightarrow \begin{pmatrix} 2x - y \\ x \end{pmatrix} = \begin{pmatrix} x \\ y \end{pmatrix}$$
$$\Leftrightarrow 2x - y = x \text{ and } x = y$$
$$\Leftrightarrow x = y.$$

Thus all points on the line $y = x$ (and only points on this line) map on to themselves. This is a line of invariant points. The invariant points can be expressed in terms of a parameter as (λ, λ).

Notice that in Example 1.9, the matrix equation $\begin{pmatrix} 2 & -1 \\ 1 & 0 \end{pmatrix}\begin{pmatrix} x \\ y \end{pmatrix} = \begin{pmatrix} x \\ y \end{pmatrix}$ led to two equations which turned out to be equivalent.

Clearly any matrix equation of this form will lead to two equations of the form $ax + by = 0$, which represent straight lines through the origin. Either these two equations are equivalent, representing the same straight line, which means that all the invariant points lie on this line, or they are not, in which case the origin is the only point which satisfies both equations, and so is the only invariant point.

e Invariant lines

A line AB is known as an *invariant line* under a transformation T if the image of each point on AB is also on AB. It is important to note that it is not necessary for points on AB to map on to themselves (as in Example 1.9) but merely that each point on AB maps to a point on AB.

Sometimes it is easy to spot which lines are invariant, for example, in a reflection, as well as the mirror line being invariant (because it is a line of invariant points), each line perpendicular to the mirror line is invariant, as shown in figure 1.27.

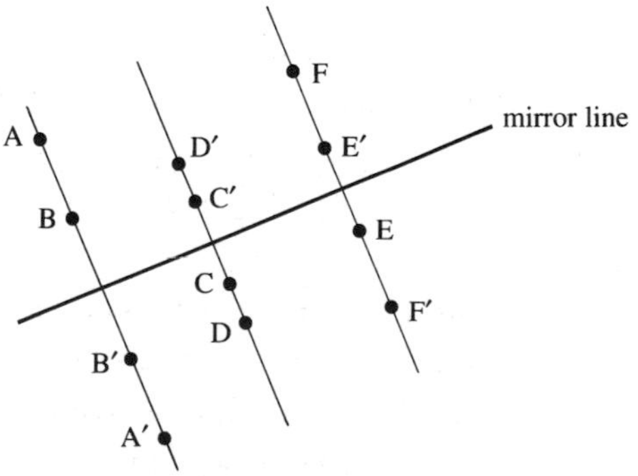

Figure 1.27

What lines, if any, are invariant in the following transformations?

(i) Enlargement, centre the origin
(ii) Rotation through 180° about the origin
(iii) Rotation through 90° about the origin
(iv) Reflection in the line $y = x$

EXERCISE 1H

1 Find the invariant points for the transformations with the following matrices.

(i) $\begin{pmatrix} 0 & -1 \\ 1 & 2 \end{pmatrix}$ **(ii)** $\begin{pmatrix} 3 & 4 \\ 1 & 2 \end{pmatrix}$ **(iii)** $\begin{pmatrix} 0.6 & 0.8 \\ 0.8 & -0.6 \end{pmatrix}$

(iv) $\begin{pmatrix} \frac{1}{\sqrt{2}} & -\frac{1}{\sqrt{2}} \\ -\frac{1}{\sqrt{2}} & \frac{1}{\sqrt{2}} \end{pmatrix}$ **(v)** $\begin{pmatrix} 4 & 1 \\ 6 & 3 \end{pmatrix}$ **(vi)** $\begin{pmatrix} 7 & -4 \\ 3 & -1 \end{pmatrix}$

2 The transformation T maps $\begin{pmatrix} x \\ y \end{pmatrix}$ to $\begin{pmatrix} a & c \\ b & d \end{pmatrix}\begin{pmatrix} x \\ y \end{pmatrix}$.

Show that invariant points other than the origin exist if $\det \mathbf{T} = a + d - 1$.

3 The matrix $\begin{pmatrix} \frac{1-m^2}{1+m^2} & \frac{2m}{1+m^2} \\ \frac{2m}{1+m^2} & \frac{m^2-1}{1+m^2} \end{pmatrix}$ represents reflection in the line $y = mx$.

Prove that the line $y = mx$ is a line of invariant points.

4 (i) $\mathbf{M}$ is a reflection of the plane such that the point (x', y') is the image of the point (x, y), where

$$\begin{pmatrix} x' \\ y' \end{pmatrix} = \begin{pmatrix} -0.6 & 0.8 \\ 0.8 & 0.6 \end{pmatrix}\begin{pmatrix} x \\ y \end{pmatrix}.$$

Find a point, other than the origin, that is invariant under this reflection. Hence find the equation of the mirror line.

(ii) T is a translation of the plane by the vector $\begin{pmatrix} a \\ b \end{pmatrix}$.

The point (X, Y) is the image of the point (x, y) under the combined transformation $\boldsymbol{TM}$ (that is $\boldsymbol{M}$ followed by $\boldsymbol{T}$) where

$$\begin{pmatrix} X \\ Y \\ 1 \end{pmatrix} = \begin{pmatrix} -0.6 & 0.8 & a \\ 0.8 & 0.6 & b \\ 0 & 0 & 1 \end{pmatrix}\begin{pmatrix} x \\ y \\ 1 \end{pmatrix}.$$

(a) Show that if $a = -4$ and $b = 2$ then $(0, 5)$ is an invariant point of $\boldsymbol{TM}$.
(b) Show that if $a = 2$ and $b = 1$ then $\boldsymbol{TM}$ has no invariant point.
(c) Find a relation between a and b that must be satisfied if $\boldsymbol{TM}$ is to have any invariant points.

[SMP]

INVESTIGATIONS

1 Investigate the sequence of matrices **I**, **M**, $\mathbf{M}^2$, $\mathbf{M}^3$, ... where $\mathbf{M} = \begin{pmatrix} 1 & 1 \\ 1 & 0 \end{pmatrix}$.

2 Mendel's genetic theory states that offspring inherit characteristics from their parents through their genes. Each characteristic is controlled by a pair of genes, which may be of two types: G or g. The three possible combinations are

GG	known as homozygous dominant, and denoted by D
Gg or gG	known as heterozygous, and denoted by H
gg	known as homozygous recessive, and denoted by R.

Offspring inherit one gene from each parent, randomly and independently. In a controlled study of a population of fruit flies, the only females allowed to mate are those known to be heterozygous.

(i) The unfinished matrix shows the probability that the offspring has combination D, H or R given the combination of genes of the male parent.

Male parent

$$\textbf{Offspring}\quad \begin{matrix} & \text{D} & \text{H} & \text{R} \\ \text{D} & \frac{1}{2} & \frac{1}{4} & 0 \\ \text{H} & \dots & \dots & \dots \\ \text{R} & \dots & \dots & \dots \end{matrix}$$

Copy and complete the matrix **M** containing this information.

(ii) Initially the proportions of the D, H and R combinations in the population are given by $\mathbf{x}_0 = \begin{pmatrix} d \\ h \\ r \end{pmatrix}$.

Show that $\mathbf{x}_1 = \mathbf{M}\mathbf{x}_0$ gives the proportions in the next generation.

(iii) Investigate what happens if the study continues over many generations.

KEY POINTS

1 The matrix $\mathbf{M} = \begin{pmatrix} a & c \\ b & d \end{pmatrix}$ represents the transformation which maps the point with position vector $\begin{pmatrix} x \\ y \end{pmatrix}$ to the point with position vector $\begin{pmatrix} x' \\ y' \end{pmatrix}$, where $\begin{cases} x' = ax + cy \\ y' = bx + dy \end{cases}$.

2 The image of $\begin{pmatrix} 1 \\ 0 \end{pmatrix}$ is the first column of **M**, the image of $\begin{pmatrix} 0 \\ 1 \end{pmatrix}$ is the second column of **M**.

3 Matrix mulitplication

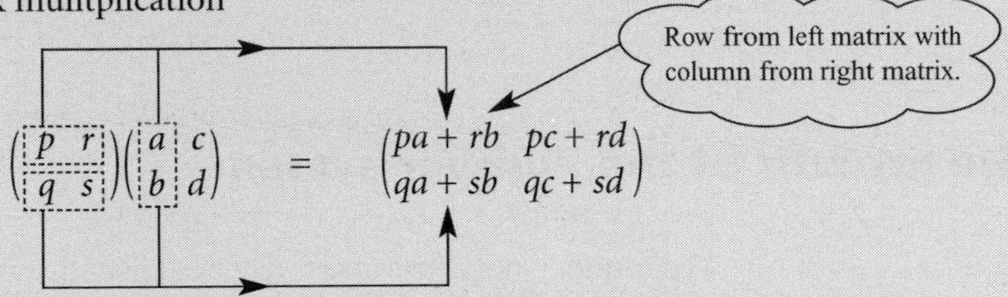
Row from left matrix with column from right matrix.

$$\begin{pmatrix} p & r \\ q & s \end{pmatrix}\begin{pmatrix} a & c \\ b & d \end{pmatrix} = \begin{pmatrix} pa + rb & pc + rd \\ qa + sb & qc + sd \end{pmatrix}$$

4 Matrix multiplication is not commutative: $\mathbf{MN} \neq \mathbf{NM}$ for all **M**, **N**.

5 Matrix multiplication is associative: $\mathbf{N}(\mathbf{ML}) = (\mathbf{NM})\mathbf{L}$.

6 The matrix $\mathbf{I} = \begin{pmatrix} 1 & 0 \\ 0 & 1 \end{pmatrix}$ is known as the *identity matrix.*

The matrix $\begin{pmatrix} 0 & 0 \\ 0 & 0 \end{pmatrix}$ is known as the *zero matrix.*

7 The composite transformation '***M*** followed by ***N***' is represented by the matrix product **NM**.

8 The determinant of the matrix $\mathbf{M} = \begin{pmatrix} a & c \\ b & d \end{pmatrix}$ is $ad - bc$.

It is denoted by $|\mathbf{M}|$, det **M** or $\begin{vmatrix} a & c \\ b & d \end{vmatrix}$.

The determinant of the matrix **M** gives the area scale factor of the associated transformation ***M***.

9 The inverse of $\mathbf{M} = \begin{pmatrix} a & c \\ b & d \end{pmatrix}$ is $\mathbf{M}^{-1} = \dfrac{1}{ad - bc}\begin{pmatrix} d & -c \\ -b & a \end{pmatrix}$, provided $ad - bc \neq 0$.

$\mathbf{MM}^{-1} = \mathbf{M}^{-1}\mathbf{M} = \mathbf{I}$.

10 When solving n simultaneous equations in n unknowns, the equations can be written as a matrix equation.

$$\mathbf{M}\begin{pmatrix} x_1 \\ x_2 \\ \dots \\ x_n \end{pmatrix} = \begin{pmatrix} a_1 \\ a_2 \\ \dots \\ a_n \end{pmatrix}$$

If det $\mathbf{M} \neq 0$, there is a unique solution which can be found by pre-multiplying by the inverse matrix $\mathbf{M}^{-1}$.
If det $\mathbf{M} = 0$, then there is either no solution or infinitely many solutions.

11 The point P is known as an invariant point under ***T*** if the image of P under ***T*** is P.

2 Complex numbers

...that wonder of analysis, that portent of the ideal world, that amphibian between being and not-being, which we call the imaginary root of negative unity.

Leibniz, 1702

The growth of the number system

The number system we use today has taken thousands of years to develop. In primitive societies all that are needed are the *counting numbers*, 1, 2, 3,... (or even just the first few of these).

The concept of a *fraction* was first recorded in a systematic way in an Egyptian papyrus of about 1650 BC. By 500 BC the Greeks had developed ways of calculating with whole numbers and their ratios (which accounts for calling fractions *rational numbers*). The followers of Pythagoras believed that everything in geometry and in applications of mathematics could be explained in terms of rational numbers.

It came as a great shock, therefore, when one of them proved that $\sqrt{2}$ was not a rational number. However, Greek thinkers gradually came to terms with the existence of such *irrational numbers*, and by 370 BC Eudoxus had devised a very careful theory of proportion which included both rational and irrational numbers.

It took about another thousand years for the next major development, when the Hindu mathematician Brahmagupta (in about AD 630) described *negative numbers* and gave the rules for dealing with negative signs. Surprisingly, the first use of a symbol for zero came even later, in AD 876. This was the final element needed to complete the set of real numbers, consisting of positive and negative rational and irrational numbers and zero.

Figure 2.1 shows the relationships between the different types of numbers.

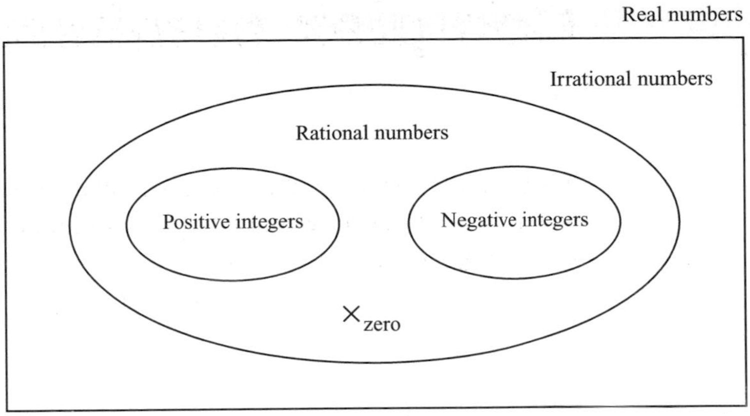

Figure 2.1

ACTIVITY 2.1 Copy figure 2.1 and write the following numbers in the correct positions.

$$3 \quad \pi \quad \frac{355}{113} \quad -1 \quad -1.4142 \quad -\sqrt{2}$$

Draw also a real number line and mark the same numbers on it.

The number system expanded in this way because people wanted to increase the range of problems they could tackle. This can be illustrated in terms of the sorts of equation that can be solved at each stage, although of course the standard algebraic way of writing these is relatively modern.

ACTIVITY 2.2 For each of these equations, make up a simple problem that would lead to the equation and say what sort of number is needed to solve the equation.

(i) $x + 7 = 10$ **(ii)** $7x = 10$

(iii) $x^2 = 10$ **(iv)** $x + 10 = 7$

(v) $x^2 + 7x = 0$ **(vi)** $x^2 + 10 = 0$

You will have hit a snag with equation **(vi)**. Since the square of every real number is positive or zero, there is no real number with a square of -10. This is a simple example of a quadratic equation with no real roots. The existence of such equations was recognised and accepted for hundreds of years, just as the Greeks had accepted that $x + 10 = 7$ had no solution.

Then two 16th century Italians, Tartaglia and Cardan, found methods of solving cubic and quartic (fourth degree) equations which forced mathematicians to take seriously the square roots of negative numbers. This required a further extension of the number system, to produce what are called *complex numbers.*

Complex numbers were regarded with great suspicion for many years. Descartes called them 'imaginary', Newton called them 'impossible', and Leibniz's mystification has already been quoted. But complex numbers turned out to be very useful, and had become accepted as an essential tool by the time Gauss first gave them a firm logical basis in 1831.

Working with complex numbers

Faced with the problem of wanting the square root of a negative number, we make the following Bold Hypothesis.

The real number system can be extended by including a new number, denoted by j, which combines with itself and the real numbers according to the usual laws of algebra, but which has the additional property that $j^2 = -1$.

The original notation for j was ι, the Greek letter iota. i is also commonly used instead of j.

The first thing to note is that we do not need further symbols for other square roots. For example, since $-196 = 196 \times (-1) = 14^2 \times j^2$, we see that -196 has two square roots, $\pm 14j$. The following example uses this idea to solve a quadratic equation with no real roots.

EXAMPLE 2.1

Solve the equation $z^2 - 6z + 58 = 0$, and check the roots.

(We use the letter z for the variable here because we want to keep x and y to stand for *real* numbers.)

SOLUTION

Using the quadratic formula:

$$
\begin{aligned}
z &= \frac{6 \pm \sqrt{6^2 - 4 \times 58}}{2} \\
&= \frac{6 \pm \sqrt{-196}}{2} \\
&= \frac{6 \pm 14j}{2} \\
&= 3 \pm 7j
\end{aligned}
$$

To check:

$$
\begin{aligned}
z = 3 + 7j \Rightarrow z^2 - 6z + 58 &= (3 + 7j)^2 - 6(3 + 7j) + 58 \\
&= 9 + 42j + 49j^2 - 18 - 42j + 58 \\
&= 9 + 42j - 49 - 18 - 42j + 58 \\
&= 0
\end{aligned}
$$

$j^2 = -1$

Notice that here 0 means $0 + 0j$.

ACTIVITY 2.3 Check the other root, $z = 3 - 7j$.

A number z of the form $x + yj$, where x and y are real, is called a *complex number*. x is called the real part of the complex number, denoted by $\text{Re}(z)$, and y is called the imaginary part, denoted by $\text{Im}(z)$. So if, for example, $z = 3 - 7j$ then $\text{Re}(z) = 3$ and $\text{Im}(z) = -7$. Notice in particular that the imaginary part is real!

In Example 2.1 you did some simple calculations with complex numbers. The general methods for addition, subtraction and multiplication are similarly straightforward.

Addition: add the real parts and add the imaginary parts.

$$(x + yj) + (u + vj) = (x + u) + (y + v)j$$

Subtraction: subtract the real parts and subtract the imaginary parts.

$$(x + yj) - (u + vj) = (x - u) + (y - v)j$$

Multiplication: multiply out the brackets in the usual way and simplify, remembering that $j^2 = -1$.

$$\begin{aligned}(x + yj)(u + vj) &= xu + xvj + yuj + yvj^2 \\ &= (xu - yv) + (xv + yu)j\end{aligned}$$

Division of complex numbers is dealt with later in the chapter.

? What are the values of j^3, j^4, j^5?

Explain how you would work out the value of j^n for any positive integer value of n.

Complex conjugates

The complex number $x - yj$ is called the *complex conjugate*, or just the *conjugate*, of $x + yj$. The complex conjugate of z is denoted by z^*. Notice from Example 2.1 that the two solutions of a quadratic equation with no real solutions are complex conjugates.

ACTIVITY 2.4

(i) Let $z = 3 + 5j$ and $w = 1 - 2j$.
Find the following.

(a) $z + z^*$ **(b)** $w + w^*$ **(c)** zz^* **(d)** ww^*

What do you notice about your answers?

(ii) Let $z = x + yj$.
Show that $z + z^*$ and zz^* are real for any values of x and y.

EXERCISE 2A

1 Express the following in the form $x + yj$.

(i) $(8 + 6j) + (6 + 4j)$ **(ii)** $(9 - 3j) + (-4 + 5j)$
(iii) $(2 + 7j) - (5 + 3j)$ **(iv)** $(5 - j) - (6 - 2j)$
(v) $3(4 + 6j) + 9(1 - 2j)$ **(vi)** $3j(7 - 4j)$
(vii) $(9 + 2j)(1 + 3j)$ **(viii)** $(4 - j)(3 + 2j)$
(ix) $(7 + 3j)^2$ **(x)** $(8 + 6j)(8 - 6j)$
(xi) $(1 + 2j)(3 - 4j)(5 + 6j)$ **(xii)** $(3 + 2j)^3$

2 Solve each of the following equations, and check the roots in each case.

(i) $z^2 + 2z + 2 = 0$ **(ii)** $z^2 - 2z + 5 = 0$
(iii) $z^2 - 4z + 13 = 0$ **(iv)** $z^2 + 6z + 34 = 0$
(v) $4z^2 - 4z + 17 = 0$ **(vi)** $z^2 + 4z + 6 = 0$

3 Given that $z = 2 + 3j$ and $w = 6 - 4j$, find the following.

(i) $\text{Re}(z)$ **(ii)** $\text{Im}(w)$
(iii) z^* **(iv)** w^*
(v) $z^* + w^*$ **(vi)** $z^* - w^*$
(vii) $\text{Im}(z + z^*)$ **(viii)** $\text{Re}(w - w^*)$
(ix) $zz^* - ww^*$ **(x)** $(z^3)^*$
(xi) $(z^*)^3$ **(xii)** $zw^* - z^*w$

4 Let $z = x + yj$.
Show that $(z^*)^* = z$.

5 Let $z_1 = x_1 + y_1j$ and $z_2 = x_2 + y_2j$.
Show that $(z_1 + z_2)^* = z_1^* + z_2^*$.

Division of complex numbers

Before tackling the slightly complicated problem of dividing by a complex number, you need to know what is meant by equality of complex numbers.

Two complex numbers $z = x + yj$ and $w = u + vj$ are equal if both $x = u$ and $y = v$. If $u \neq x$ or $v \neq y$, or both, then z and w are not equal.

You may feel that this is making a fuss about something which is obvious. However, think about the similar question of the equality of rational numbers. The rational numbers $\frac{x}{y}$ and $\frac{u}{v}$ are equal if $x = u$ and $y = v$.

? Is it possible for the rational numbers $\frac{x}{y}$ and $\frac{u}{v}$ to be equal if $u \neq x$ and $v \neq y$?

So for two complex numbers to be equal, the real parts must be equal and the imaginary parts must be equal. When we use this result we say that we are *equating real and imaginary parts.*

Equating real and imaginary parts is a very useful method which often yields 'two for the price of one' when working with complex numbers. The following example illustrates this.

EXAMPLE 2.2 Find real numbers p and q such that $p + q\text{j} = \dfrac{1}{3 + 5\text{j}}$.

SOLUTION

You need to find real numbers p and q such that

$$(p + q\text{j})(3 + 5\text{j}) = 1.$$

Expanding gives

$$3p - 5q + (5p + 3q)\text{j} = 1.$$

Equating real and imaginary parts gives

$$\begin{aligned} &\text{Real:} && 3p - 5q = 1 \\ &\text{Imaginary:} && 5p + 3q = 0. \end{aligned}$$

These simultaneous equations give $p = \frac{3}{34}$, $q = -\frac{5}{34}$ and so

$$\frac{1}{3 + 5\text{j}} = \frac{3}{34} - \frac{5}{34}\text{j}.$$

ACTIVITY 2.5 By writing $\dfrac{1}{x + y\text{j}} = p + q\text{j}$, show that $\dfrac{1}{x + y\text{j}} = \dfrac{x - y\text{j}}{x^2 + y^2}$.

This result shows that there is an easier way to find the reciprocal of a complex number. First, notice that

$$\begin{aligned} (x + y\text{j})(x - y\text{j}) &= x^2 - y^2\text{j}^2 \\ &= x^2 + y^2 \end{aligned}$$

which is real.

So to find the reciprocal of a complex number you multiply numerator and denominator by the complex conjugate of the denominator.

EXAMPLE 2.3 Find the real and imaginary parts of $\dfrac{1}{5 + 2\text{j}}$.

SOLUTION

Multiply numerator and denominator by $5 - 2\text{j}$.

$5 - 2\text{j}$ is the conjugate of the denominator, $5 + 2\text{j}$.

$$\begin{aligned} \frac{1}{5 + 2\text{j}} &= \frac{5 - 2\text{j}}{(5 + 2\text{j})(5 - 2\text{j})} \\ &= \frac{5 - 2\text{j}}{25 + 4} \\ &= \frac{5 - 2\text{j}}{29} \end{aligned}$$

so the real part is $\frac{5}{29}$, and the imaginary part is $-\frac{2}{29}$.

Note

You may have noticed that this process is very similar to the process of rationalising a denominator, which you met in C1. To make the denominator of $\frac{1}{3 + \sqrt{2}}$ rational you had to multiply the numerator and denominator by $3 - \sqrt{2}$.

Similarly, division of complex numbers is carried out by multiplying both numerator and denominator by the conjugate of the denominator, as in the next example.

EXAMPLE 2.4

Express $\frac{9 - 4\text{j}}{2 + 3\text{j}}$ as a complex number in the form $x + y\text{j}$.

SOLUTION

$$\begin{aligned}\frac{9 - 4\text{j}}{2 + 3\text{j}} &= \frac{9 - 4\text{j}}{2 + 3\text{j}} \times \frac{2 - 3\text{j}}{2 - 3\text{j}} \\ &= \frac{18 - 27\text{j} - 8\text{j} + 12\text{j}^2}{2^2 + 3^2} \\ &= \frac{6 - 35\text{j}}{13} \\ &= \tfrac{6}{13} - \tfrac{35}{13}\text{j}\end{aligned}$$

The corresponding general result is obtained in the same way:

$$\frac{x + y\text{j}}{u + v\text{j}} = \frac{(x + y\text{j})(u - v\text{j})}{(u + v\text{j})(u - v\text{j})} = \frac{xu + yv}{u^2 + v^2} + \frac{yu - xv}{u^2 + v^2}\text{j}$$

unless $u = v = 0$, in which case the division is impossible, not surprisingly, since the denominator is then zero.

? What are the values of $\frac{1}{\text{j}}$, $\frac{1}{\text{j}^2}$ and $\frac{1}{\text{j}^3}$?

Explain how you would work out the value of $\frac{1}{\text{j}^n}$ for any positive integer value of n.

The collapse of a Bold Hypothesis

You have just avoided a mathematical inconvenience (that –1 has no real square root) by introducing a new mathematical object, j, which has the property that you want: $\text{j}^2 = -1$.

What happens if you try the same approach to get rid of the equally inconvenient ban on dividing by zero? The problem here is that there is no real number equal to $1 \div 0$. So try making the Bold Hypothesis that you can introduce a new mathematical object which equals $1 \div 0$ but otherwise behaves like a real number. Denote this new object by ∞.

Then $1 \div 0 = \infty$, and so $1 = 0 \times \infty$.

But then you soon meet a contradiction:

$$
\begin{aligned}
& & 2 \times 0 &= 3 \times 0 \\
&\Rightarrow & (2 \times 0) \times \infty &= (3 \times 0) \times \infty \\
&\Rightarrow & 2 \times (0 \times \infty) &= 3 \times (0 \times \infty) \\
&\Rightarrow & 2 \times 1 &= 3 \times 1 \\
&\Rightarrow & 2 &= 3 \qquad \text{which is impossible.}
\end{aligned}
$$

So this Bold Hypothesis quickly leads to trouble. How can you be sure that the same will never happen with complex numbers? For the moment you will just have to take on trust that there is an answer, and that all is well.

EXERCISE 2B

1 Express these complex numbers in the form $x + y\text{j}$.

(i) $\dfrac{1}{3+\text{j}}$ **(ii)** $\dfrac{1}{6-\text{j}}$

(iii) $\dfrac{5\text{j}}{6-2\text{j}}$ **(iv)** $\dfrac{7+5\text{j}}{6-2\text{j}}$

(v) $\dfrac{3+2\text{j}}{1+\text{j}}$ **(vi)** $\dfrac{47-23\text{j}}{6+\text{j}}$

(vii) $\dfrac{2-3\text{j}}{3+2\text{j}}$ **(viii)** $\dfrac{5-3\text{j}}{4+3\text{j}}$

(ix) $\dfrac{6+\text{j}}{2-5\text{j}}$ **(x)** $\dfrac{12-8\text{j}}{(2+2\text{j})^2}$

2 Find real numbers a and b with $a > 0$ such that

(i) $(a + b\text{j})^2 = 21 + 20\text{j}$ **(ii)** $(a + b\text{j})^2 = -40 - 42\text{j}$

(iii) $(a + b\text{j})^2 = -5 - 12\text{j}$ **(iv)** $(a + b\text{j})^2 = -9 + 40\text{j}$

(v) $(a + b\text{j})^2 = 1 - 1.875\text{j}$ **(vi)** $(a + b\text{j})^2 = \text{j}$.

3 Find real numbers a and b such that

$$\frac{a}{3+\text{j}} + \frac{b}{1+2\text{j}} = 1 - \text{j}.$$

4 Solve these equations.

(i) $(1 + \text{j})z = 3 + \text{j}$

(ii) $(3 - 4\text{j})(z - 1) = 10 - 5\text{j}$

(iii) $(2 + \text{j})(z - 7 + 3\text{j}) = 15 - 10\text{j}$

(iv) $(3 + 5\text{j})(z + 2 - 5\text{j}) = 6 + 3\text{j}$

5 Find all the complex numbers z for which $z^2 = 2z^*$.

6 For $z = x + y\text{j}$, find $\dfrac{1}{z} + \dfrac{1}{z^*}$ in terms of x and y.

7 Show that

(i) $\text{Re}(z) = \dfrac{z + z^*}{2}$ **(ii)** $\text{Im}(z) = \dfrac{z - z^*}{2\text{j}}$.

8 **(i)** Expand and simplify $(a + bj)^3$.
(ii) Deduce that if $(a + bj)^3$ is real then either $b = 0$ or $b^2 = 3a^2$.
(iii) Hence find all the complex numbers z for which $z^3 = 1$.

9 **(i)** Expand and simplify $(z - \alpha)(z - \beta)$.
Deduce that the quadratic equation with roots α and β is

$$z^2 - (\alpha + \beta)z + \alpha\beta = 0,$$

that is:

$$z^2 - (\text{sum of roots})z + \text{product of roots} = 0.$$

(ii) Using the result from part **(i)**, find quadratic equations in the form $az^2 + bz + c = 0$ with the following roots.

(a) $7 + 4j, 7 - 4j$ **(b)** $\frac{5j}{3}, -\frac{5j}{3}$

(c) $-2 + \sqrt{8}j, -2 - \sqrt{8}j$ **(d)** $2 + j, 3 + 2j$

10 ☆ Find an example to show that non-real numbers p and q may be found such that the equation $z^2 + pz + q = 0$ has a real root.
Is it possible for the equation to have two real roots if p and q are non-real?

11 ☆ **(i)** Evaluate the following.
(a) $(1 + j)^2$
(b) $(1 + j)^4$
(c) $(1 + j)^{4k}$, where k is a positive integer

(ii) By considering the binomial expansion of $(1 + j)^{4k}$, prove that

$${}^{4k}C_0 - {}^{4k}C_2 + {}^{4k}C_4 - {}^{4k}C_6 + \ldots + {}^{4k}C_{4k} = (-4)^k.$$

(iii) Check this numerically in the following cases.
(a) $k = 3$ **(b)** $k = 4$

(iv) Investigate in a similar way the value of

$${}^{4k+2}C_1 - {}^{4k+2}C_3 + {}^{4k+2}C_5 - {}^{4k+2}C_7 + \ldots + {}^{4k+2}C_{4k+1}.$$

e *The remaining questions relate to enrichment material.*

12 The complex numbers z and w satisfy the following simultaneous equations.

$$z + jw = 13$$
$$3z - 4w = 2j$$

Find z and w, giving your answers in the form $a + bj$.

[MEI, *part*]

13 Given that $z = 2 + 3j$ is a solution of the equation

$$z^2 + (a - j)z + 16 + bj = 0$$

where a and b are real, find a, b and the other solution of the equation.

Representing complex numbers geometrically

Since each complex number $x + yj$ can be defined by the ordered pair of real numbers (x, y), it is natural to represent $x + yj$ by the point with cartesian co-ordinates (x, y).

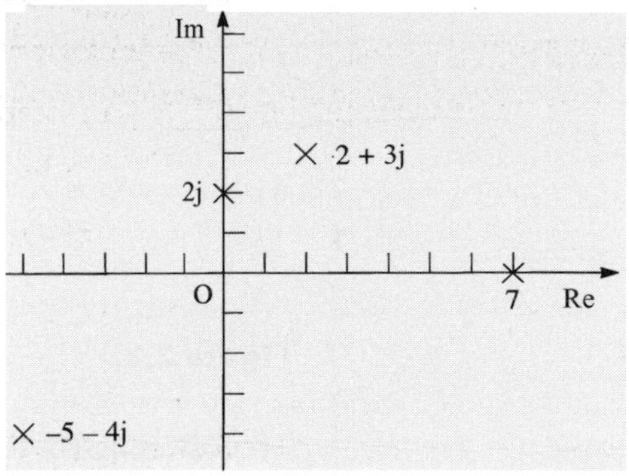

Figure 2.2

For example, in figure 2.2,

$2 + 3j$	is represented by	$(2, 3)$
$-5 - 4j$	is represented by	$(-5, -4)$
$2j$	is represented by	$(0, 2)$
7	is represented by	$(7, 0)$.

All real numbers are represented by points on the x axis, which is therefore called the *real axis*. Pure imaginary numbers (of the form $0 + yj$) give points on the y axis, which is called the *imaginary axis*. It is useful to label these Re and Im respectively. This geometrical illustration of complex numbers is called the *complex plane* or the *Argand diagram* after Jean-Robert Argand (1768–1822), a self-taught Swiss book-keeper who published an account of it in 1806.

ACTIVITY 2.6

(i) Copy figure 2.2.
For each of the four given points z mark also the point $-z$.
Describe the geometrical transformation which maps the point representing z to the point representing $-z$.

(ii) For each of the points z mark the point z^*, the complex conjugate of z.
Describe the geometrical transformation which maps the point representing z to the point representing z^*.

You will have seen in this activity that the points representing z and $-z$ have half-turn symmetry about the origin, and that the points representing z and z^* are reflections of each other in the real axis.

? How would you describe points that are reflections of each other in the imaginary axis?

Representing the sum and difference of complex numbers

Several mathematicians before Argand had used the complex plane representation. In particular, a Norwegian surveyor, Caspar Wessel (1745–1818), wrote a paper in 1797 (largely ignored until it was republished in French a century later) in which the complex number $x + yj$ is represented by the position vector $\begin{pmatrix} x \\ y \end{pmatrix}$, shown in figure 2.3.

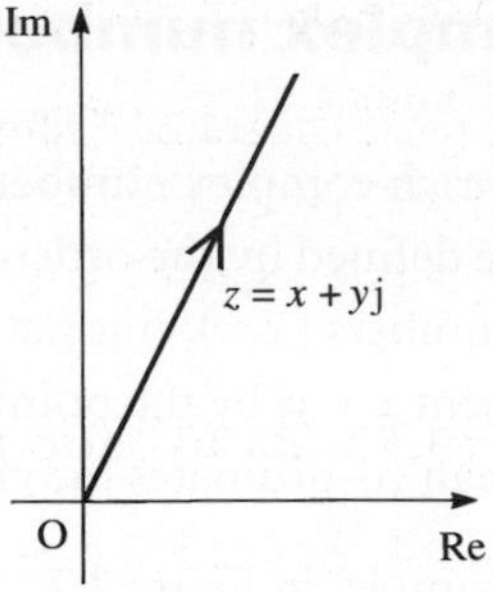

Figure 2.3

The advantage of this is that the addition of complex numbers can then be shown by the addition of the corresponding vectors.

$$\begin{pmatrix} x_1 \\ y_1 \end{pmatrix} + \begin{pmatrix} x_2 \\ y_2 \end{pmatrix} = \begin{pmatrix} x_1 + x_2 \\ y_1 + y_2 \end{pmatrix}$$

In an Argand diagram the position vectors representing z_1 and z_2 form two sides of a parallelogram, the diagonal of which is the vector $z_1 + z_2$ (see figure 2.4).

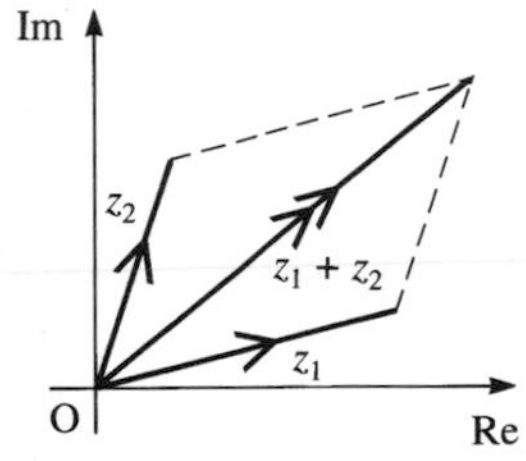

Figure 2.4

You can also represent z by any other directed line segment with components $\begin{pmatrix} x \\ y \end{pmatrix}$, not anchored at the origin as a position vector. Then addition can be shown as a triangle of vectors (see figure 2.5).

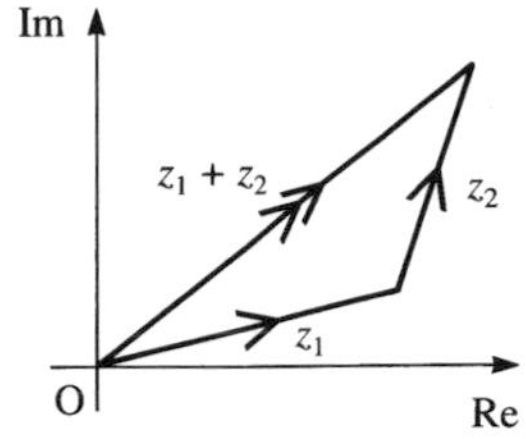

Figure 2.5

If you draw the other diagonal of the parallelogram, and let it represent the complex number w (see figure 2.6), then

$$z_2 + w = z_1 \Rightarrow w = z_1 - z_2.$$

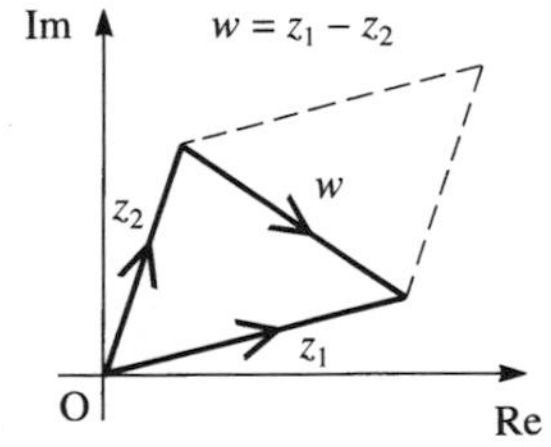

Figure 2.6

This gives a useful illustration of subtraction: the complex number $z_1 - z_2$ is represented by the vector from the point representing z_2 to the point representing z_1, as shown in figure 2.7. Notice the order of the points: the vector $z_1 - z_2$ starts at the point z_2 and goes to the point z_1.

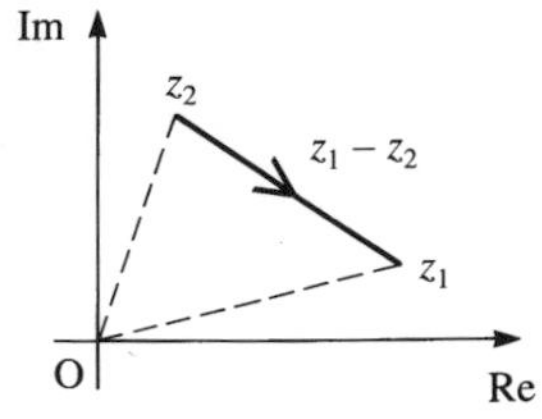

Figure 2.7

ACTIVITY 2.7

(i) Draw a diagram to illustrate $z_2 - z_1$.

(ii) Draw a diagram to illustrate that $z_1 - z_2 = z_1 + (-z_2)$.
Show that $z_1 + (-z_2)$ gives the same vector, $z_1 - z_2$ as before, but represented by a line segment in a different place.

The modulus of a complex number

Figure 2.8 shows the point representing $z = x + y\text{j}$ on an Argand diagram.

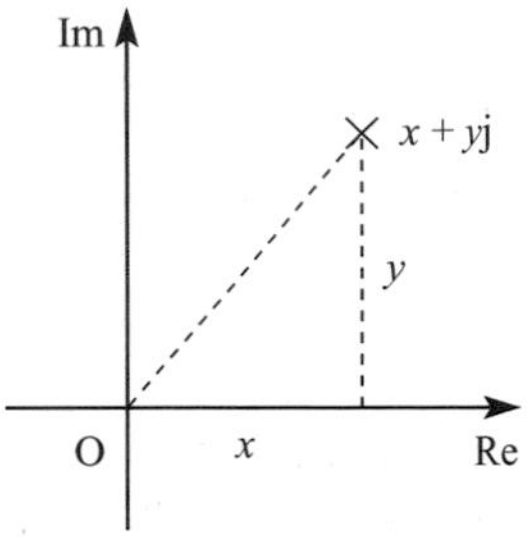

Figure 2.8

Using Pythagoras' theorem, you can see that the distance of this point from the origin is $\sqrt{x^2 + y^2}$. This distance is called the modulus of z, and is denoted by $|z|$.

So for the complex number $z = x + y\text{j}$, $|z| = \sqrt{x^2 + y^2}$.

If z is real, $z = x$ say, then $|z| = \sqrt{x^2}$, which is the absolute value of x, i.e. $|x|$. So the use of the modulus sign with complex numbers fits with its previous meaning for real numbers.

EXERCISE 2C

1 Represent each of the following complex numbers on a single Argand diagram, and find the modulus of each complex number.

(i) $3 + 2\text{j}$ **(ii)** 4j **(iii)** $-5 + \text{j}$

(iv) -2 **(v)** $-6 - 5\text{j}$ **(vi)** $4 - 3\text{j}$

2 Given that $z = 2 - 4\text{j}$, represent the following by points on a single Argand diagram.

(i) z **(ii)** $-z$ **(iii)** z^*

(iv) $-z^*$ **(v)** $\text{j}z$ **(vi)** $-\text{j}z$

(vii) $\text{j}z^*$ **(viii)** $(\text{j}z)^*$

3 Given that $z = 10 + 5\text{j}$ and $w = 1 + 2\text{j}$, represent the following complex numbers on an Argand diagram.

(i) z **(ii)** w **(iii)** $z + w$

(iv) $z - w$ **(v)** $w - z$

4 Given that $z = 3 + 4j$ and $w = 5 - 12j$, find the following.

(i) $|z|$ **(ii)** $|w|$ **(iii)** $|zw|$

(iv) $\left|\frac{z}{w}\right|$ **(v)** $\left|\frac{w}{z}\right|$

What do you notice?

5 Let $z = 1 + j$.

(i) Find z^n and $|z^n|$ for $n = -1, 0, 1, 2, 3, 4, 5$.

(ii) Plot each of the points z^n from part **(i)** on a single Argand diagram. Join each point to its predecessor and to the origin.

(iii) What do you notice?

6 Give a geometrical proof that $(-z)^* = -(z^*)$.

Sets of points in an Argand diagram

? In the last section, you saw that $|z|$ is the distance of the point representing z from the origin in the Argand diagram.

What do you think that $|z_2 - z_1|$ represents?

If $z_1 = x_1 + y_1 j$ and $z_2 = x_2 + y_2 j$, then $z_2 - z_1 = x_2 - x_1 + (y_2 - y_1)j$.

So $|z_2 - z_1| = \sqrt{(x_2 - x_1)^2 + (y_2 - y_1)^2}$.

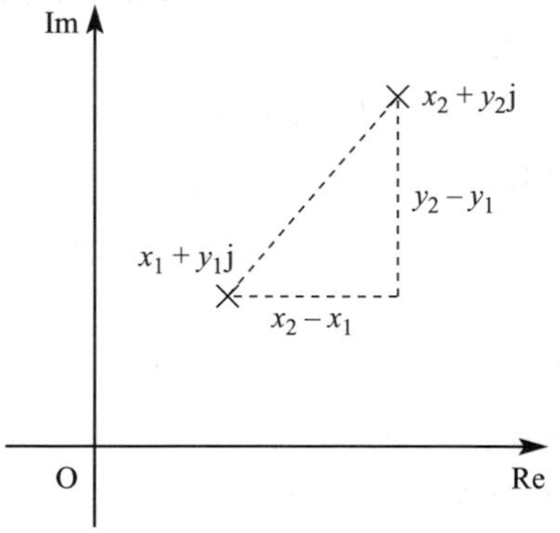

Figure 2.9

Figure 2.9 shows an Argand diagram with the points representing the complex numbers $z_1 = x_1 + y_1 j$ and $z_2 = x_2 + y_2 j$ marked.

Using Pythagoras' theorem, you can see that the distance between z_1 and z_2 is given by $\sqrt{(x_2 - x_1)^2 + (y_2 - y_1)^2}$.

So $|z_2 - z_1|$ is the distance between the points z_1 and z_2.

This is the key to solving many questions about sets of points in an Argand diagram, as in the following examples.

EXAMPLE 2.5

Draw an Argand diagram showing the set of points z for which $|z - 3 - 4j| = 5$.

SOLUTION

$|z - 3 - 4j|$ can be written as $|z - (3 + 4j)|$, and this is the distance from the point $3 + 4j$ to the point z.

This equals 5 if the point z lies on the circle with centre $3 + 4j$ and radius 5 (see figure 2.10).

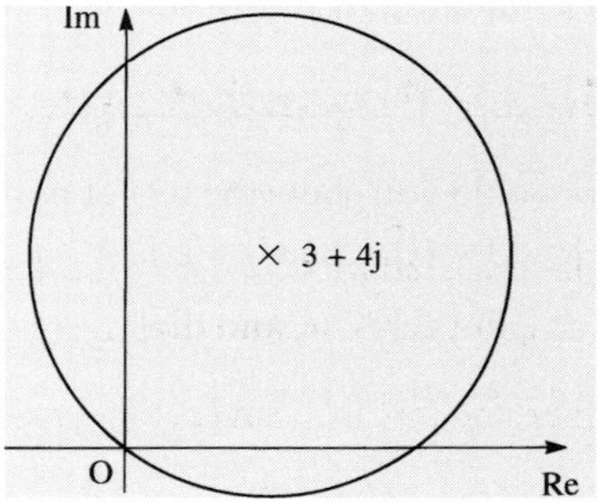

Figure 2.10

? How would you show the sets of points for which

(i) $|z - 3 - 4j| \leqslant 5$

(ii) $|z - 3 - 4j| < 5$

(iii) $|z - 3 - 4j| \geqslant 5$?

EXAMPLE 2.6

e *This example is enrichment material.*

Draw an Argand diagram showing the set of points z for which $|z - 3 - 4j| \leqslant |z + 1 - 2j|$.

SOLUTION

The condition can be written as $|z - (3 + 4j)| \leqslant |z - (-1 + 2j)|$.

$|z - (3 + 4j)|$ is the distance of point z from the point $3 + 4j$, point A in figure 2.11, and $|z - (-1 + 2j)|$ is the distance of point z from the point $-1 + 2j$, point B in figure 2.11.

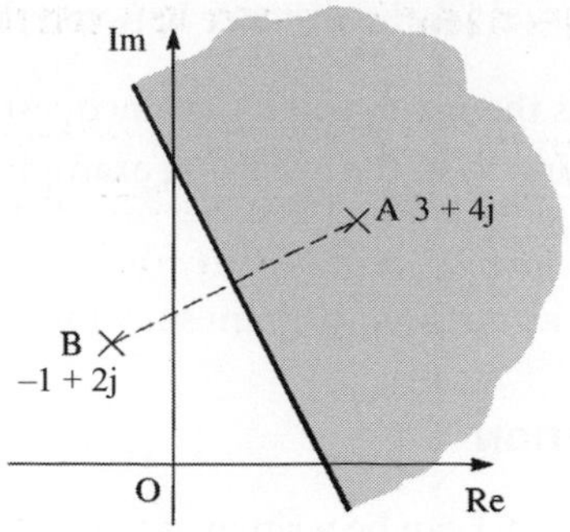

Figure 2.11

These distances are equal if z is on the perpendicular bisector of AB.

So the given condition holds if z is on this bisector or in the half plane on the side of it containing A, shown shaded in figure 2.11.

How would you show the sets of points for which

(i) $|z - 3 - 4j| = |z + 1 - 2j|$

(ii) $|z - 3 - 4j| < |z + 1 - 2j|$

(iii) $|z - 3 - 4j| > |z + 1 - 2j|$?

EXERCISE 2D

1 For each of parts **(i)** to **(viii)**, draw an Argand diagram showing the set of points z for which the given condition is true.

(i) $|z| = 2$ **(ii)** $|z - 4| \leqslant 3$

(iii) $|z - 5j| = 6$ **(iv)** $|z + 3 - 4j| < 5$

(v) $|6 - j - z| \geqslant 2$ **(vi)** $|z + 2 + 4j| = 0$

(vii) $2 \leqslant |z - 1 + j| \leqslant 3$ **(viii)** $\text{Re}(z) = -2$

2 Draw an Argand diagram showing the set of points z for which $|z - 12 + 5j| \leqslant 7$. Use the diagram to prove that, for these z, $6 \leqslant |z| \leqslant 20$.

3 ☆☆ What are the greatest and least values of $|z + 3 - 2j|$ if

$$|z - 5 + 4j| \leqslant 3?$$

4 ☆☆ By using an Argand diagram see if it is possible to find values of z for which $|z - 2 + j| \geqslant 10$ and $|z + 4 + 2j| \leqslant 2$ simultaneously.

The remaining question relates to enrichment material.

5 For each of parts **(i)** to **(iv)**, draw an Argand diagram showing the set of points z for which the given condition is true.

(i) $|z| = |z - 4|$ **(ii)** $|z| \geqslant |z - 2j|$

(iii) $|z + 1 - j| = |z - 1 + j|$ **(iv)** $|z + 5 + 7j| \leqslant |z - 2 - 6j|$

The modulus–argument form of complex numbers

The position of the point z in an Argand diagram can be described by means of the length of the line connecting this point to the origin, and the angle which this line makes with the positive real axis (see figure 2.12).

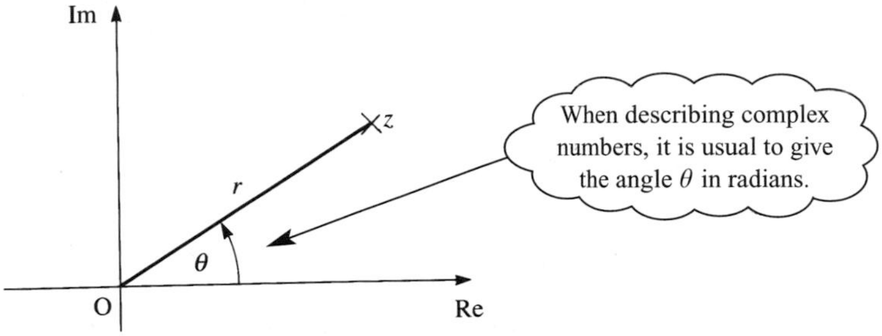

Figure 2.12

The distance r is of course $|z|$, the modulus of z as defined on page 57.

The angle θ is slightly more complicated: it is measured anticlockwise from the positive real axis, normally in radians. However, it is not uniquely defined since adding any multiple of 2π to θ gives the same direction. To avoid confusion, it is usual to choose that value of θ for which $-\pi < \theta \leqslant \pi$. This is called the *principal argument* of z, denoted by arg z. Then every complex number except zero has a unique principal argument. The argument of zero is undefined.

For example, with reference to figure 2.13,

$$\arg(-4) = \pi$$

$$\arg(-2j) = -\frac{\pi}{2}$$

$$\arg(1.5) = 0$$

$$\arg(-3 + 3j) = \frac{3\pi}{4}$$

Remember that π radians = 180°.

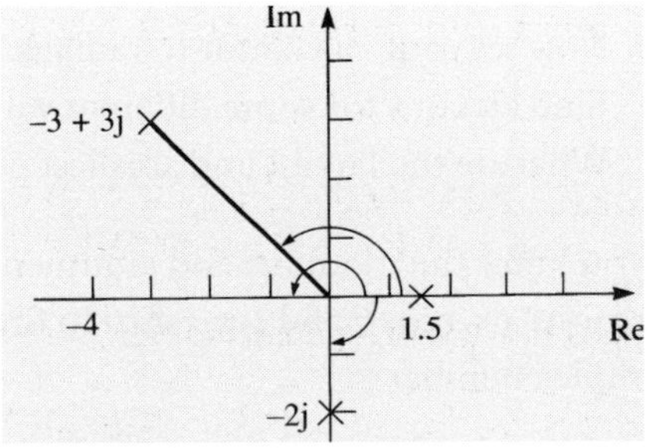

Figure 2.13

? Without using your calculator, state the values of the following.

(i) arg j **(ii)** arg (–4 – 4j) **(iii)** arg (2 – 2j)

You can see from figure 2.14 that

$$x = r\cos\theta \qquad y = r\sin\theta$$

$$r = \sqrt{x^2 + y^2} \qquad \tan\theta = \frac{y}{x}$$

and the same relations hold in the other quadrants too.

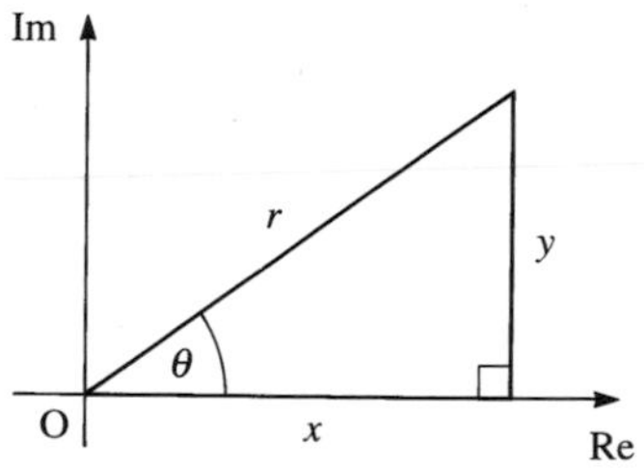

Figure 2.14

Since $x = r\cos\theta$ and $y = r\sin\theta$, we can write the complex number $z = x + y\text{j}$ in the form

$$z = r(\cos\theta + \text{j}\sin\theta).$$

This is called the *modulus–argument* form.

ACTIVITY 2.8

(i) Set your calculator to degrees and use it to find the following.

(a) arctan 1 **(b)** arctan 2 **(c)** arctan 100

(d) arctan (–2) **(e)** arctan (–50) **(f)** arctan (–200)

(Note: your calculator may use $\tan^{-1}x$ or inv tan x to mean arctan x.)

What are the largest and smallest possible values, in degrees, of arctan x?

(ii) Now set your calculator to radians.
Find arctan x for some different values of x.
What are the largest and smallest possible values, in radians, of arctan x?

If you know the modulus and argument of a complex number, it is easy to use the relations $x = r\cos\theta$ and $y = r\sin\theta$ to find the real and imaginary parts of the complex number.

Similarly, if you know the real and imaginary parts, you can find the modulus and argument of the complex number using the relations $r = \sqrt{x^2 + y^2}$ and $\tan\theta = \frac{y}{x}$, but you do have to be quite careful in finding the argument. It is tempting to say that $\theta = \arctan\left(\frac{y}{x}\right)$, but, as you saw in the last activity, this gives a value between $-\frac{\pi}{2}$ and $\frac{\pi}{2}$, which is correct only if z is in the first or fourth quadrants.

For example, suppose that the point $z_1 = 2 - 3j$ has argument θ_1, and the point $z_2 = -2 + 3j$ has argument θ_2.
It is true to say that $\tan\theta_1 = \tan\theta_2 = -\frac{3}{2}$. In the case of z_1, which is in the fourth quadrant, θ_1 is correctly given by $\arctan\left(-\frac{3}{2}\right) \approx -0.98$ rad ($\approx -56°$). However, in the case of z_2, which is in the second quadrant, θ_2 is given by $\left(-\frac{3}{2}\right) + \pi \approx 2.16$ rad ($\approx 124°$) These two points are illustrated in figure 2.15.

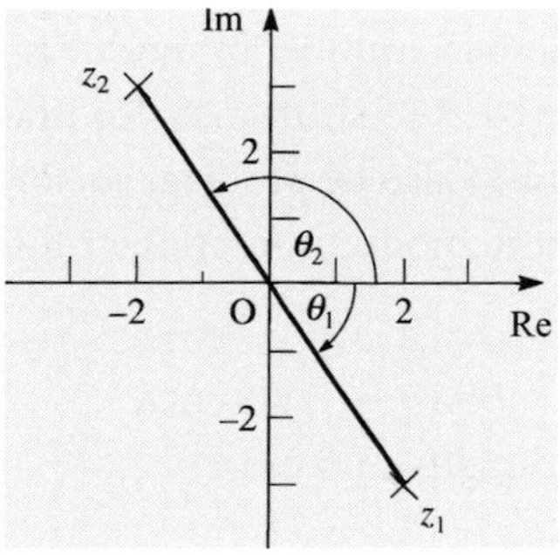

Figure 2.15

Figure 2.16 shows the values of the argument in each quadrant. It is wise always to draw a sketch diagram when finding the argument of a complex number.

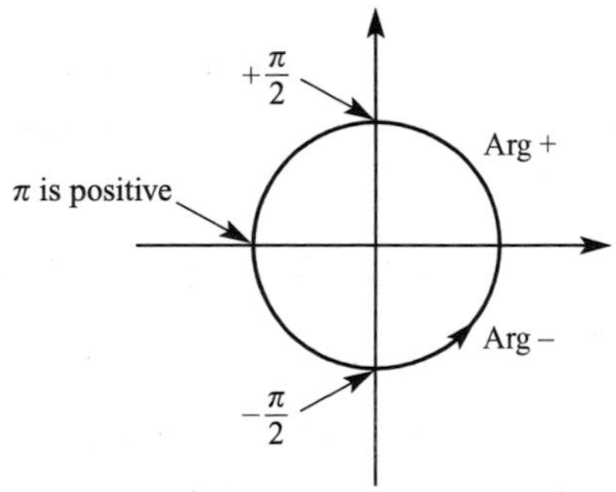

Figure 2.16

ACTIVITY 2.9 Mark the points $1 + j$, $1 - j$, $-1 + j$, $-1 - j$ on an Argand diagram.
Find $\arg z$ for each of these, and check that your answers are consistent with figure 2.16.

Note

The modulus–argument form of a complex number is sometimes called the *polar* form, as the modulus of a complex number is its distance from the origin, sometimes called the *pole*. Equations of curves can be given in polar form: this is covered in FP2.

ACTIVITY 2.10 Most calculators can convert from (x, y) to (r, θ) (called *rectangular* to *polar*, and often shown as R → P) and from (r, θ) to (x, y) (polar to rectangular, P → R). Find out how to use these facilities on your calculator, and compare with other available types of calculator.
Does your calculator always give the correct θ, or do you sometimes have to add or subtract π (or 180°)?

A complex number in modulus–argument form must be given in the form $z = r(\cos\theta + \mathrm{j}\sin\theta)$, not, for example, in the form $z = r(\cos\theta - \mathrm{j}\sin\theta)$. The value of r must also be positive. So, for example, the complex number $-2(\cos\alpha + \mathrm{j}\sin\alpha)$ is not in modulus–argument form. However, by using some of the relationships

$$\cos(\pi - \alpha) = -\cos\alpha \qquad \sin(\pi - \alpha) = \sin\alpha$$
$$\cos(\alpha - \pi) = -\cos\alpha \qquad \sin(\alpha - \pi) = -\sin\alpha$$
$$\cos(-\alpha) = \cos\alpha \qquad \sin(-\alpha) = -\sin\alpha$$

you can rewrite the complex number, for example

$$\begin{aligned}-2(\cos\alpha + \mathrm{j}\sin\alpha) &= 2(-\cos\alpha - \mathrm{j}\sin\alpha)\\ &= 2(\cos(\alpha - \pi) + \mathrm{j}\sin(\alpha - \pi)).\end{aligned}$$

This is now written correctly in modulus–argument form. The modulus is 2 and the argument is $\alpha - \pi$.

? How would you rewrite the following in modulus–argument form?
(i) $-2(\cos\alpha - \mathrm{j}\sin\alpha)$ **(ii)** $2(\cos\alpha - \mathrm{j}\sin\alpha)$

When you use the modulus–argument form of a complex number, remember to give the argument in radians, and to use a simple rational multiple of π where possible.

ACTIVITY 2.11 Copy and complete this table.
Give your answers in terms of $\sqrt{2}$ or $\sqrt{3}$ where appropriate, rather than as decimals. You may find figure 2.17 helpful.

	$\frac{\pi}{4}$	$\frac{\pi}{6}$	$\frac{\pi}{3}$
tan			
sin			
cos			

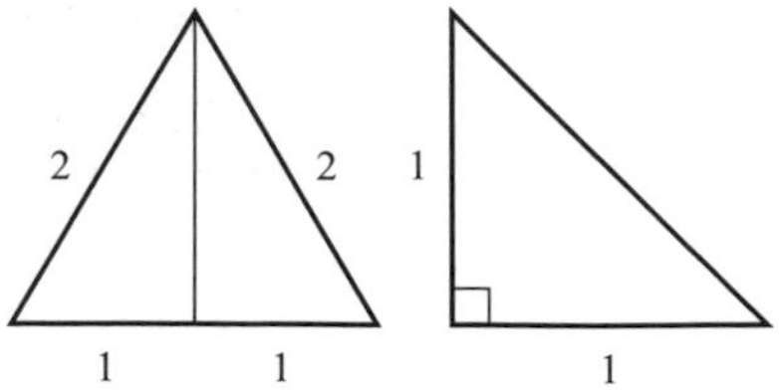

Figure 2.17

EXAMPLE 2.7

Write the following complex numbers in modulus–argument form.

(i) $4 + 3j$ **(ii)** $-1 + j$ **(iii)** $-1 - \sqrt{3}j$

SOLUTION

(i) $x = 4, y = 3$

Modulus $= \sqrt{3^2 + 4^2} = 5$

Since $4 + 3j$ lies in the first quadrant, the argument $= \arctan \frac{3}{4}$.

$4 + 3j = 5(\cos\alpha + j\sin\alpha)$, where $\alpha = \arctan\frac{3}{4} \approx 0.644$ radians

(ii) $x = -1, y = 1$

Modulus $= \sqrt{1^2 + 1^2} = \sqrt{2}$

Since $-1 + j$ lies in the second quadrant,

$$\begin{aligned}\text{argument} &= \arctan(-1) + \pi \\ &= -\frac{\pi}{4} + \pi = \frac{3\pi}{4}.\end{aligned}$$

$$-1 + j = \sqrt{2}\left(\cos\frac{3\pi}{4} + j\sin\frac{3\pi}{4}\right)$$

(iii) $x = -1, y = -\sqrt{3}$

Modulus $= \sqrt{1 + 3} = 2$

Since $-1 - \sqrt{3}j$ lies in the third quadrant,

$$\begin{aligned}\text{argument} &= \arctan\sqrt{3} - \pi \\ &= \frac{\pi}{3} - \pi = -\frac{2\pi}{3}.\end{aligned}$$

$$-1 - \sqrt{3}j = 2\left(\cos\left(-\frac{2\pi}{3}\right) + j\sin\left(-\frac{2\pi}{3}\right)\right)$$

ACTIVITY 2.12 **e** *This activity is enrichment material.*

The complex numbers w and z are given by $w = 1 + j$ and $z = 1 - \sqrt{3}j$.

(i) Find **(a)** wz **(b)** $\frac{w}{z}$.

(ii) Find the modulus and argument of the following.

(a) w **(b)** z **(c)** wz **(d)** $\frac{w}{z}$

(iii) What are the relationships between $|w|$, $|z|$, $|wz|$ and $\left|\frac{w}{z}\right|$?

What are the relationships between $\arg w$, $\arg z$, $\arg wz$ and $\arg \frac{w}{z}$?

(iv) Now let $w = r_1(\cos\theta_1 + j\sin\theta_1)$ and $z = r_2(\cos\theta_2 + j\sin\theta_2)$.

(a) Find expressions for wz and $\frac{w}{z}$ and use the expressions you found for $\sin(\alpha + \beta)$, $\cos(\alpha + \beta)$, $\sin(\alpha - \beta)$ and $\cos(\alpha - \beta)$ in Activity 1.10 on page 25 to write these in modulus–argument form.

(b) Hence find expressions for $|wz|$, $\left|\frac{w}{z}\right|$, $\arg wz$ and $\arg \frac{w}{z}$.

EXERCISE 2E

1 Write down the values of the modulus and the principal argument of each of these complex numbers.

(i) $8\left(\cos\frac{\pi}{5} + j\sin\frac{\pi}{5}\right)$ **(ii)** $\frac{\cos 2.3 + j\sin 2.3}{4}$

(iii) $4\left(\cos\frac{\pi}{5} - j\sin\frac{\pi}{3}\right)$ **(iv)** $-3(\cos(-3) + j\sin(-3))$

2 For each complex number, find the modulus and principal argument, and hence write the complex number in modulus–argument form.
Give the argument in radians, either as a simple rational multiple of π or correct to 3 decimal places.

(i) 1 **(ii)** -2 **(iii)** $3j$
(iv) $-4j$ **(v)** $1 + j$ **(vi)** $-5 - 5j$
(vii) $1 - \sqrt{3}j$ **(viii)** $6\sqrt{3} + 6j$ **(ix)** $3 - 4j$
(x) $-12 + 5j$ **(xi)** $4 + 7j$ **(xii)** $-58 - 93j$

3 Write each complex number with the given modulus and argument in the form $x + yj$, giving surds in your answer where appropriate.

(i) $|z| = 2$, $\arg z = \frac{\pi}{2}$ **(ii)** $|z| = 3$, $\arg z = \frac{\pi}{3}$

(iii) $|z| = 7$, $\arg z = \frac{5\pi}{6}$ **(iv)** $|z| = 1$, $\arg z = -\frac{\pi}{4}$

(v) $|z| = 5$, $\arg z = -\frac{2\pi}{3}$ **(vi)** $|z| = 6$, $\arg z = -2$

4 Given that $\arg(5 + 2j) = \alpha$, find the principal argument of each of the following in terms of α.

(i) $-5 - 2j$ **(ii)** $5 - 2j$ **(iii)** $-5 + 2j$
(iv) $2 + 5j$ **(v)** $-2 + 5j$

Sets of points using the modulus–argument form

? You already know that $\arg z$ gives the angle between the line connecting the point z with the origin and the real axis.

What do you think $\arg(z_2 - z_1)$ represents?

If $z_1 = x_1 + y_1\text{j}$ and $z_2 = x_2 + y_2\text{j}$, then $z_2 - z_1 = x_2 - x_1 + (y_2 - y_1)\text{j}$.

$$\arg(z_2 - z_1) = \arctan\frac{y_2 - y_1}{x_2 - x_1}$$

Figure 2.18 shows an Argand diagram with the points representing the complex numbers $z_1 = x_1 + y_1\text{j}$ and $z_2 = x_2 + y_2\text{j}$ marked.

The angle between the line joining z_1 and z_2 and a line parallel to the real axis is given by

$$\arctan\frac{y_2 - y_1}{x_2 - x_1}.$$

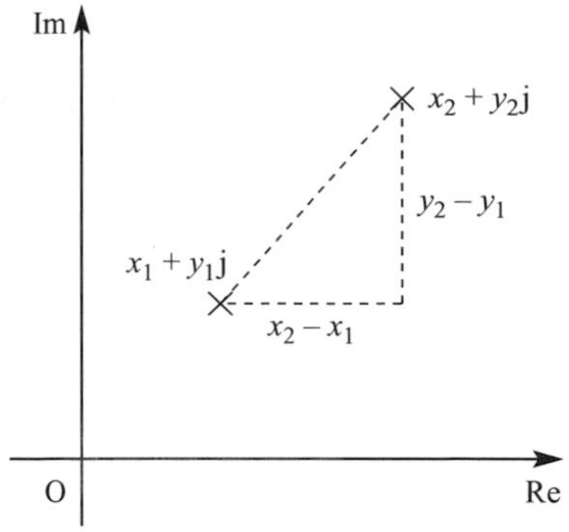

Figure 2.18

So $\arg(z_1 - z_2)$ is the angle between the line joining z_1 and z_2 and a line parallel to the real axis.

EXAMPLE 2.8

Draw Argand diagrams showing the sets of points z for which

(i) $\arg z = \frac{\pi}{4}$

(ii) $\arg(z - \text{j}) = \frac{\pi}{4}$

(iii) $0 \leqslant \arg(z - \text{j}) \leqslant \frac{\pi}{4}$.

SOLUTION

(i) $\arg z = \frac{\pi}{4} \Leftrightarrow$ the line joining the origin to the point z has direction $\frac{\pi}{4}$

$\Leftrightarrow z$ lies on the half-line from the origin in the $\frac{\pi}{4}$ direction, see figure 2.19.

(Note that the origin is not included, since $\arg 0$ is undefined.)

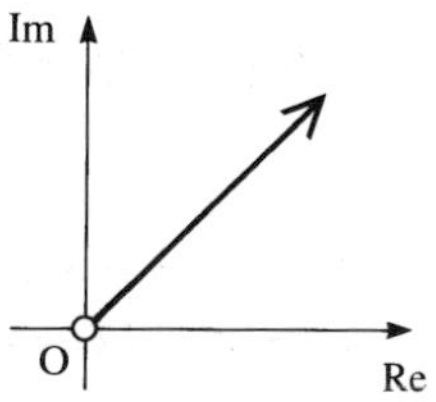

Figure 2.19

(ii) $\arg(z-\mathrm{j}) = \frac{\pi}{4} \Leftrightarrow$ the line joining the point j to the point z has direction $\frac{\pi}{4}$

$\Leftrightarrow z$ lies on the half-line from the point j in the $\frac{\pi}{4}$ direction, see figure 2.20.

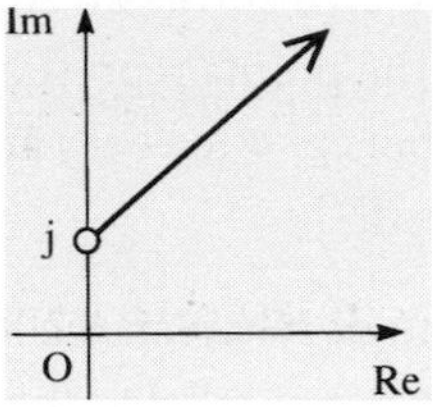

Figure 2.20

(iii) $0 \leqslant \arg(z-\mathrm{j}) \leqslant \frac{\pi}{4} \Leftrightarrow$ the line joining the point j to the point z has direction between 0 and $\frac{\pi}{4}$ (inclusive)

$\Leftrightarrow z$ lies in the one-eighth plane shown in figure 2.21.

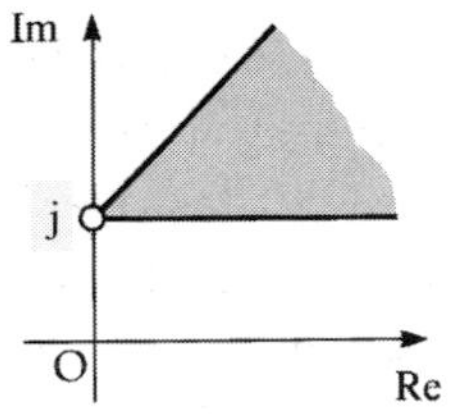

Figure 2.21

EXERCISE 2F

1 For each of parts **(i)** to **(vi)** draw an Argand diagram showing the set of points z for which the given condition is true.

(i) $\arg z = -\frac{\pi}{3}$

(ii) $\arg(z-4\mathrm{j}) = 0$

(iii) $\arg(z+3) \geqslant \frac{\pi}{2}$

(iv) $\arg(z+1+2\mathrm{j}) = \frac{3\pi}{4}$

(v) $\arg(z-3+\mathrm{j}) \leqslant -\frac{\pi}{6}$

(vi) $-\frac{\pi}{4} \leqslant \arg(z+5-3\mathrm{j}) \leqslant \frac{\pi}{3}$

2 Find the least and greatest possible values of $\arg z$ if $|z-8\mathrm{j}| \leqslant 4$.

3 You are given the complex number $w = -\sqrt{3} + 3\mathrm{j}$.

(i) Find $\arg w$ and $|w-2\mathrm{j}|$.

(ii) On an Argand diagram, shade the region representing complex numbers z which satisfy both of these inequalities.

$$|z-2\mathrm{j}| \leqslant 2 \quad \text{and} \quad \tfrac{1}{2}\pi \leqslant \arg z \leqslant \tfrac{2}{3}\pi.$$

Indicate the point on your diagram which corresponds to w.

(iii) Given that z satisfies both the inequalities in part **(ii)**, find the greatest possible value of $|z - w|$.

[MEI, *part*]

4 (i) If k is positive and $|z| \leqslant k$, prove that $0 \leqslant |z + k| \leqslant 2k$ and $-\frac{\pi}{2} < \arg(z + k) < \frac{\pi}{2}$.

☆☆☆ **(ii)** Find the least and greatest values of $|z + 2k|$ and $\arg(z + 2k)$.

Complex numbers and equations

The reason for inventing complex numbers was to provide solutions for quadratic equations which have no real roots, i.e. to solve $az^2 + bz + c = 0$ when the discriminant $b^2 - 4ac$ is negative. This is straightforward since if $b^2 - 4ac = -k^2$ (where k is real) then the formula for solving quadratic equations gives $z = \frac{-b \pm k\text{j}}{2a}$. These are the two complex roots of the equation. Notice that these roots are a pair of *conjugate* complex numbers.

It would be natural to think that to solve cubic equations would require a further extension of the number system to give some sort of 'super-complex' numbers, with ever more extensions to deal with higher degree equations. But luckily things are much simpler. It turns out that *all* polynomial equations (even those with complex coefficients) can be solved by means of complex numbers. This was realised as early as 1629 by Albert Girard, who stated that an nth degree polynomial equation has precisely n roots, including complex roots and taking into account repeated roots. (For example, the fifth degree equation $(z - 2)(z - 4)^2(z^2 + 9) = 0$ has five roots: 2, 4 (twice), 3j and –3j.) Many great mathematicians tried to prove this. The chief difficulty is to show that every polynomial equation must have at least *one* root: this is called the *Fundamental Theorem of Algebra* and was first proved by Gauss (again!) in 1799.

The Fundamental Theorem, which is too difficult to prove here, is an example of an *existence theorem*: it tells us that a solution exists, but does not say what it is. To find the solution of a particular equation you may be able to use an exact method, such as the formula for the roots of a quadratic equation. (There are much more complicated formulae for solving cubic or quartic equations, but not in general for equations of degree five or more.) Alternatively, there are good approximate methods for finding roots to any required accuracy, and your calculator probably has this facility.

ACTIVITY 2.13 Find out how to use your calculator to solve polynomial equations.

You have already noted that the complex roots of a quadratic equation occur as a conjugate pair. The same is true of the complex roots of any polynomial equation with real coefficients. This is very useful in solving polynomial equations with complex roots, as shown in the following examples.

EXAMPLE 2.9

Given that $1 + 2j$ is a root of $4z^3 - 11z^2 + 26z - 15 = 0$, find the other roots.

SOLUTION

Since the coefficients are real, the conjugate $1 - 2j$ is also a root.

Therefore $[z - (1 + 2j)]$ and $[z - (1 - 2j)]$ are both factors of $4z^3 - 11z^2 + 26z - 15 = 0$.

This means that $(z - 1 - 2j)(z - 1 + 2j)$ is a factor of $4z^3 - 11z^2 + 26z - 15 = 0$.

$$\begin{aligned}(z - 1 - 2j)(z - 1 + 2j) &= [(z - 1) - 2j][(z - 1) + 2j] \\ &= (z - 1)^2 + 4 \\ &= z^2 - 2z + 5\end{aligned}$$

By looking at the coefficient of z^3 and the constant term, you can see that the remaining factor is $4z - 3$.

$$4z^3 - 11z^2 + 26z - 15 = (z^2 - 2z + 5)(4z - 3)$$

The third root is therefore $\frac{3}{4}$.

EXAMPLE 2.10

Given that $-2 + j$ is a root of the equation $z^4 + az^3 + bz^2 + 10z + 25 = 0$, find the values of a and b, and solve the equation.

SOLUTION

$z = -2 + j$

$z^2 = (-2 + j)^2 = 4 - 4j + (j)^2 = 4 - 4j - 1 = 3 - 4j$

$z^3 = (-2 + j)z^2 = (-2 + j)(3 - 4j) = -6 + 11j + 4 = -2 + 11j$

$z^4 = (-2 + j)z^3 = (-2 + j)(-2 + 11j) = 4 - 24j - 11 = -7 - 24j$

Now substitute these into the equation.

$$-7 - 24j + a(-2 + 11j) + b(3 - 4j) + 10(-2 + j) + 25 = 0$$

$$(-7 - 2a + 3b - 20 + 25) + (-24 + 11a - 4b + 10)j = 0$$

Equating real and imaginary parts gives

$$-2a + 3b - 2 = 0$$

$$11a - 4b - 14 = 0.$$

Solving these equations simultaneously gives $a = 2$, $b = 2$.

The equation is $z^4 + 2z^3 + 2z^2 + 10z + 25 = 0$.

Since $-2 + j$ is one root, $-2 - j$ is another root.

So $(z + 2 - j)(z + 2 + j) = (z + 2)^2 + 1$
$= z^2 + 4z + 5$ is a factor.

Using polynomial division or by inspection

$$z^4 + 2z^3 + 2z^2 + 10z + 25 = (z^2 + 4z + 5)(z^2 - 2z + 5).$$

The other two roots are the solutions of the quadratic equation $z^2 - 2z + 5 = 0$.

Using the quadratic formula

$$\begin{aligned} z &= \frac{2 \pm \sqrt{4 - 4 \times 5}}{2} \\ &= \frac{2 \pm \sqrt{-16}}{2} \\ &= \frac{2 \pm 4\text{j}}{2} \\ &= 1 \pm 2\text{j}. \end{aligned}$$

The roots of the equation are $-2 \pm \text{j}$ and $1 \pm 2\text{j}$.

EXERCISE 2G

1 Check that $2 + \text{j}$ is a root of $z^3 - z^2 - 7z + 15 = 0$, and find the other roots.

2 One root of $z^3 - 15z^2 + 76z - 140 = 0$ is an integer.
Solve the equation.

3 Given that $1 - \text{j}$ is a root of $z^3 + pz^2 + qz + 12 = 0$, find the real numbers p and q, and the other roots.

4 One root of $z^4 - 10z^3 + 42z^2 - 82z + 65 = 0$ is $3 + 2\text{j}$.
Solve the equation.

5 The equation $z^4 - 8z^3 + 20z^2 - 72z + 99 = 0$ has a pure imaginary root.
Solve the equation.

6 You are given the complex number $w = 1 - \text{j}$.

(i) Express w^2, w^3 and w^4 in the form $a + b\text{j}$.

(ii) Given that $w^4 + 3w^3 + pw^2 + qw + 8 = 0$, where p and q are real numbers, find the values of p and q.

(iii) Write down two roots of the equation $z^4 + 3z^3 + pz^2 + qz + 8 = 0$, where p and q are the real numbers found in part **(ii)**.

[MEI, *part*]

7 (i) Given that $\alpha = -1 + 2\text{j}$, express α^2 and α^3 in the form $a + b\text{j}$.
Hence show that α is a root of the cubic equation

$$z^3 + 7z^2 + 15z + 25 = 0.$$

(ii) Find the other two roots of this cubic equation.

(iii) Illustrate the three roots of the cubic equation on an Argand diagram, and find the modulus and argument of each root.

(iv) L is the locus of points in the Argand diagram representing complex numbers z for which $\left|z + \frac{5}{2}\right| = \frac{5}{2}$. Show that all three roots of the cubic equation lie on L and draw the locus L on your diagram.

[MEI]

8 The cubic equation $z^3 + 6z^2 + 12z + 16 = 0$ has one real root α and two complex roots β, γ.

(i) Verify that $\alpha = -4$, and find β and γ in the form $a + bj$. (Take β to be the root with positive imaginary part.)

(ii) Find $\frac{1}{\beta}$ and $\frac{1}{\gamma}$ in the form $a + bj$.

(iii) Find the modulus and argument of each of α, β and γ.

(iv) Illustrate the six complex numbers $\alpha, \beta, \gamma, \frac{1}{\alpha}, \frac{1}{\beta}, \frac{1}{\gamma}$ on an Argand diagram, making clear any geometrical relationships between the points.

[MEI, *part*]

9 You are given that the complex number $\alpha = 1 + 4j$ satisfies the cubic equation

$$z^3 + 5z^2 + kz + m = 0,$$

where k and m are real constants.

(i) Find α^2 and α^3 in the form $a + bj$.

(ii) Find the value of k and show that $m = 119$.

(iii) Find the other two roots of the cubic equation. Give the arguments of all three roots.

(iv) Verify that there is a constant c such that all three roots of the cubic equation satisfy

$$|z + 2| = c.$$

Draw an Argand diagram showing the locus of points representing all complex numbers z for which $|z + 2| = c$.
Mark the points corresponding to the three roots of the cubic equation.

[MEI]

10 In this question, α is the complex number $-1 + 3j$.

(i) Find α^2 and α^3.

It is given that λ and μ are real numbers such that $\lambda\alpha^3 + 8\alpha^2 + 34\alpha + \mu = 0$.

(ii) Show that $\lambda = 3$, and find the value of μ.

(iii) Solve the equation $\lambda z^3 + 8z^2 + 34z + \mu = 0$, where λ and μ are as in part **(ii)**. Find the modulus and argument of each root, and illustrate the three roots on an Argand diagram.

[MEI, *part*]

11 The cubic equation $z^3 + z^2 + 4z - 48 = 0$ has one real root α and two complex roots β and γ.

(i) Verify that $\alpha = 3$ and find β and γ in the form $a + bj$. Take β to be the root with positive imaginary part, and give your answers in an exact form.

(ii) Find the modulus and argument of each of the numbers $\alpha, \beta, \gamma, \frac{\beta}{\gamma}$, giving the arguments in radians between $-\pi$ and π.

Illustrate these four numbers on an Argand diagram.

(iii) On your Argand diagram, draw the locus of points representing complex numbers z such that

$$\arg(z - \alpha) = \arg\beta.$$

[MEI, *part*]

KEY POINTS

1 Complex numbers are of the form $z = x + y\mathrm{j}$ with $\mathrm{j}^2 = -1$.
x is called the real part, $\mathrm{Re}(z)$, and y is called the imaginary part, $\mathrm{Im}(z)$.

2 The conjugate of z is $z^* = x - y\mathrm{j}$.

3 To add or subtract complex numbers, add or subtract the real and imaginary parts separately.

$$(x_1 + y_1\mathrm{j}) \pm (x_2 + y_2\mathrm{j}) = (x_1 \pm x_2) + (y_1 \pm y_2)\mathrm{j}$$

4 Multiplication:

$$(x_1 + y_1\mathrm{j})(x_2 + y_2\mathrm{j}) = (x_1x_2 - y_1y_2) + (x_1y_2 + x_2y_1)\mathrm{j}$$

5 Division – multiply top and bottom by the conjugate of the bottom.

$$\frac{x_1 + y_1\mathrm{j}}{x_2 + y_2} = \frac{(x_1x_2 + y_1y_2) + (x_2y_1 - x_1y_2)\mathrm{j}}{x_2^2 + y_2^2}$$

6 The complex number z can be represented geometrically as the point (x, y). This is known as an Argand diagram.

7 The modulus of $z = x + y\mathrm{j}$ is $|z| = \sqrt{x^2 + y^2}$.
This is the distance of the point z from the origin.

8 The distance between the points z_1 and z_2 in an Argand diagram is $|z_1 - z_2|$.

9 Modulus properties:

$$|z|^2 = zz^* \qquad |z_1 + z_2| \leqslant |z_1| + |z_2|$$

10 The principal argument of z, $\arg z$, is the angle θ, $-\pi < \theta \leqslant \pi$, between the line connecting the origin and the point z and the positive real axis.

11 The modulus–argument form of z is $z = r(\cos\theta + \mathrm{j}\sin\theta)$, where $r = |z|$ and $\theta = \arg z$.

12 $x = r\cos\theta \qquad y = r\sin\theta$

$r = \sqrt{x^2 + y^2} \qquad \tan\theta = \dfrac{y}{x}$

13 A polynomial equation of degree n has n roots, taking into account complex roots and repeated roots. In the case of polynomial equations with real coefficients, complex roots always occur in conjugate pairs.

3 Graphs and inequalities

Every picture is worth a thousand words.

Traditional Chinese proverb

The graph in figure 3.1 shows how the population of rabbits on a small island changes over time after a small group is introduced to the island.

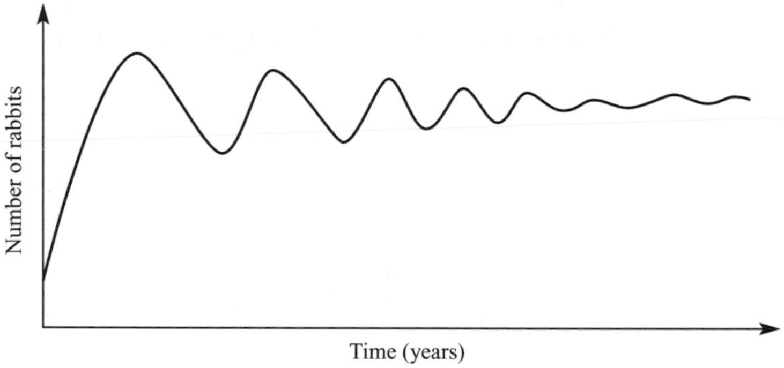

Figure 3.1

❓ What can you conclude from the graph?

Good diagrams not only help writers to communicate ideas efficiently, but they also help students and researchers to discover and understand relationships.

Sketching graphs has been introduced in C1 and C2. If you have already covered this work, you will know that a sketch graph should show the essential features of the graph, such as where it cuts the axes, the nature and position of turning points, any symmetry, and the behaviour of the graph as x or y tends to infinity. Approximate locations rather than exact positions are often used.

In this chapter you will learn to find the key features of a curve by looking at its equation, and to use them to sketch the curve. Although calculus methods (introduced in C2) are available, they are often not needed.

Throughout this chapter you will find it helpful to use a graphic calculator or computer graph-drawing package to check your sketches. However, you should aim to be able to produce your own sketch graphs without being dependent on technology. To be able to sketch the graph of a function accurately without using a machine demonstrates a good appreciation of the behaviour of that function. Learning to draw such sketches will help you realise how various functions behave, and why they behave like that.

Graphic calculators and computer graph-drawing packages draw graphs rapidly, many using 'dot-to-dot' methods. Sometimes the operator has the opportunity to adjust the *resolution* (or step between successive dots): smaller steps produce more accurate graphs. Even when using small steps the display should be interpreted carefully as some packages wrongly connect together separate branches of a curve.

ACTIVITY 3.1

Use a graphic calculator or computer graph-drawing package to draw the graph of $y = \frac{1}{x}$ from $x = -4$ to $x = 4$ and compare the display with the diagrams in figure 3.2. Try changing the x range, or the resolution.

The incorrect diagram is the output from a computer graph-drawing package.

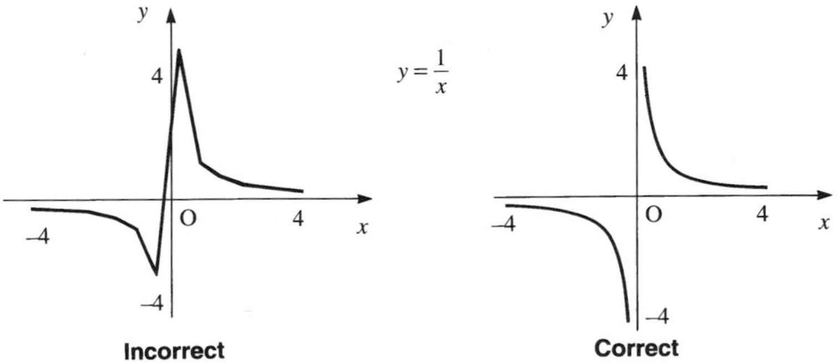

Figure 3.2

(i) Why is it wrong to join the two branches of $y = \frac{1}{x}$?

(ii) Is it better to join points with straight lines or with curves?

(iii) Why do graphic calculators not display smooth curves?

Even if your graphic calculator does produce less than perfect graphs, don't throw it away! Ability to control and correctly interpret its display turns it into a valuable tool. Adjusting the range of the display – effectively adjusting the width and height of the window through which the graph is viewed – changes the horizontal and vertical scales. Most calculators allow you to zoom in or out. Some allow you to scroll horizontally or vertically. Unfortunately the controls are not yet standardised across the various makes of calculator, so it is inappropriate to describe them in detail here. But do experiment with them, so that you learn to use them to advantage, paying particular attention to the range controls.

Graphs of rational functions

A rational number is defined as a number which can be expressed as $\frac{n}{d}$ where the numerator, n, and the denominator, d, are integers, and $d \neq 0$. In a similar way a *rational function* is defined as a function which can be expressed in the form $\frac{\mathrm{N}(x)}{\mathrm{D}(x)}$, where the numerator, $\mathrm{N}(x)$, and denominator, $\mathrm{D}(x)$, are polynomials, and $\mathrm{D}(x)$ is not the zero polynomial. This section concentrates on how to sketch graphs of rational functions.

Think about the graph of $y = \frac{1}{x}$. If you translate it three units to the right and two units up you obtain the graph of $y = \frac{1}{x-3} + 2$ which can be rearranged as $y = \frac{2x-5}{x-3}$ (see figure 3.3).

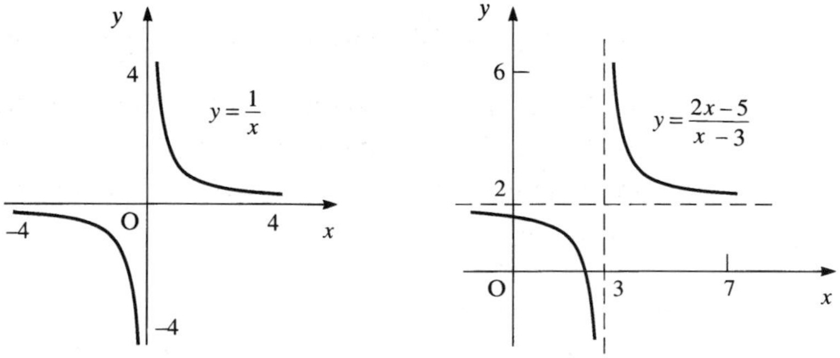

Figure 3.3

Asymptotes

Imagine yourself moving along the curve $y = \frac{2x-5}{x-3}$ from the left. As your x co-ordinate gets close to 3, your y co-ordinate tends to $-\infty$, and you get closer and closer to the vertical line $x = 3$, shown dashed.

If you move along the curve again, letting your x co-ordinate increase without limit, you get closer and closer to the horizontal line $y = 2$, also shown dashed.

These dashed lines are examples of *asymptotes*. An asymptote is a straight line which a curve approaches tangentially as x and/or y tends to infinity. The line $x = 3$ is a vertical asymptote; the line $y = 2$ is a horizontal asymptote. It is usual for asymptotes to be shown by dashed lines in books. In their own work, people often use a different colour for asymptotes.

In general the line $x = a$ is a vertical asymptote for the curve $y = \frac{\mathrm{N}(x)}{\mathrm{D}(x)}$ if $\mathrm{D}(a) = 0$ and $\mathrm{N}(a) \neq 0$. The signs of the numerator $\mathrm{N}(x)$ and the denominator $\mathrm{D}(x)$ when x is close to a enable us to determine whether y tends to positive or negative infinity as x tends to a from left or from right. This is shown in Step **2** below.

❓ What are the vertical asymptotes of the graphs of the following?

(i) $y = \dfrac{1}{x+2}$ **(ii)** $y = \dfrac{x-2}{(x-1)(x+2)}$ **(iii)** $y = \dfrac{2}{(2x-1)(x^2+1)}$

Check your answers by sketching each graph using a computer or graphic calculator.

The essential features of a sketch graph

Shown below are the steps used in building up a sketch graph of $y = \dfrac{x+2}{(x-2)(x+1)}$.

Step 1 Find where the graph cuts the axes

The y *intercept* is where the graph cuts the y axis. You find it by evaluating y when $x = 0$. In the case of the equation $y = \dfrac{x+2}{(x-2)(x+1)}$, the y intercept is $(0, -1)$.

The x intercept is where the graph cuts the x axis. To find it, you put $y = 0$, and solve the resulting equation, getting, in this case, just one root, $x = -2$. You now know that this graph passes through $(0, -1)$ and $(-2, 0)$ and does not cut the axes anywhere else.

❓ Where does the graph of $y = \dfrac{3x+1}{x-2}$ cut the axes?

Step 2 Find the vertical asymptotes and examine the behaviour of the graph either side of them

The denominator of $\dfrac{x+2}{(x-2)(x+1)}$ is zero when $x = -1$ or 2, but these values do not make the numerator zero, so the vertical asymptotes are the lines $x = -1$ and $x = 2$.

Behaviour of the graph either side of the asymptote x = –1

To examine the behaviour near $x = -1$, we look at the three terms $(x + 2)$, $(x - 2)$ and $(x + 1)$, paying particular attention to their signs (see figure 3.4).

When x is slightly less than -1

$\begin{cases} (x+2) \text{ is positive} \\ (x-2) \text{ is negative} \\ (x+1) \text{ is negative and close to zero} \end{cases}$

so that $y = \dfrac{(x+2)}{(x-2)(x+1)}$ is large and positive.

You can make y as large as you like by taking x sufficiently close to -1

$\Rightarrow$ as x tends to -1 from the left $y \to +\infty$.

Vertical asymptotes

When x is slightly more than -1

$\begin{cases} (x+2) \text{ is positive} \\ (x-2) \text{ is negative} \\ (x+1) \text{ is positive and close to zero so that} \end{cases}$

$y = \dfrac{(x+2)}{(x-2)(x+1)}$ is numerically large but negative.

You can make $|y|$ as large as you like by taking x sufficiently close to -1

$\Rightarrow$ as x tends to -1 from the right $y \to -\infty$.

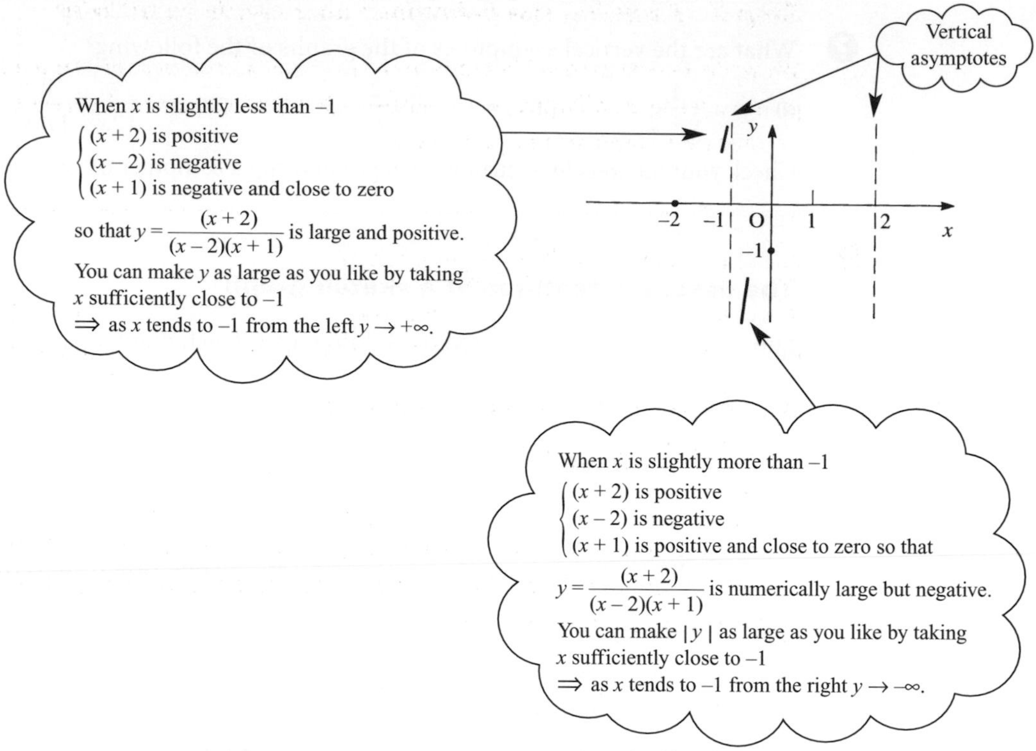

Figure 3.4

Behaviour of the graph either side of the asymptote $x = 2$

You can use a similar method to examine the behaviour of the graph as it approaches its other vertical asymptote, $x = 2$. You will find that $y \to -\infty$ as $x \to 2$ from the left and $y \to +\infty$ as $x \to 2$ from the right. Figure 3.5 shows the details obtained so far.

$y \to +\infty$ as $x \to 2$ from the right.

$y \to -\infty$ as $x \to 2$ from the left.

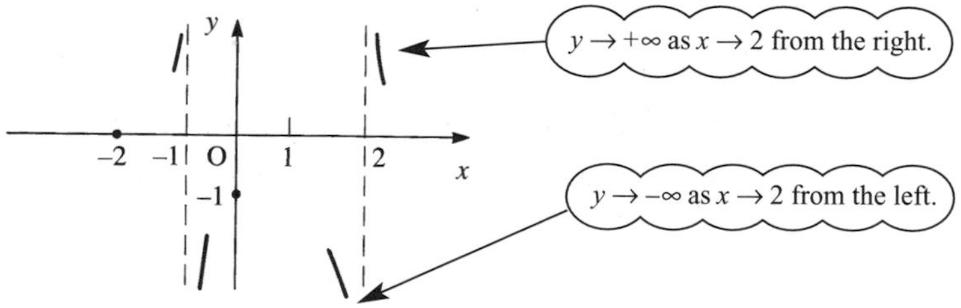

Figure 3.5

❓ What is the vertical asymptote of the graph of $y = \dfrac{3x+1}{x-2}$?

Describe the behaviour of the graph on each side of the asymptote.

Step 3 Examine the behaviour as x tends to infinity

We write $x \to \infty$ to mean 'x tends to infinity', i.e. x becomes very large in a positive sense. Similarly $x \to -\infty$ means 'x tends to negative infinity', i.e. x becomes very large in a negative sense.

? Find the value of $y = \dfrac{x+2}{(x-2)(x+1)}$ when x is

(i) 100 **(ii)** 1000 **(iii)** 10 000

(iv) −100 **(v)** −1000 **(vi)** −10 000

What do you think happens to y as $x \to \infty$?
What happens to y as $x \to -\infty$?

When x is numerically very large (either positive or negative) the 2 in the numerator and the −2 and the 1 in the denominator become negligible compared to the values of x. So as $x \to \pm\infty$,

$$y = \frac{x+2}{(x-2)(x+1)} \to \frac{x}{x^2} = \frac{1}{x} \to 0.$$

This means that the line $y = 0$ is a horizontal asymptote.

? **(i)** What are the signs of $(x + 2)$, $(x - 2)$ and $(x + 1)$ for
(a) large, positive values of x
(b) large, negative values of x?

(ii) What is the sign of y for
(a) large, positive values of x
(b) large, negative values of x?

From the discussion point above, we now know that $y \to 0$ from above as $x \to \infty$, and $y \to 0$ from below as $x \to -\infty$. This additional information is shown in figure 3.6.

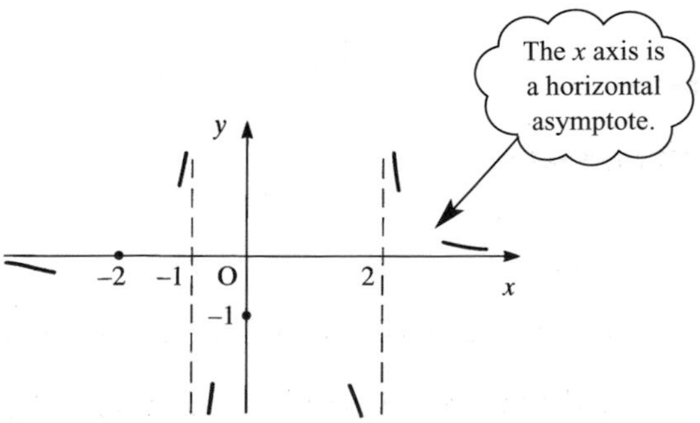

Figure 3.6

In the same way, if the numerator of any rational function is of lower degree than the denominator, then $y = 0$ is a horizontal asymptote.

If the numerator has the same degree as the denominator, then as $x \to \pm\infty$, y tends to a fixed rational number. So there is a horizontal asymptote of the form $y = c$.

❓ How does the graph of $y = \dfrac{3x + 1}{x - 2}$ behave as $x \to \pm\infty$?

Step 4 Complete the sketch

The sketch is completed in figure 3.7. Notice that this leads us to conclude that there is a local maximum between $x = -1$ and $x = 2$, and a local minimum to the left of $x = -2$. We do not know the exact x co-ordinate or the y co-ordinate of either the minimum or the maximum. Nor have we shown that there are no other turning points (see below for more on that subject).

If you need to locate the stationary points precisely you can differentiate; then solve $\dfrac{dy}{dx} = 0$. This would tell you that there are only two turning points, at $x = 0$ and at $x = -4$.

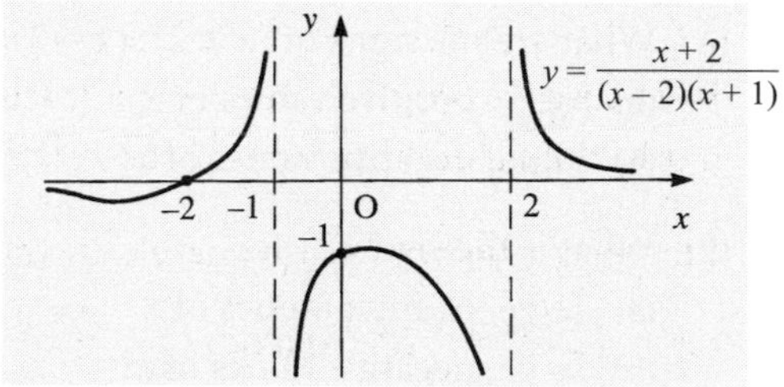

Figure 3.7

ACTIVITY 3.2 Use your answers from the earlier discussion points to sketch the graph of $y = \dfrac{3x + 1}{x - 2}$. Check your sketch using a computer or graphic calculator.

How many turning points?

The sketch of $y = \dfrac{x+2}{(x-2)(x+1)}$ was based on the information shown here in figure 3.8(a).

Can you be sure that there are only two turning points, as we chose to sketch it – see figure 3.8(b)?

How do you know that figure 3.8(c), with additional turning points, is wrong?

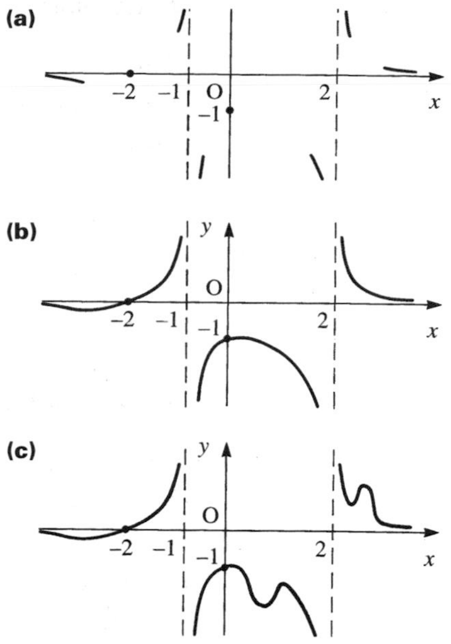

Figure 3.8

One way to do this would be to differentiate $y = \dfrac{x+2}{(x-2)(x+1)}$ and then put $\dfrac{dy}{dx} = 0$.

However, you may not have met differentiating rational functions (this is covered in C3), and furthermore there is usually no need to find the actual co-ordinates of the turning points. An easier approach is to think about how many times the graph could meet a horizontal line with equation $y = c$, where c is a constant.

The x co-ordinate of the points where the graph of $y = \dfrac{x+2}{(x-2)(x+1)}$ meets the line $y = c$ satisfies the equation $\dfrac{x+2}{(x-2)(x+1)} = c$.

To solve this equation, you could multiply both sides by $(x-2)(x+1)$, getting

$$x + 2 = c(x-2)(x+1)$$

which is a quadratic equation in x (unless $c = 0$).

It may have

- no real roots, corresponding to line A in figure 3.9 not meeting the curve
- or one real root, (i.e. repeated roots) – see line B
- or two distinct real roots – see lines C and D.

The quadratic equation cannot have more than two roots: a horizontal line cannot meet the curve in more than two places. But lines E and F each meet the curve four times, a clear contradiction.

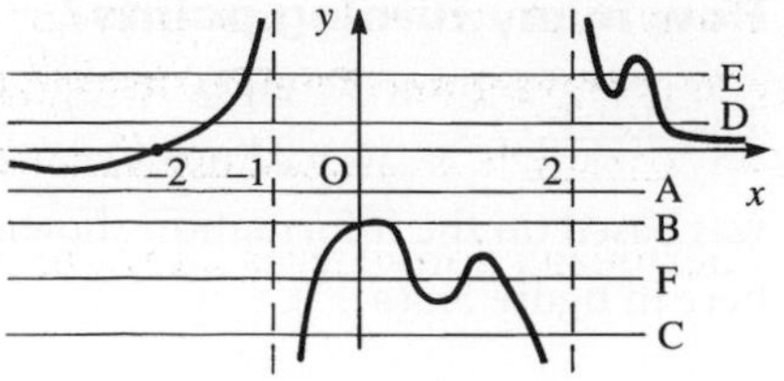

Figure 3.9

You already know that you have a (local) maximum between $x = -1$ and $x = 2$ and a (local) minimum to the left of $x = -2$. Each additional turning point increases (by 2) the number of times the curve meets a horizontal line which already intersects the curve. So you cannot have additional turning points.

? Explain how this argument also tells you that the local maximum point on the curve must be lower than the local minimum point.

EXAMPLE 3.1

Sketch the graph of $y = \dfrac{(x-2)(6-x)}{(x+1)(x-4)}$.

SOLUTION

Step 1

When $x = 0$, $y = \dfrac{-2 \times 6}{1 \times -4} = 3$

When $y = 0$, $x = 2$ or 6

The graph cuts the axes at (0, 3), (2, 0) and (6, 0).

Step 2

The vertical asymptotes of the curve are $x = -1$ and $x = 4$.

To look at the behaviour near the asymptotes, a table like the one below may be helpful.

	x slightly less than -1	x slightly more than -1	x slightly less than 4	x slightly more than 4
$(x-2)$	$-$	$-$	$+$	$+$
$(6-x)$	$+$	$+$	$+$	$+$
$(x+1)$	$-$	$+$	$+$	$+$
$(x-4)$	$-$	$-$	$-$	$+$
$\dfrac{(x-2)(6-x)}{(x+1)(x+4)}$	$\dfrac{-\times+}{-\times-} = -$	$\dfrac{-\times+}{+\times-} = +$	$\dfrac{+\times+}{+\times-} = -$	$\dfrac{+\times+}{+\times+} = +$

The table shows that y is negative immediately to the left of the asymptote $x = -1$, and positive immediately to its right; and y is negative immediately to the left of the asymptote $x = 4$, and positive immediately to its right.

The information so far is shown in figure 3.10.

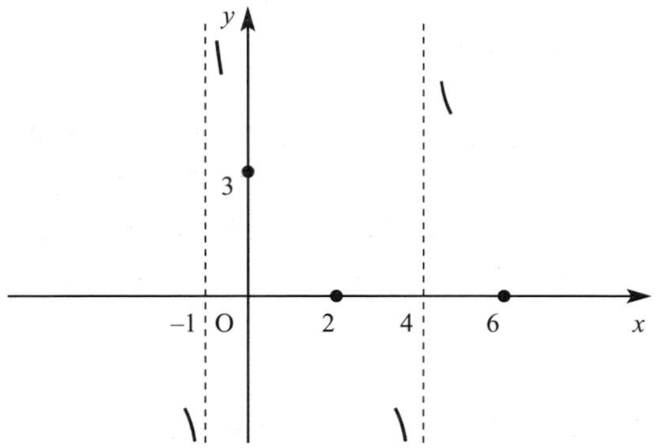

Figure 3.10

Step 3

As $x \to \pm\infty$, $y = \dfrac{(x-2)(6-x)}{(x+1)(x-4)} \to \dfrac{-x^2}{x^2} = -1$.

So $y = -1$ is a horizontal asymptote.

For large positive values of x (e.g. try $x = 100$) $y > -1$, so $y \to -1$ from above as $x \to \infty$.

For large negative values of x (e.g. try $x = -100$) $y < -1$, so $y \to -1$ from below as $x \to -\infty$.

Figure 3.11 shows this additional information.

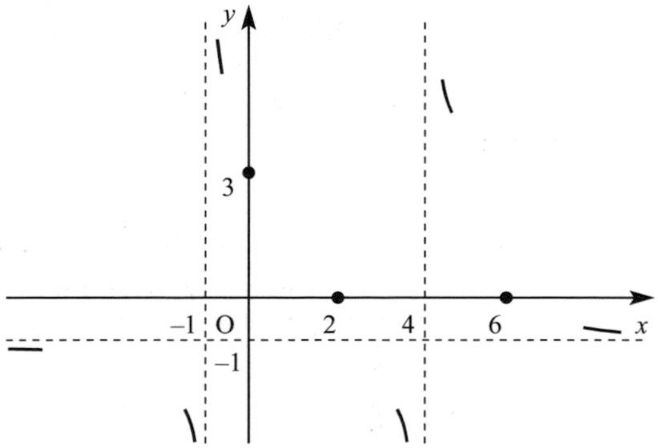

Figure 3.11

Step 4

The sketch is completed in figure 3.12.

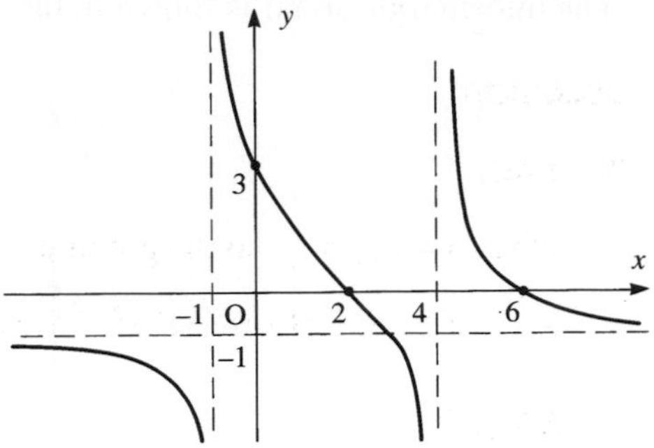

Figure 3.12

The equation $y = \dfrac{(x-2)(6-x)}{(x+1)(x-4)}$ is equivalent to a quadratic in x, so each horizontal line (except the asymptote $y = -1$) will cross the graph at most twice. There cannot be any stationary points.

? In Example 3.1, was all the information obtained from steps 1, 2 and 3 necessary?

Could you have drawn the sketch without all this information?

Using symmetry

Recognising symmetry can help you to draw a sketch.

If $f(x) = f(-x)$ the graph of $y = f(x)$ is symmetrical about the y axis, and f is an *even* function (see C3, Chapter 3). Functions containing only even powers of x are even functions.

If $f(x) = -f(-x)$ the graph of $y = f(x)$ has rotational symmetry of order 2 about the origin; in this case f is an *odd* function.

? Find an example of an even function and an odd function, and sketch their graphs.

EXAMPLE 3.2

(i) Sketch the graph of $y = f(x)$, where $f(x) = \frac{x^2+1}{x^2+2}$.

(ii) The equation $f(x) = k$ has no real solutions.

What can you say about the value of k?

SOLUTION

(i) ***Step 1***

When $x = 0$, $y = \frac{1}{2}$, so the graph passes through $\left(0, \frac{1}{2}\right)$.

No (real) value of x makes $x^2 + 1 = 0$, so the graph does not cut the x axis.

Step 2

No (real) value of x makes $x^2 + 2 = 0$, so there are no vertical asymptotes.

Step 3

As $x \to \pm\infty$, $y = \frac{x^2+1}{x^2+2} \to \frac{x^2}{x^2} = 1$

So $y = 1$ is a horizontal asymptote.

Since the denominator is larger than the numerator for all values of x, $y < 1$ for all x.

So $y \to 1$ from below as $x \to \pm\infty$.

As $f(x)$ contains only even powers of x, f is an even function and the graph is symmetrical about the y axis (see figure 3.13).

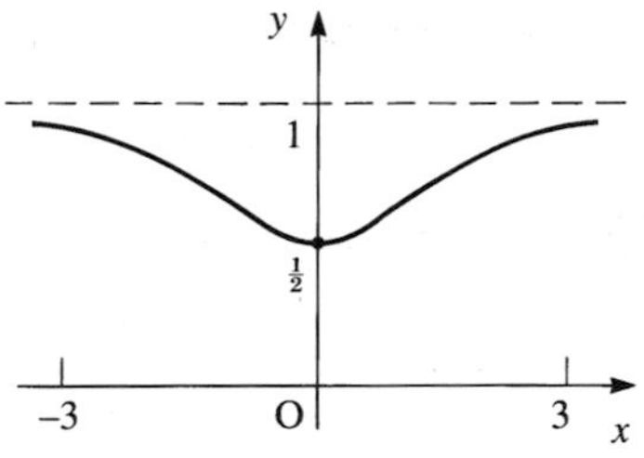

Figure 3.13

Symmetry considerations tell you that the graph is stationary at $\left(0, \frac{1}{2}\right)$.
As $y = \frac{x^2+1}{x^2+2}$, no horizontal line will cross the graph more than twice, so you cannot have any more turning points.
(Differentiation will also confirm that $\left(0, \frac{1}{2}\right)$ is the only stationary point.)

(ii) Solutions of the equation $f(x) = k$ occur where the horizontal line $y = k$ meets the curve $y = f(x)$.

From the sketch of $y = f(x)$, you can see that if $k < \frac{1}{2}$ or $k \geqslant 1$, then the line $y = k$ will not meet the curve and so there are no solutions to the equation $f(x) = k$.

EXERCISE 3A

Follow the steps below for each of questions 1 to 12.

Step 1 Find the co-ordinates of the point(s) where the graph cuts the axes.
Step 2 Find the vertical asymptote(s).
Step 3 State the behaviour of the graph as $x \to \pm\infty$.
Step 4 Sketch the graph.

1 $y = \dfrac{2}{x-3}$

2 $y = \dfrac{2}{(x-3)^2}$

3 $y = \dfrac{1}{x^2+1}$

4 $y = \dfrac{x}{x^2-4}$

5 $y = \dfrac{2-x}{x+3}$

6 $y = \dfrac{x-5}{(x+2)(x-3)}$

7 $y = \dfrac{3-x}{(2-x)(4-x)}$

8 $y = \dfrac{x}{x^2+3}$

9 $y = \dfrac{x-3}{(x-4)^2}$

10 $y = \dfrac{(2x-3)(5x+2)}{(x+1)(x-4)}$

11 $y = \dfrac{x^2-6x+9}{x^2+1}$

12 $y = \dfrac{x^2-5x-6}{(x+1)(x-4)}$

(Be careful!)

13 **(i)** Sketch the graph of $y = \dfrac{4-x^2}{4+x^2}$.

(ii) The equation $\dfrac{4-x^2}{4+x^2} = k$ has no real solutions.

What can you say about the value of k?

14 **(i)** Sketch the graph of $y = \dfrac{1}{(x+1)(3-x)}$.

(ii) Write down the equation of the line of symmetry of the graph, and hence find the co-ordinates of the local minimum point.

(iii) For what values of k does the equation $\dfrac{1}{(x+1)(3-x)} = k$ have

(a) two real distinct solutions

(b) one real solution

(c) no real solutions?

15 **(i)** Sketch the graph of $y = \dfrac{x}{x^2-9}$.

(ii) Show how the equation can be rearranged as a quadratic equation in x, provided $y \neq 0$.

(iii) If y is given (and is not zero), how many values of x can be found?

(iv) Explain why the graph has no turning points anywhere.

16 Without using calculus explain why the graph of $y = \dfrac{x-2}{x+3}$ has no turning points.

17 ☆ **(i)** Show that $y = \dfrac{x-b}{(x-a)(x-c)}$ has no turning points if $a < b < c$.

☆ **(ii)** What happens if $a = c$ and $b < a$?

18 **(i)** ☆ Describe the symmetry of the graph of $y = \dfrac{x^4 - x^2 + 2}{x^4 + 1}$ and locate any ☆ asymptotes.

☆ **(ii)** Sketch the graph.

Inequalities

An *inequality* is a statement involving one of the relationships $<$, $>$, $\leqslant$ or $\geqslant$.

There are two types of inequality:

- those whose truth depend on the value of the variable involved
- those which are always true.

For example: the statement $x^2 > 4$ is true if and only if $x < -2$ or $x > 2$, whereas the statement $(x - 3)^2 + y^2 \geqslant 0$ is true for all real values of x and y.

This section deals with the first type of inequality, in which the task is to find the set of values for which the inequality is true. This is called *solving the inequality.*

There are some basic rules for manipulating inequalities.

Rule	Example (based on 'is greater than')
1 You may add the same number to each side of an inequality.	$x > y \Leftrightarrow x + a > y + a$
2 You may multiply (or divide) both sides of an inequality by the same positive number.	If p is positive: $x > y \Leftrightarrow px > py$
3 If both sides of an inequality are multiplied (or divided) by the same negative number the inequality is reversed.	If n is negative: $x > y \Leftrightarrow nx < ny$
4 You may add (but not subtract) corresponding sides of inequalities of the same type.	$a > b$ and $x > y \Rightarrow a + x > b + y$
5 Inequalities of the same type are *transitive.*	$x > y$ and $y > z \Rightarrow x > z$

The same basic rules apply to each of the inequalities $>$, $<$, $\geqslant$ and $\leqslant$.

? Give an example to show that inequalities may not be subtracted.

An obvious method of solving an inequality such as $f(x) > 0$ is to use the graph of $y = f(x)$: the solution is then the set of values of x for which the graph is above the x axis. If you have already drawn the graph, or it is required for another purpose, this is a quick and easy method. However, if a graph is not required, it may be quicker to use an algebraic method. Example 3.3 shows two different approaches to the same problem; one graphical and the other algebraic.

EXAMPLE 3.3

Solve the inequality $\dfrac{x+2}{(x-2)(x+1)} \leqslant 0$.

SOLUTION 1

The graph of $y = \dfrac{x+2}{(x-2)(x+1)}$ was sketched on page 80.

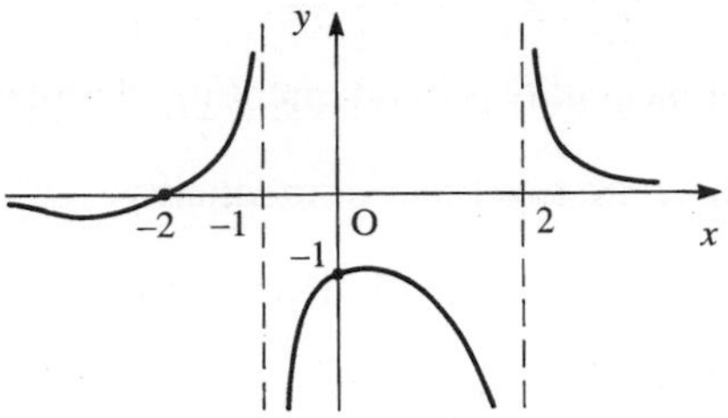
y
x
–2
–1
O
2
–1

Figure 3.14

From figure 3.14, you can see that the graph lies below the x axis for values of x less than -2, and also for values of x between the two vertical asymptotes, $x = -1$ and $x = 2$.

The solution is $x \leqslant -2$ or $-1 < x < 2$.

This solution is shown in figure 3.15.

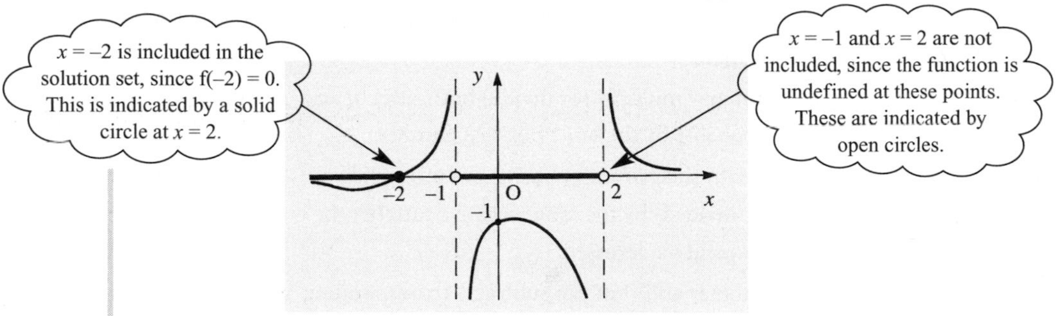
x = –2 is included in the solution set, since f(–2) = 0. This is indicated by a solid circle at x = 2.
x = –1 and x = 2 are not included, since the function is undefined at these points. These are indicated by open circles.
y
x
–2
–1
O
2
–1

Figure 3.15

SOLUTION 2

As the value of x changes, a function $f(x)$ can only change its sign as x passes through a value where $f(x) = 0$ or where $f(x)$ is undefined. These values of x are known as critical points. In the case of a function of the form $f(x) = \dfrac{g(x)}{h(x)}$, the critical points occur when $g(x) = 0$ or $h(x) = 0$. You can then find out whether each factor is positive or negative in each region, and hence whether or not the inequality is true in each region.

In this case, the critical points are $x = -2$ (where the numerator is zero), $x = -1$ and $x = 2$ (where the denominator is zero). First note that $x = -2$ is included in the solution set, but $x = -1$ and $x = 2$ are not.

	$x<-2$	$-2<x<-1$	$-1<x<2$	$x>2$
$(x+2)$	$-$	$+$	$+$	$+$
$(x-2)$	$-$	$-$	$-$	$+$
$(x+1)$	$-$	$-$	$+$	$+$
$\dfrac{x+2}{(x-2)(x+1)}$	$\dfrac{-}{-\times-}=-$	$\dfrac{+}{-\times-}=+$	$\dfrac{+}{-\times+}=-$	$\dfrac{+}{+\times+}=+$

The solution is $x \leqslant -2$ or $-1 < x < 2$.

Inequalities of the form $g(x) \leqslant h(x)$

To solve $g(x) \leqslant h(x)$, you could draw the graphs of $y = g(x)$ and $y = h(x)$ and find the values of x where the graph of $g(x)$ intersects or is lower than the graph of $h(x)$.

Alternatively, you can rearrange the inequality so that it is all on the left-hand side; then use either a graphical or algebraic method. In the next example, three different methods are shown.

EXAMPLE 3.4

Solve the inequality $x + 2 \geqslant \dfrac{3}{x}$.

SOLUTION 1

Since both sides of the inequality are simple functions, it is easy to sketch graphs of $y = x + 2$ and $y = \dfrac{3}{x}$.

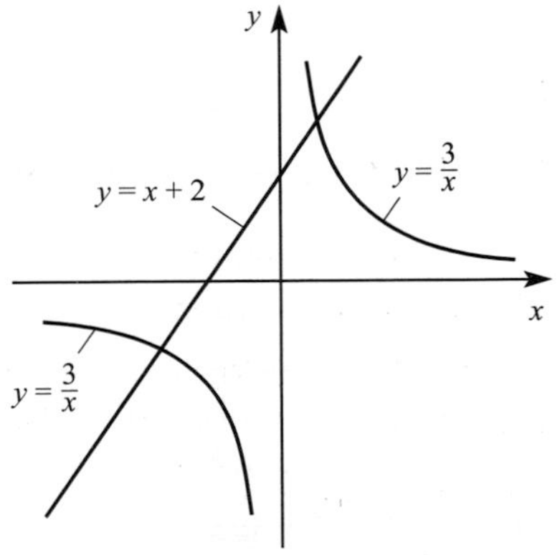

Figure 3.16

To find the points where the graphs intersect, solve the equation $x + 2 = \dfrac{3}{x}$.

$$x(x+2) = 3$$
$$x^2 + 2x - 3 = 0$$
$$(x+3)(x-1) = 0$$
$$x = -3 \text{ or } 1$$

Note that $x = 0$ is not included in the solution set, since $\frac{3}{x}$ is undefined at this point.

From the graph, the solution is $-3 \leqslant x < 0$ or $x \geqslant 1$.

SOLUTION 2

$$x + 2 \geqslant \frac{3}{x}$$

$$\Leftrightarrow x + 2 - \frac{3}{x} \geqslant 0$$

$$\Leftrightarrow \frac{x^2 + 2x - 3}{x} \geqslant 0$$

$$\Leftrightarrow \frac{(x+3)(x-1)}{x} \geqslant 0$$

The critical points are $x = -3$, $x = 1$ and $x = 0$. Notice that $x = -3$ and $x = 1$ are included in the solution set, but $x = 0$ is not.

	$x < -3$	$-3 < x < 0$	$0 < x < 1$	$x > 1$
$(x+3)$	$-$	$+$	$+$	$+$
$(x-1)$	$-$	$-$	$-$	$+$
x	$-$	$-$	$+$	$+$
$\frac{(x+3)(x-1)}{x}$	$\frac{-\times-}{-} = -$	$\frac{+\times-}{-} = +$	$\frac{+\times-}{+} = -$	$\frac{+\times+}{+} = +$

The solution is $-3 \leqslant x < 0$ and $x \geqslant 1$.

SOLUTION 3

As in Solution 2, rearrange the inequality to obtain $\frac{(x+3)(x-1)}{x} \geqslant 0$.

If this were an equation, you could multiply both sides by x, provided that $x \neq 0$. However, as this is an inequality, multiplying both sides by x is a problem; x could be positive or negative, and if it is negative you must reverse the inequality. You could consider the two cases separately, but this is rather cumbersome; a better method is to multiply both sides by x^2, which is always positive, provided that $x \neq 0$.

Multiplying by x^2 gives $x(x+3)(x-1) \geqslant 0$, $x \neq 0$.

This cubic graph is easy to sketch.

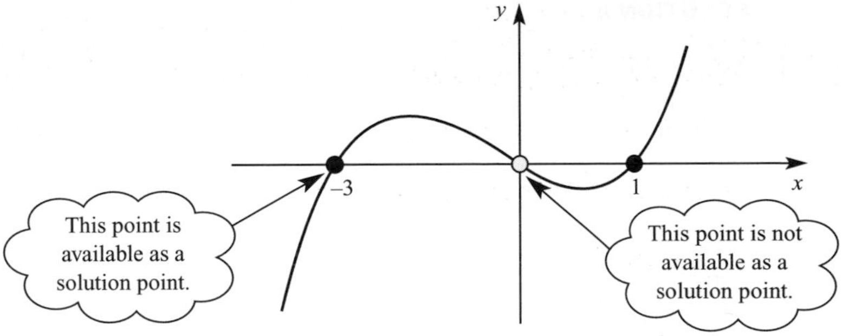

Figure 3.17

From the graph the solution is $-3 \leqslant x < 0$ or $x \geqslant 1$.

In the next example, both sides of the inequality are rather more complicated expressions, so sketching graphs of both functions would involve quite a lot of work. However, either of the methods shown in Solution 2 and Solution 3 of Example 3.4 work well.

EXAMPLE 3.5

Solve the inequality $\dfrac{2x-1}{x-1} \leqslant \dfrac{9}{x+1}$.

SOLUTION 1

$$\frac{2x-1}{x-1} \leqslant \frac{9}{x+1} \Leftrightarrow \frac{2x-1}{x-1} - \frac{9}{x+1} \leqslant 0$$

$$\Leftrightarrow \frac{(2x-1)(x+1)-9(x-1)}{(x-1)(x+1)} \leqslant 0$$

$$\Leftrightarrow \frac{2x^2-8x+8}{(x-1)(x+1)} \leqslant 0$$

$$\Leftrightarrow \frac{2(x-2)^2}{(x-1)(x+1)} \leqslant 0$$

The critical points are $x = 2$, $x = 1$ and $x = -1$. Note that $x = 2$ is included in the solution but $x = 1$ and $x = -1$ are not.

	$x < -1$	$-1 < x < 1$	$1 < x < 2$	$x > 2$
$(x-2)^2$	+	+	+	+
$(x-1)$	−	−	+	+
$(x+1)$	−	+	+	+
$\dfrac{2(x-2)^2}{(x-1)(x+1)}$	$\dfrac{+}{-\times-} = +$	$\dfrac{+}{-\times+} = -$	$\dfrac{+}{+\times+} = +$	$\dfrac{+}{+\times+} = +$

The solution is $-1 < x < 1$ or $x = 2$.

SOLUTION 2

As in Solution 1, rearrange the inequality to obtain $\dfrac{2(x-2)^2}{(x-1)(x+1)} \leqslant 0$.

Multiply by $(x-1)^2(x+1)^2$, provided $x \neq \pm 1$:

$$2(x-1)(x+1)(x-2)^2 \leqslant 0$$

A sketch of $y = 2(x-1)(x+1)(x-2)^2$ gives you the solution $-1 < x < 1$ or $x = 2$.

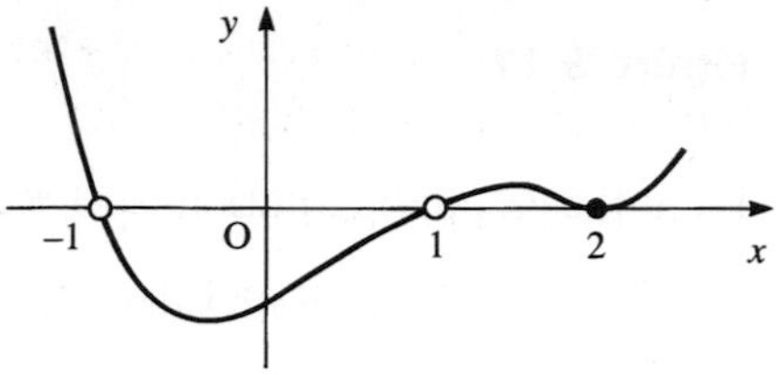

Figure 3.18

EXERCISE 3B

1 **(i)** Sketch the graph of $y = (x+3)(x-1)(2x-7)$.
(ii) Solve the inequality $(x+3)(x-1)(2x-7) > 0$.

2 **(i)** Sketch the graph of $y = \dfrac{x+2}{x-1}$.
(ii) Solve the inequality $\dfrac{x+2}{x-1} \geqslant 0$.

3 **(i)** Sketch the graphs of $y = x^2$ and $y = 2x + 3$ on the same axes.
(ii) Solve the inequality $x^2 < 2x + 3$.

4 **(i)** Sketch the graphs of $y = \dfrac{8}{x}$ and $y = x^2$ on the same axes.
(ii) Solve the inequality $x^2 \geqslant \dfrac{8}{x}$.

5 **(i)** Sketch the graphs of $y = x^3$ and $y = \dfrac{1}{x}$ on the same axes.
(ii) Solve the inequality $x^3 \leqslant \dfrac{1}{x}$.

6 Solve the following inequalities.

(i) $(x-1)(x-2)^2(x-3)^3 > 0$
(ii) $x^3 < x(3x+10)$
(iii) $\dfrac{(x-5)(x-2)}{x+1} \leqslant 0$
(iv) $\dfrac{5x-2}{(x+1)(x-2)} \geqslant 0$
(v) $\dfrac{(x+2)(x-4)}{x(x-2)^2} \geqslant 0$
(vi) $\dfrac{x^3-4}{x-2} \leqslant x+2$
(vii) $\dfrac{2x+3}{x-2} \leqslant 1$
(viii) $\dfrac{1}{x+6} \leqslant \dfrac{2}{2-3x}$

7 **(i)** Solve the inequality $(x+2)(x-3) < 4x$.
(ii) Solve the inequality $x + 2 < \dfrac{4x}{x-3}$.

8 Solve these inequalities.

(i) $\dfrac{x+3}{2x-1} \geqslant 2$ **(ii)** $\dfrac{2x-1}{x+3} \leqslant \dfrac{1}{2}$

[MEI, *part*]

e The range of values taken by a function

On pages 81 to 82 you saw that it is possible to justify the number of turning points on a graph by considering the number of places where the graph meets a horizontal line of the form $y = c$.

It is possible to extend this idea to find the range of possible values of a function, and hence to find the co-ordinates of turning points without using calculus.

At the beginning of this chapter the graph of $y = \dfrac{x+2}{(x-2)(x+1)}$ was sketched, see figure 3.19.

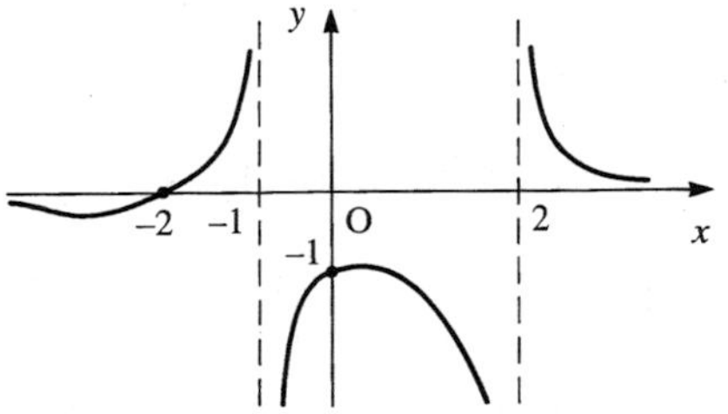

Figure 3.19

This graph meets the horizontal line $y = c$ where $c = \dfrac{x+2}{(x-2)(x+1)}$

$$\Rightarrow \quad c(x-2)(x+1) = x+2$$
$$\Rightarrow \quad cx^2 - cx - 2c = x+2$$
$$\Rightarrow \quad cx^2 - (c+1)x - 2c - 2 = 0$$

? How many roots can this equation have?

The condition for the quadratic equation $cx^2 - (c+1)x - 2c - 2 = 0$ to have real roots is

$$(c+1)^2 - 4c(-2c-2) \geqslant 0$$
$$c^2 + 2c + 1 + 8c^2 + 8c \geqslant 0$$
$$9c^2 + 10c + 1 \geqslant 0$$
$$(c+1)(9c+1) \geqslant 0$$
$$c \leqslant -1 \text{ or } c \geqslant -\tfrac{1}{9}$$

The expression $\frac{x+2}{(x-2)(x+1)}$ cannot take any values between –1 and $-\frac{1}{9}$. If you drew the lines $y = -1$ and $y = -\frac{1}{9}$ on the sketch graph, the line $y = -1$ would touch the local maximum, and the line $y = -\frac{1}{9}$ would touch the local minimum. Therefore the local maximum has y co-ordinate –1, and the local minimum has y co-ordinate $-\frac{1}{9}$.

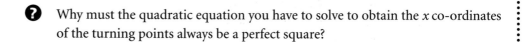

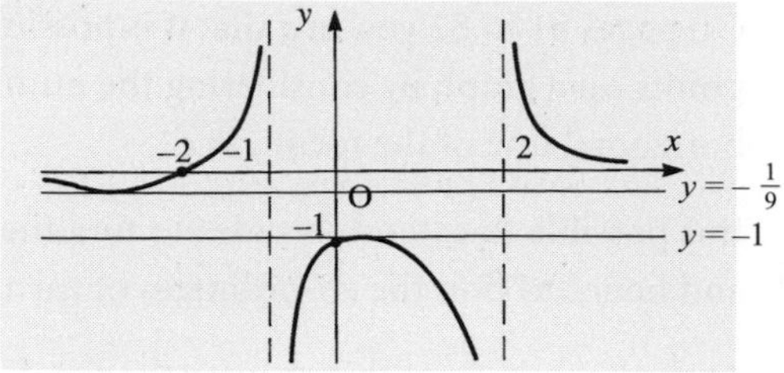

Figure 3.20

You can then find the x co-ordinate of each turning point by substituting the y co-ordinates into the quadratic equation $yx^2 - (y+1)x - 2y - 2 = 0$.

For the local maximum $y = -1$ $\Rightarrow (-1)x^2 - (-1+1)x - (2 \times -1) - 2 = 0$

$\Rightarrow x^2 = 0$

The local maximum has co-ordinates (0, 1).

For the local minimum $y = -\frac{1}{9}$

$$\Rightarrow -\tfrac{1}{9}x^2 - \left(-\tfrac{1}{9} + 1\right)x + \tfrac{2}{9} - 2 = 0$$
$$\Rightarrow -\tfrac{1}{9}x^2 - \tfrac{8}{9}x - \tfrac{16}{9} = 0$$
$$\Rightarrow x^2 + 8x + 16 = 0$$
$$\Rightarrow (x+4)^2 = 0$$
$$\Rightarrow x = -4$$

The local minimum has co-ordinates $\left(-4, -\frac{1}{9}\right)$.

? Why must the quadratic equation you have to solve to obtain the x co-ordinates of the turning points always be a perfect square?

EXERCISE 3C

The questions in this exercise relate to enrichment material

1 (i) Rearrange $y = \dfrac{(x-2)(x+1)}{x^2}$ as a quadratic equation in x.

(ii) Write down the condition for this equation to have real roots, and deduce the maximum value of y for real x.

(iii) Find the value of x corresponding to this value of y.

(iv) Sketch the graph of $y = \dfrac{(x-2)(x+1)}{x^2}$, showing the co-ordinates of the turning point.

2 (i) Use the method of question 1 parts **(i)** and **(ii)** to show that

$$1 \leqslant \frac{9x^2 + 8x + 3}{x^2 + 1} \leqslant 11.$$

(ii) Sketch the graph of $y = \dfrac{9x^2 + 8x + 3}{x^2 + 1}$, giving the co-ordinates of the turning points.

3 (i) Find the set of possible values of $\dfrac{6x + 6}{x^2 + 3}$ for real x.

(ii) Sketch the graph of $y = \dfrac{6x + 6}{x^2 + 3}$, giving the co-ordinates of the turning points.

INVESTIGATIONS

1 Given that a, b, c, d and k are constants, investigate

(i) the form of the graph of $y = \dfrac{(x-a)(x-b)}{(x-c)(x-d)}$

(ii) the number and location of roots of the equation

$$\frac{(x-a)(x-b)}{(x-c)(x-d)} = k.$$

2 Investigate the shape of the graph of $y = \dfrac{ax^2 + bx + c}{Ax^2 + Bx + C}$ when

(i) $b^2 < 4ac$ and $B^2 = 4AC$

(ii) $b^2 \geqslant 4ac$ and $B^2 < 4AC$

(iii) $b^2 < 4ac$ and $B^2 > 4AC$

KEY POINTS

1 A rational function is a function which can be expressed in the form $\frac{N(x)}{D(x)}$, where the numerator, $N(x)$, and denominator, $D(x)$, are polynomials, and $D(x)$ is not the zero polynomial.

2 To sketch the graph of $y = \frac{N(x)}{D(x)}$ follow these steps.

Step 1 Find the intercepts, that is where the graph cuts the axes.
Step 2 Examine the behaviour of the graph near the vertical asymptotes; these are the lines $x = a$ if $D(a) = 0$ and $N(a) \neq 0$.
Step 3 Examine the behaviour as $x \to \pm\infty$.
Step 4 Show what you have found in Steps 1, 2 and 3 on a sketch graph and complete the sketch.

3 Inequalities of the form $f(x) > 0$ (or $f(x) < 0$) can be solved by sketching the graph of $y = f(x)$ and finding those parts of the graph which are above (or below) the x axis.

4 If you want to multiply (or divide) both sides of an inequality by some number you need to know its sign:

- if p is positive: $x > y \Leftrightarrow px > py$
- if n is negative: $x > y \Leftrightarrow nx > ny$.

When multiplying or dividing by a negative number, reverse the inequality.

5 Inequalities of the form $f(x) < 0$ or $f(x) > 0$ can also be solved by finding the critical points (the points where the function is either zero or undefined) and testing whether the inequality is true in each region.

6 An alternative approach to solving an inequality involving a rational function is to multiply by the square of the denominator (as this is automatically positive).

4 Algebra: Identities and roots of equations

In mathematics it is new ways of looking at old things that seem to be the most prolific sources of far-reaching discoveries.

Eric Temple Bell, 1951

? Figure 4.1(a) shows a cube of side x from which another cube of side y has been removed. Figure 4.1(b) is an exploded view of the same solid.

Write down an expression for the volume of each section of the exploded view.

Use this to show that

$$x^3 - y^3 \equiv (x - y)(x^2 + xy + y^2).$$

Is this true for all possible values of x and y?

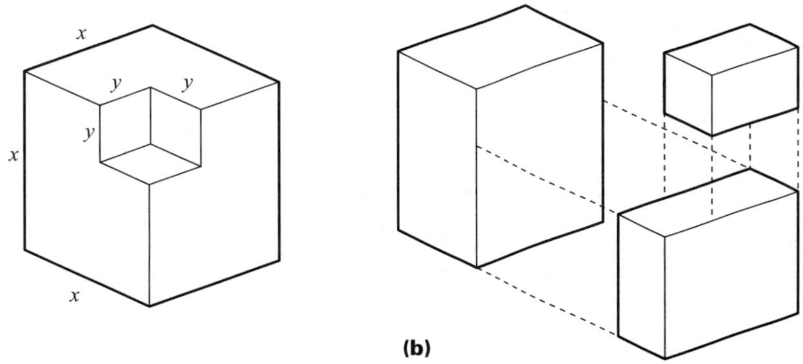

Figure 4.1

Identities

During your work in mathematics you will have seen and used statements known as *identities*, such as the one above: $x^3 - y^3 \equiv (x - y)(x^2 + xy + y^2)$.

You may not, perhaps, have used the symbol $\equiv$ before. This symbol means 'is identically equal to', and is used to emphasise that a statement is true for all values of the variables for which the expressions involved are defined.

Here are some more examples of identities:

1 $-(1-x) \equiv x-1$

2 $(x+y)^2 \equiv x^2 + 2xy + y^2$

3 $\dfrac{a^2-b^2}{a+b} \equiv a-b$

Statements 1 and 2 are true for all values of x and y. Statement 3 is true for all values of a and b, provided $a + b \neq 0$, as in that case the left-hand side of the identity is undefined.

It is important to make sure that you can tell the difference between equations and identities.

- In an identity, all possible values of the variable (or variables) will satisfy the identity, provided only that the functions are defined for these values. For example, the identity $(x-1)^2 \equiv x^2 - 2x + 1$ is true for all values of x. It does not make sense to try to solve this!
- In an equation, not all values of the variable (or variables) satisfy the equation. For example, the equation $x^2 - 7x + 12 = 0$ is only satisfied by $x = 3$ or $x = 4$.

? What happens if you try to solve $(x-1)^2 = x^2 - 2x + 1$?

EXAMPLE 4.1

Find the values of the constants A, B and C in the identity

$$2x^2 - 5x - 3 \equiv (Ax + B)(x-2) + C.$$

SOLUTION 1

One method to solve this problem is to multiply out the brackets and compare the two sides of the identity.

$$\begin{aligned} 2x^2 - 5x - 3 &\equiv (Ax + B)(x-2) + C \\ &\equiv Ax^2 - 2Ax + Bx - 2B + C \\ &\equiv Ax^2 + (-2A + B)x - 2B + C \end{aligned}$$

Since the identity is true for all values of x, the coefficient of x^2 on the right of the identity must be the same as the coefficient of x^2 on the left of the identity. Similarly, the coefficient of x on the right-hand side must be the same as the coefficient of x on the left-hand side, and the constant term must be the same on each side.

Comparing coefficients of x^2: $2 = A$

Comparing coefficients of x: $-5 = -2A + B \Rightarrow -5 = -4 + B$

$\Rightarrow -1 = B$

Comparing constant terms: $-3 = -2B + C \Rightarrow -3 = 2 + C$

$\Rightarrow -5 = C$

This method is called *equating coefficients*.

$A = 2$, $B = -1$, $C = -5$.

SOLUTION 2

An alternative method is to substitute any three values for x into the identity, giving three equations in A, B and C, which you can then solve. By choosing the values of x carefully, you can often make this very easy. In this example, using $x = 2$ gives an equation involving C only, and using $x = 0$ gives an equation involving B and C only. Any value of x can be used for the third equation.

$$2x^2 - 5x - 3 \equiv (Ax + B)(x - 2) + C$$

Substitute $x = 2$: $8 - 10 - 3 = 0 + C \Rightarrow C = -5$

Substitute $x = 0$: $-3 = -2B + C \Rightarrow -3 = -2B - 5$

$\Rightarrow 2 = -2B$

$\Rightarrow -1 = B$

Substitute $x = 1$: $2 - 5 - 3 = (A + B)(-1) + C \Rightarrow -6 = -A + 1 - 5$

$\Rightarrow A = 2$

$A = 2$, $B = -1$, $C = -5$.

You can also use a combination of these two methods: in this example you might notice, without multiplying out, that the only term in x^2 on the right of the identity is Ax^2, so x must be 2. You can then substitute $x = 2$ and $x = 0$ to find B and C.

Note

The identity symbol, $\equiv$, is not always used in writing down identities. It is generally used only when it may not be clear whether or not an expression is an identity. A lot of identities occur in trigonometry; you may have already met one or two, such as $\sin^2\theta + \cos^2\theta = 1$ and $\tan\theta = \frac{\sin\theta}{\cos\theta}$. These identities are sometimes written using the identity symbol, and sometimes using the equals symbol.

ACTIVITY 4.1

Find a textbook which covers some trigonometry work, or your formula book. Find some identities involving $\sin\theta$, $\cos\theta$ or $\tan\theta$, for example the compound angle formulae or the factor formulae.

Use your calculator to check that these identities are true for several different values of θ.

EXERCISE 4A

1 Which of the following are identities?
For those which are identities, rewrite them using the identity symbol.
For those which are not identities, give a value of the variable(s) which do not satisfy the equation.

(i) $(x+2)^2 = x^2 + 2x + 2$ **(ii)** $(x+2)^2 = x^2 + 4x + 4$

(iii) $(x+y)(x-y) = x^2 - y^2$ **(iv)** $\dfrac{4x-2}{1-2x} = -2$

(v) $2x^2 + x + 4 = (x-1)^2 + 3$ **(vi)** $x^2 + 6x + 1 = (x+3)^2 - 8$

2 Find the values of A and B in the identity $x^2 + 4x + 1 \equiv (x+A)^2 + B$.

3 Find the values of A, B and C in the identity
$2x^2 + 3x - 1 \equiv A(x+1)^2 + B(x-3) + C$.

4 Find the values of P, Q and R in the identity
$2x + 3 \equiv P(x-1)^2 + Q(x-1)(x-2) + R(x-2)$.

5 Find the values of L, M and N in the identity
$3x^2 + 2x - 1 \equiv L(x+M)^2 + N$.

6 Find the values of A, B, C and D in the identity
$x^3 - 1 \equiv (x-2)(Ax^2 + Bx + C) + D$.

7 ☆☆☆ Find the values of A and B in the identity

$$\frac{1}{(x-1)(x+2)} \equiv \frac{A}{x-1} + \frac{B}{x+2}.$$

8 ☆☆☆ Find the values of A, B and C in the identity

$$\frac{2x+1}{(x^2+1)(2x-1)} \equiv \frac{Ax+B}{x^2+1} + \frac{C}{2x-1}.$$

Properties of the roots of polynomial equations

In the work which follows, z is used as the variable (or unknown) instead of x to emphasise that these results apply regardless of whether the roots are complex or real.

Quadratic equations

ACTIVITY 4.2

Solve each of the following quadratic equations by factorising.
Write down the sum of the roots and the product of the roots.
What do you notice?

(i) $x^2 - 3x + 2 = 0$ **(ii)** $x^2 + x - 6 = 0$ **(iii)** $x^2 - 6x + 8 = 0$

(iv) $x^2 - 3x - 10 = 0$ **(v)** $2x^2 - 3x + 1 = 0$ **(vi)** $2x^2 - 5x + 3 = 0$

The roots of polynomial equations are usually denoted by Greek letters. The two roots of a quadratic equation are denoted by the first two letters of the Greek alphabet, α (alpha) and β (beta).

You can write the equation

$$az^2 + bz + c = 0,$$

where $a \neq 0$, in factorised form as

$$a(z - \alpha)(z - \beta) = 0.$$

This gives the identity

$$az^2 + bz + c \equiv a(z - \alpha)(z - \beta).$$

Multiplying out:

$$\begin{aligned} az^2 + bz + c &\equiv a(z^2 - \alpha z - \beta z + \alpha\beta) \\ &\equiv az^2 - a(\alpha + \beta)z + a\alpha\beta \end{aligned}$$

Equating coefficients of z:

$$b = -a(\alpha + \beta) \quad \Rightarrow \quad \alpha + \beta = -\frac{b}{a}$$

Equating constant terms:

$$c = a\alpha\beta \qquad \Rightarrow \quad \alpha\beta = \frac{c}{a}$$

So the sum of the roots, $\alpha + \beta = -\frac{b}{a}$

and the product of the roots, $\alpha\beta = \frac{c}{a}$.

From these results you can obtain information about the roots without actually solving the equation.

? What happens if you try to find the values of α and β by solving the equations $\alpha + \beta = -\frac{b}{a}$ and $\alpha\beta = \frac{c}{a}$ as a pair of simultaneous equations?

ACTIVITY 4.3 The quadratic formula gives the roots of the quadratic equation $az^2 + bz + c = 0$ as

$$\alpha = \frac{-b + \sqrt{b^2 - 4ac}}{2a}, \qquad \beta = \frac{-b - \sqrt{b^2 - 4ac}}{2a},$$

Use these expressions to prove that $\alpha + \beta = -\frac{b}{a}$ and $\alpha\beta = \frac{c}{a}$.

EXAMPLE 4.2

Find a quadratic equation with roots 5 and –3.

SOLUTION

The sum of the roots is 2 $\Rightarrow -\frac{b}{a} = 2.$

The product of the roots is –15 $\Rightarrow \frac{c}{a} = -15.$

Taking a to be 1 gives $b = -2$ and $c = -15$.

A quadratic equation with roots 5 and –3 is $z^2 - 2z - 15 = 0$.

Note

There are an infinite number of possible answers to this question. For example, if you take a to be 2, you obtain the equation $2z^2 - 4z - 30 = 0$, which has the same roots. However, taking a to be 1 gives the simplest equation, unless either b or c turn out to be fractions, in which case you might choose a suitable value of a to make the coefficients integers.

Using these properties of the roots of an equation sometimes allows you to form a new equation with roots that are related to the roots of the original equation. Example 4.3 illustrates this.

EXAMPLE 4.3

The roots of the equation $2z^2 + 3z + 5 = 0$ are α and β.

(i) Find the values of $\alpha + \beta$ and $\alpha\beta$.

(ii) Find the quadratic equation with roots 2α and 2β.

(iii) Find the quadratic equation with roots $\alpha + 1$ and $\beta + 1$.

SOLUTION

(i) $\alpha + \beta = -\frac{b}{a} = -\frac{3}{2}$

$\alpha\beta = \frac{c}{a} = \frac{5}{2}$

(ii) The sum of the roots of the new equation

$$\begin{aligned} &= 2\alpha + 2\beta \\ &= 2(\alpha + \beta) \\ &= 2 \times -\frac{3}{2} = -3. \end{aligned}$$

The product of the roots of the new equation

$$\begin{aligned} &= 2\alpha \times 2\beta \\ &= 4\alpha\beta \\ &= 4 \times \frac{5}{2} = 10. \end{aligned}$$

In the new equation, $-\frac{b}{a} = -3$ and $\frac{c}{a} = 10$.

Taking a to be 1 gives $b = 3$ and $c = 10$.

The required equation is $z^2 + 3z + 10 = 0$.

(iii) The sum of the roots of the new equation

$$= \alpha + 1 + \beta + 1$$
$$= \alpha + \beta + 2$$
$$= -\frac{3}{2} + 2 = \frac{1}{2}.$$

The product of the roots of the new equation

$$= (\alpha + 1)(\beta + 1)$$
$$= \alpha\beta + \alpha + \beta + 1$$
$$= \frac{5}{2} - \frac{3}{2} + 1 = 2.$$

In the new equation, $-\frac{b}{a} = \frac{1}{2}$ and $\frac{c}{a} = 2$.

Taking a to be 2 gives $b = -1$ and $c = 4$.

The required equation is $2z^2 - z + 4 = 0$.

? Why do you take a to be 1 in part **(ii)** and 2 in part **(iii)**?

ACTIVITY 4.4 Solve the quadratic equations $2z^2 + 3z + 5 = 0$, $z^2 + 3z + 10 = 0$ and $2z^2 - z + 4 = 0$ from Example 4.3 and check that the relationships between the roots of these equations are correct.

e *More on quadratic equations*

Sometimes a little more work is needed to find a new equation with roots that are related to the roots of the original equation. Two solutions are given to Example 4.4, showing different techniques which may be helpful.

EXAMPLE 4.4 The roots of the equation $z^2 - 4z - 2 = 0$ are α and β.

Find the quadratic equation with roots α^2 and β^2.

SOLUTION 1

$\alpha + \beta = 4$
$\alpha\beta = -2$

We need to find $\alpha^2 + \beta^2$ and $\alpha^2\beta^2$.

$$(\alpha + \beta)^2 = \alpha^2 + 2\alpha\beta + \beta^2 \quad \Rightarrow \quad 4^2 = \alpha^2 + \beta^2 + 2 \times -2$$
$$\Rightarrow \quad \alpha^2 + \beta^2 = 16 + 4 = 20$$

$$\alpha^2\beta^2 = (\alpha\beta)^2 = (-2)^2 = 4$$

The required equation is $z^2 - 20z + 4 = 0$.

SOLUTION 2

Here is an alternative method of finding $\alpha^2 + \beta^2$.

α is a root of $z^2 - 4z - 2 = 0 \quad \Rightarrow \quad \alpha^2 - 4\alpha - 2 = 0$

β is a root of $z^2 - 4z - 2 = 0 \quad \Rightarrow \quad \beta^2 - 4\beta - 2 = 0$

Adding: $\quad \alpha^2 + \beta^2 - 4(\alpha + \beta) - 4 = 0$

$$\Rightarrow \quad \alpha^2 + \beta^2 = 4(\alpha + \beta) + 4$$
$$= 4 \times 4 + 4 = 20$$

Then proceed as in Solution 1.

EXERCISE 4B

1 Write down the sum and product of the roots of each of these quadratic equations.

(i) $2z^2 + 7z + 6 = 0$ **(ii)** $5z^2 - z - 1 = 0$

(iii) $7z^2 + 2 = 0$ **(iv)** $5z^2 + 24z = 0$

(v) $z(z + 8) = 4 - 3z$ **(vi)** $3z^2 + 8z - 6 = 0$

2 Write down quadratic equations (with integer coefficients) with the following roots.

(i) 7, 3 **(ii)** 4, –1

(iii) –5, –4.5 **(iv)** 5, 0

(v) 3 repeated **(vi)** $3 - 2j$, $3 + 2j$

3 The roots of $2z^2 + 5z - 9 = 0$ are α and β.
Find quadratic equations with these roots.

(i) 3α and 3β **(ii)** $-\alpha$ and $-\beta$

(iii) $\alpha - 2$ and $\beta - 2$ **(iv)** $1 - 2\alpha$ and $1 - 2\beta$

4 Using the fact that $\alpha + \beta = -\frac{b}{a}$, $\alpha\beta = \frac{c}{a}$, what can you say about the roots α and β of $az^2 + bz + c = 0$ if you also know that

(i) a, b, c are all positive and $b^2 - 4ac > 0$

(ii) $b = 0$

(iii) $c = 0$

(iv) a and c have opposite signs?

5 One root of $az^2 + bz + c = 0$ is twice the other. Prove that $2b^2 = 9ac$.

6 ☆ The roots of $az^2 + bz + c = 0$ are α and β.
Find quadratic equations with these roots.

(i) $k\alpha$ and $k\beta$ **(ii)** $k + \alpha$ and $k + \beta$

e *The remaining questions relate to enrichment material*

7 The roots of $z^2 - 2z + 3 = 0$ are α and β.

(i) Write down the values of $\alpha + \beta$ and $\alpha\beta$.

(ii) Write $\frac{1}{\alpha} + \frac{1}{\beta}$ and $\frac{1}{\alpha} \times \frac{1}{\beta}$ as single fractions and use your answer to part **(i)** to find their values.

(iii) Write down an equation (with integer coefficients) whose roots are $\frac{1}{\alpha}, \frac{1}{\beta}$.

(iv) Find the equation with roots that are the reciprocals of the roots of $az^2 + bz + c = 0$.

8 The roots of $z^2 + 8z - 2 = 0$ are α and β.
Find quadratic equations with these roots.

(i) α^2 and β^2

(ii) $2\alpha + \beta$ and $\alpha + 2\beta$

(iii) $\alpha^2\beta$ and $\alpha\beta^2$

(iv) $\frac{\alpha}{\beta}$ and $\frac{\beta}{\alpha}$

Cubic equations

There are corresponding properties for the roots of cubic and quartic equations (as well as equations of higher degree).

Since a cubic equation has three roots, these are denoted by α, β and γ (gamma, the third letter of the Greek alphabet). As before, you can write the cubic equation

$$az^3 + bz^2 + cz + d = 0$$

in factorised form as

$$a(z - \alpha)(z - \beta)(z - \gamma) = 0.$$

This gives the identity

$$az^3 + bz^2 + cz + d \equiv a(z - \alpha)(z - \beta)(z - \gamma).$$

Multiplying out:

$$\begin{aligned} az^3 + bz^2 + cz + d &\equiv a(z - \alpha)(z - \beta)(z - \gamma) \\ &\equiv az^3 - a(\alpha + \beta + \gamma)z^2 + a(\alpha\beta + \alpha\gamma + \beta\gamma)z - a\alpha\beta\gamma \end{aligned}$$

? Check this for yourself.

Equating coefficients of z^2:

$$b = -a(\alpha + \beta + \gamma) \quad \Rightarrow \quad \alpha + \beta + \gamma = -\frac{b}{a}$$

Equating coefficients of z:

$$c = a(\alpha\beta + \beta\gamma + \gamma\alpha) \quad \Rightarrow \quad \alpha\beta + \beta\gamma + \gamma\alpha = \frac{c}{a}$$

Equating constant terms:

$$d = -a\alpha\beta\gamma \quad \Rightarrow \quad \alpha\beta\gamma = -\frac{d}{a}$$

So the sum of the roots, $\alpha + \beta + \gamma = -\frac{b}{a}$

the sum of the products of roots in pairs, $\alpha\beta + \beta\gamma + \gamma\alpha = \frac{c}{a}$

and the product of the roots, $\alpha\beta\gamma = -\frac{d}{a}$.

As with the roots of quadratic equations, you cannot find the roots directly from these equations. If you attempt to solve them as simultaneous equations, you will just get back to the original cubic equation (with α, β or γ in place of z). But if you have additional information about the roots (as in Example 4.5 perhaps), these equations can provide a quick and easy method of solution.

Note

$\Sigma\alpha$ and $\Sigma\alpha\beta$ are often used to denote $\alpha + \beta + \gamma$ and $\alpha\beta + \beta\gamma + \gamma\alpha$ respectively. Provided you know the degree of the equation you are working with (e.g. cubic, quartic) it should be clear what this means. Functions like these are called symmetric functions of the roots, because exchanging any two of α, β, γ does not change the value of the function. Similar notation is used to denote other symmetric functions of the roots. For example, for a cubic with roots α, β and γ, $\Sigma\alpha^2\beta$ means

$$\alpha^2\beta + \alpha\beta^2 + \alpha^2\gamma + \alpha\gamma^2 + \beta^2\gamma + \beta\gamma^2 .$$

EXAMPLE 4.5

The roots of the equation

$$2z^3 - 9z^2 - 27z + 54 = 0$$

form a geometric progression (i.e. they may be written as $\frac{a}{r}$, a, ar).
Solve the equation.

SOLUTION

$$\alpha\beta\gamma = -\frac{d}{a} \quad\Rightarrow\quad \frac{a}{r} \times a \times ar = -\frac{54}{2}$$

$$\Rightarrow\quad a^3 = -27$$

$$\Rightarrow\quad a = -3$$

$$\Sigma\alpha = -\frac{b}{a} \quad\Rightarrow\quad \frac{a}{r} + a + ar = \frac{9}{2}$$

$$\Rightarrow\quad -3\left(\frac{1}{r} + 1 + r\right) = \frac{9}{2}$$

$$\Rightarrow\quad 2\left(\frac{1}{r} + 1 + r\right) = -3$$

$$\Rightarrow\quad 2 + 2r + 2r^2 = -3r$$

$$\Rightarrow\quad 2r^2 + 5r + 2 = 0$$

$$\Rightarrow\quad (2r + 1)(r + 2) = 0$$

$$\Rightarrow\quad r = -2 \text{ or } r = -\tfrac{1}{2}$$

Either value of r gives the three roots $\frac{3}{2}$, -3, 6.

In the next example, you are asked to form a new equation with roots that are related to the roots of the original equation. You can use a similar approach to the one you used for quadratic equations (as in Example 4.3). Not surprisingly, this is rather more complicated when a cubic equation is involved. A second solution is also given, using the method of substitution, which can be simpler to use.

EXAMPLE 4.6

The roots of the cubic equation $2z^3 + 5z^2 - 3z - 2 = 0$ are α, β, γ.
Find the cubic equation with roots $2\alpha + 1, 2\beta + 1, 2\gamma + 1$.

SOLUTION 1

$$\alpha + \beta + \gamma = -\frac{b}{a} = -\frac{5}{2}$$

$$\alpha\beta + \beta\gamma + \gamma\alpha = \frac{c}{a} = -\frac{3}{2}$$

$$\alpha\beta\gamma = -\frac{d}{a} = 1$$

For the new equation:

$$\begin{aligned}\text{Sum of roots} &= 2\alpha + 1 + 2\beta + 1 + 2\gamma + 1 \\ &= 2(\alpha + \beta + \gamma) + 3 \\ &= -5 + 3 = -2\end{aligned}$$

$$\begin{aligned}\text{Product of roots in pairs} &= (2\alpha + 1)(2\beta + 1) + (2\beta + 1)(2\gamma + 1) + (2\gamma + 1)(2\alpha + 1) \\ &= [4\alpha\beta + 2(\alpha + \beta) + 1] + [4\beta\gamma + 2(\beta + \gamma) + 1] + \\ &\quad [4\gamma\alpha + 2(\gamma + \alpha) + 1] \\ &= 4(\alpha\beta + \beta\gamma + \gamma\alpha) + 4(\alpha + \beta + \gamma) + 3 \\ &= 4 \times -\tfrac{3}{2} + 4 \times -\tfrac{5}{2} + 3 \\ &= -13\end{aligned}$$

? Check this for yourself.

$$\begin{aligned}\text{Product of roots} &= (2\alpha + 1)(2\beta + 1)(2\gamma + 1) \\ &= 8\alpha\beta\gamma + 4(\alpha\beta + \beta\gamma + \gamma\alpha) + 2(\alpha + \beta + \gamma) + 1 \\ &= 8 \times 1 + 4 \times -\tfrac{3}{2} + 2 \times -\tfrac{5}{2} + 1 \\ &= -2\end{aligned}$$

In the new equation, $-\frac{b}{a} = -2, \frac{c}{a} = -13, -\frac{d}{a} = -2$.

The new equation is $z^3 + 2z^2 - 13z + 2 = 0$.

SOLUTION 2 (Substitution method)

Let $w = 2z + 1$ so that $z = \dfrac{w - 1}{2}$.

α, β, γ are the roots of $2z^3 + 5z^2 - 3z - 2 = 0$

$\Leftrightarrow 2\alpha + 1, 2\beta + 1, 2\gamma + 1$ are the roots of $2\left(\frac{w-1}{2}\right)^3 + 5\left(\frac{w-1}{2}\right)^2 - 3\left(\frac{w-1}{2}\right) - 2 = 0$.

$$\begin{aligned}\Leftrightarrow \quad & (w - 1)^3 + 5(w - 1)^2 - 6(w - 1) - 8 = 0 \\ \Leftrightarrow \quad & w^3 - 3w^2 + 3w - 1 + 5w^2 - 10w + 5 - 6w + 6 - 8 = 0 \\ \Leftrightarrow \quad & w^3 + 2w^2 - 13w + 2 = 0\end{aligned}$$

You can see from the above that the substitution method can be very efficient.

e More on cubic equations

The substitution method is also used in the next example.

EXAMPLE 4.7

The roots of the cubic equation $az^3 + bz^2 + cz + d = 0$ are α, β, γ.

Find the cubic equation with roots $\frac{1}{\alpha}, \frac{1}{\beta}, \frac{1}{\gamma}$.

SOLUTION

Let $w = \frac{1}{z}$ so that $z = \frac{1}{w}$.

α, β, γ are the roots of $az^3 + bz^2 + cz + d = 0$

$\Leftrightarrow \frac{1}{\alpha}, \frac{1}{\beta}, \frac{1}{\gamma}$ are the roots of $\frac{a}{w^3} + \frac{b}{w^2} + \frac{c}{w} + d = 0$

$\Leftrightarrow a + bw + cw^2 + dw^3 = 0$

Notice that taking the reciprocal of each root reverses the coefficients of the equation. This property applies to polynomial equations of all degrees, provided that none of the roots is zero.

ACTIVITY 4.5

The cubic equation $az^3 + bz^2 + cz + d = 0$ has roots α, β, γ.

Explain why substituting $-\frac{d}{aw}$ for z in $az^3 + bz^2 + cz + d = 0$ forms an equation with roots $\alpha\beta, \beta\gamma, \gamma\alpha$.

Simplify the resulting equation as much as possible and show that your result is valid even if one of α, β, γ is zero.

Not all problems involving finding a new equation can be solved using the substitution method. If substitution cannot be used, you will need to find the sum of the roots, the product of the roots in pairs, and the product of the three roots of the new equation from the information you have, as in Example 4.6 Solution 1. This can involve some fairly complicated algebra. The following identities are sometimes useful.

(i) $(\Sigma\alpha)^2 = \Sigma\alpha^2 + 2\Sigma\alpha\beta$

(ii) $(\Sigma\alpha\beta)^2 = \Sigma(\alpha\beta)^2 + 2\alpha\beta\gamma\Sigma\alpha$

(iii) $\alpha\beta\gamma\Sigma\frac{1}{\alpha} = \Sigma\alpha\beta$

ACTIVITY 4.6

Write the above identities out in full, and prove them.

EXAMPLE 4.8

The cubic equation $2x^3 - 3x^2 - 12x - 4 = 0$ has roots α, β and γ.

(i) Write down the values of $\alpha + \beta + \gamma$, $\beta\gamma + \gamma\alpha + \alpha\beta$ and $\alpha\beta\gamma$.

(ii) Find $\alpha^2 + \beta^2 + \gamma^2$ and $(\alpha\beta)^2 + (\beta\gamma)^2 + (\gamma\alpha)^2$.

(iii) Find a cubic equation with integer coefficients which has these roots.

$$\frac{\alpha\beta}{\gamma}, \frac{\beta\gamma}{\alpha} \text{ and } \frac{\gamma\alpha}{\beta}.$$

SOLUTION

(i) $\alpha + \beta + \gamma = \frac{3}{2}$

$\beta\gamma + \gamma\alpha + \alpha\beta = -6$

$\alpha\beta\gamma = 2$

(ii) Using identity **(i)** from Activity 4.6:

$$\begin{aligned}\alpha^2 + \beta^2 + \gamma^2 &= (\alpha + \beta + \gamma)^2 - 2(\alpha\beta + \beta\gamma + \gamma\alpha)\\ &= \tfrac{9}{4} + 12\\ &= \tfrac{57}{4}\end{aligned}$$

Using identity **(ii)** from Activity 4.6:

$$\begin{aligned}(\alpha\beta)^2 + (\beta\gamma)^2 + (\gamma\alpha)^2 &= (\alpha\beta + \beta\gamma + \gamma\alpha)^2 - 2\alpha\beta\gamma(\alpha + \beta + \gamma)\\ &= (-6)^2 - 2 \times 2 \times \tfrac{3}{2}\\ &= 30\end{aligned}$$

(iii) For the new equation:

$$\begin{aligned}\text{Sum of roots} &= \frac{\alpha\beta}{\gamma} + \frac{\beta\gamma}{\alpha} + \frac{\gamma\alpha}{\beta}\\ &= \frac{(\alpha\beta)^2 + (\beta\gamma)^2 + (\gamma\alpha)^2}{\alpha\beta\gamma}\\ &= \frac{30}{2} = 15\end{aligned}$$

$$\begin{aligned}\text{Product of roots in pairs} &= \frac{\alpha\beta\beta\gamma}{\gamma\alpha} + \frac{\beta\gamma\gamma\alpha}{\alpha\beta} + \frac{\gamma\alpha\alpha\beta}{\beta\gamma}\\ &= \beta^2 + \gamma^2 + \alpha^2\\ &= \tfrac{57}{4}\end{aligned}$$

$$\begin{aligned}\text{Product of roots} &= \frac{\alpha\beta\beta\gamma\gamma\alpha}{\alpha\beta\gamma}\\ &= \alpha\beta\gamma\\ &= 2\end{aligned}$$

For the new equation, $-\frac{b}{a} = 15$, $\frac{c}{a} = \frac{57}{4}$, $-\frac{d}{a} = 2$

Taking $a = 4 \Rightarrow b = -60$, $c = 57$, $d = -8$

The new equation is $4z^3 - 60z^2 + 57z - 8 = 0$

EXERCISE 4C

1 The roots of the cubic equation are $2z^3 + 3z^2 - z + 7 = 0$ are α, β, γ.
Find the following.

(i) $\Sigma\alpha$ **(ii)** $\Sigma\alpha\beta$ **(iii)** $\alpha\beta\gamma$

2 Find cubic equations (with integer coefficients) with the following roots.

(i) 1, 2, 4 **(ii)** 2, –2, 3
(iii) 0, –2, –1.5 **(iv)** 2 (repeated), 2.5
(v) –2, –3, 5 **(vi)** 1, 2 + j, 2 – j

3 The roots of each of these equations are in arithmetic progression (i.e. they may be written as $\alpha - d, \alpha, \alpha + d$).
Solve each equation.

(i) $z^3 - 15z^2 + 66z - 80 = 0$ **(ii)** $9z^3 - 18z^2 - 4z + 8 = 0$
(iii) $z^3 - 6z^2 + 16 = 0$ **(iv)** $54z^3 - 189z^2 + 207z - 70 = 0$

4 The roots of the equation $2z^3 - 12z^2 + kz - 15 = 0$ are in arithmetic progression.
Solve the equation and find k.

5 Solve $32z^3 - 14z + 3 = 0$ given that one root is twice another.

6 The roots of the equation $2z^3 + 4z^2 - 3z + 1 = 0$ are α, β, γ.
Find cubic equations with these roots.

(i) $2\alpha, 2\beta, 2\gamma$ **(ii)** $\alpha + 3, \beta + 3, \gamma + 3$
(iii) $2 - \alpha, 2 - \beta, 2 - \gamma$ **(iv)** $3\alpha - 2, 3\beta - 2, 3\gamma - 2$

7 The equation $z^3 + pz^2 + 2pz + q = 0$ has roots $\alpha, 2\alpha, 4\alpha$.
Find all the possible values of p, q, α.

8 The roots of $z^3 + pz^2 + qz + r = 0$ are $\alpha, -\alpha, \beta$, and $r \neq 0$.
Show that $r = pq$, and find all three roots in terms of p and q.

9 The cubic equation $8x^3 + px^2 + qx + r = 0$ has roots $\alpha, \dfrac{1}{2\alpha}$ and β.

(i) Express p, q and r in terms of α and β.
(ii) Show that $2r^2 - pr + 4q = 16$.
(iii) Given that $p = 6$ and $q = -23$, find the two possible values of r and, in each case, solve the equation $8x^3 + 6x^2 - 23x + r = 0$.

[MEI]

10 ☆☆☆☆ Show that one root of $az^3 + bz^2 + cz + d = 0$ is the reciprocal of another root if and only if $a^2 - d^2 = ac - bd$.
Verify that this condition is satisfied for the equation $21z^3 - 16z^2 - 95z + 42 = 0$ and hence solve the equation.

11 ☆☆☆☆☆ Find a formula connecting a, b, c and d which is a necessary and sufficient condition for the roots of the equation $az^3 + bz^2 + cz + d = 0$ to be in geometric progression.
Show that this condition is satisfied for the equation $8z^3 - 52z^2 + 78z - 27 = 0$ and hence solve the equation.

The remaining questions relate to enrichment material.

12 The roots of the cubic equation $x^3 - 5x^2 - 6x - 4 = 0$ are α, β, γ.

(i) Write down the values of $\alpha + \beta + \gamma$, $\alpha\beta + \beta\gamma + \gamma\alpha$ and $\alpha\beta\gamma$.

(ii) Find the value of $\alpha^2 + \beta^2 + \gamma^2$.

(iii) Show that $(\alpha\beta)^2 + (\beta\gamma)^2 + (\gamma\alpha)^2 = -4$. Deduce that α, β, γ are not all real.

(iv) Find a cubic equation with integer coefficients whose roots are $\frac{\beta\gamma}{\alpha}$, $\frac{\gamma\alpha}{\beta}$ and $\frac{\alpha\beta}{\gamma}$.

[MEI]

13 The cubic equation $16x^3 + kx^2 + 27 = 0$ (where k is a real constant) has roots α, β and γ.

(i) Write down the values of $\beta\gamma + \gamma\alpha + \alpha\beta$ and $\alpha\beta\gamma$, and express k in terms of α, β and γ.

(ii) For the case where there is a repeated root, say $\beta = \gamma$, solve the cubic equation and find the value of k.

(iii) For the case $k = 9$, find a cubic equation with integer coefficients which has these roots.

$$\frac{1}{\alpha} + 1, \frac{1}{\beta} + 1, \frac{1}{\gamma} + 1$$

[MEI]

Quartic equations

Quartic equations have four roots, denoted by α, β, γ and δ (delta, the fourth letter of the Greek alphabet).

? So far you have learnt two properties of the roots of quadratic equations, and three properties of the roots of cubic equations.

Predict the four properties of the roots $\alpha, \beta, \gamma, \delta$ of the quartic equation $az^4 + bz^3 + cz^2 + dz + e = 0$

As before, the quartic equation

$$az^4 + bz^3 + cz^2 + dz + e = 0$$

can be written in factorised form as

$$a(z - \alpha)(z - \beta)(z - \gamma)(z - \delta) = 0.$$

This gives the identity

$$az^4 + bz^3 + cz^2 + dz + e \equiv a(z - \alpha)(z - \beta)(z - \gamma)(z - \delta).$$

ACTIVITY 4.7 Multiply out the right-hand side of the identity above to show that

$$az^4 + bz^3 + cz^2 + dz + e \equiv az^4 - a(\alpha + \beta + \gamma + \delta)z^3 + a(\alpha\beta + \alpha\gamma + \alpha\delta + \beta\gamma + \gamma\delta + \delta\alpha)z^2 - a(\alpha\beta\gamma + \beta\gamma\delta + \gamma\delta\alpha + \delta\alpha\beta)z + a\alpha\beta\gamma\delta$$

Equating coefficients shows that:

$$\sum\alpha = \alpha + \beta + \gamma + \delta = -\frac{b}{a}$$

(The sum of the individual roots)

$$\sum\alpha\beta = \alpha\beta + \alpha\gamma + \alpha\delta + \beta\gamma + \beta\delta + \gamma\delta = \frac{c}{a}$$

(The sum of the product of roots in pairs)

$$\sum\alpha\beta\gamma = \alpha\beta\gamma + \beta\gamma\delta + \gamma\delta\alpha + \delta\alpha\beta = -\frac{d}{a}$$

(The sum of the product of roots in threes)

$$\alpha\beta\gamma\delta = \frac{e}{a}$$

(The product of the roots)

EXAMPLE 4.9

The roots of the quartic equation $4z^4 + pz^3 + qz^2 - z + 3 = 0$ are $\alpha, -\alpha, \alpha + \lambda, \alpha - \lambda$, where α and λ are real numbers.

(i) Express p and q in terms of α and λ.

(ii) Show that $\alpha = \frac{1}{2}$, and find the values of p and q.
Give the roots of the quartic equation.

SOLUTION

(i) $\sum\alpha = \alpha - \alpha + \alpha + \lambda + \alpha - \lambda = -\frac{p}{4}$

(Use the sum of the individual roots to find an expression for p.)

$$\Rightarrow \quad 2\alpha = -\frac{p}{4}$$

$$\Rightarrow \quad p = -8\alpha$$

$$\sum\alpha\beta = -\alpha^2 + \alpha(\alpha + \lambda) + \alpha(\alpha - \lambda) - \alpha(\alpha + \lambda) - \alpha(\alpha - \lambda) + (\alpha + \lambda)(\alpha - \lambda) = \frac{q}{4}$$

$$\Rightarrow \quad -\lambda^2 = \frac{q}{4}$$

$$\Rightarrow \quad q = -4\lambda^2$$

(Use the sum of the product of the roots in pairs to find an expression for q.)

(ii) $\sum\alpha\beta\gamma = -\alpha^2(\alpha + \lambda) - \alpha(\alpha + \lambda)(\alpha - \lambda) + \alpha(\alpha + \lambda)(\alpha - \lambda) - \alpha^2(\alpha - \lambda) = \frac{1}{4}$

$$\Rightarrow \quad -2\alpha^3 = \frac{1}{4}$$

$$\Rightarrow \quad \alpha^3 = -\frac{1}{8}$$

$$\Rightarrow \quad \alpha = -\frac{1}{2}$$

(Use the sum of the product of the roots in threes to find α (λ cancels out) and hence find p, using your answer to part **(i)**.)

$$p = -8\alpha = -8 \times -\frac{1}{2} = 4$$

$$\alpha\beta\gamma\delta = -\alpha^2(\alpha + \lambda)(\alpha - \lambda) = \frac{3}{4}$$

(Use the sum of the product of the roots and the value for α to find λ, and hence find q, using your answer to part **(i)**.)

$$\Rightarrow \quad -\alpha^2(\alpha^2 - \lambda^2) = \frac{3}{4}$$

$$\Rightarrow \quad -\frac{1}{4}\left(\frac{1}{4} - \lambda^2\right) = \frac{3}{4}$$

$$\Rightarrow \quad \frac{1}{4} - \lambda^2 = -3$$

$$\Rightarrow \quad \lambda^2 = \frac{13}{4}$$

$$q = -4\lambda^2 = -4 \times \frac{13}{4} = -13$$

(Substitute the values for α and λ to give the roots.)

The roots of the equation are $\frac{1}{2}, -\frac{1}{2}, -\frac{1}{2} + \frac{1}{2}\sqrt{13}, -\frac{1}{2} - \frac{1}{2}\sqrt{13}$.

e Quintic equations

? Predict the five properties of the roots $\alpha, \beta, \gamma, \delta, \varepsilon$ of the quintic

$$az^5 + bz^4 + cz^3 + dz^2 + ez + f = 0.$$

EXERCISE 4D

1 The roots of $2z^4 + 3z^3 + 6z^2 - 5z + 4 = 0$ are $\alpha, \beta, \gamma, \delta$.
Write down the values of the following.

(i) $\sum\alpha$ **(ii)** $\sum\alpha\beta$ **(iii)** $\sum\alpha\beta\gamma$ **(iv)** $\alpha\beta\gamma\delta$

2 Find quartic equations (with integer coefficients) with these roots.

(i) $1, -1, 2, 4$
(ii) $0, 1.5, -2.5, -4$
(iii) 1.5 (repeated), -3 (repeated)
(iv) $1, -3, 1 + \text{j}, 1 - \text{j}$

3 The roots of the quartic equation $2z^4 + 4z^3 - 3z^2 - z + 6 = 0$ are $\alpha, \beta, \gamma, \delta$.
Find quartic equations with these roots.

(i) $2\alpha, 2\beta, 2\gamma, 2\delta$
(ii) $\alpha - 1, \beta - 1, \gamma - 1, \delta - 1$

4 The roots of the quartic equation $x^4 + 8x^3 + 20x^2 + 16x + 4 = 0$ are α, β, γ and δ.

(i) By making a suitable substitution, find a quartic equation with these roots.
$\alpha + 2, \beta + 2, \gamma + 2$ and $\delta + 2$

(ii) Solve the equation found in part **(i)**, and hence find the values of α, β, γ and δ.

[MEI, *part*]

5 The quartic equation $9x^4 + px^3 - 32x + q = 0$, where p and q are real, has roots $\alpha, 3\alpha, \beta, -\beta$.

(i) By considering the coefficients of x^2 and x, find α and β, where $\beta > 0$.

(ii) Show that $p = 24$, and find the value of q.

(iii) By making the substitution $y = x - k$, for a suitable value of k, find a cubic equation with integer coefficients which has roots $-2\alpha, \beta - 3\alpha, -\beta - 3\alpha$.

[MEI]

KEY POINTS

1 An identity is true for all values of the variable(s); an equation is true only for certain values.

2 If α and β are the roots of the quadratic equation $az^2 + bz + c = 0$, then

$$\alpha + \beta = -\frac{b}{a},$$

$$\alpha\beta = \frac{c}{a}.$$

3 If α, β and γ are the roots of the cubic equation $az^3 + bz^2 + cz + d = 0$, then

$$\sum\alpha = \alpha + \beta + \gamma = -\frac{b}{a},$$

$$\sum\alpha\beta = \alpha\beta + \beta\gamma + \gamma\alpha = \frac{c}{a},$$

$$\alpha\beta\gamma = -\frac{d}{a}.$$

4 If α, β, γ and δ are the roots of the quartic equation $az^4 + bz^3 + cz^2 + dz + e = 0$, then

$$\sum\alpha = \alpha + \beta + \gamma + \delta = -\frac{b}{a},$$

$$\sum\alpha\beta = \alpha\beta + \alpha\gamma + \beta\delta + \beta\gamma + \gamma\delta + \delta\alpha = \frac{c}{a},$$

$$\sum\alpha\beta\gamma = \alpha\beta\gamma + \beta\gamma\delta + \gamma\delta\alpha + \delta\alpha\beta = -\frac{d}{a},$$

$$\alpha\beta\gamma\delta = \frac{e}{a}.$$

5 Induction and series

The distance does not matter; it is only the first step that is difficult.

Marquise du Deffand (1763)

Induction in mathematics

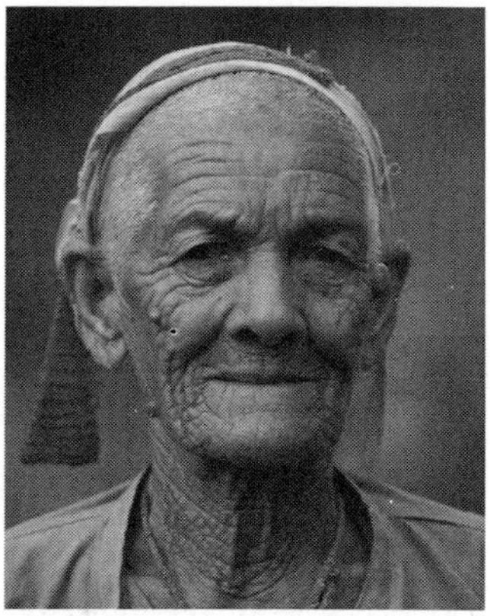

This old woman lives in the mountains of Nepal.

It is her birthday and she says she is 100 years old. No records were kept at the time of her birth. When asked how she knows she is 100, she says 'Because I was 99 last year'.

? How do you know how old you are?

Can you be sure that the old woman really is 100?

ACTIVITY 5.1 Work out the first four terms of this pattern.

$$\frac{1}{1\times 2} =$$

$$\frac{1}{1\times 2} + \frac{1}{2\times 3} =$$

$$\frac{1}{1\times 2} + \frac{1}{2\times 3} + \frac{1}{3\times 4} =$$

...

Look carefully at your answers and *predict* the next two terms. Then check your predictions.

Activity 5.1 illustrates one common way of making progress in mathematics. Looking at a number of particular cases suggests a pattern, which can usually be written algebraically to form a *conjecture* (i.e. a guess) about a more general result.

The conjecture can then be tested in further particular cases. If you find a *counter-example* (a case where the conjecture is not true) then the conjecture is definitely disproved. If, on the other hand, the further cases agree with the conjecture you may feel that you are on the right lines, but you can never be certain that trying another particular case might not reveal a counter-example: the conjecture has been confirmed, but not proved.

Activity 5.1 involves the sum of a sequence of numbers. The nth term in the sequence can be written as

$$\frac{1}{n(n+1)}.$$

If there are n numbers in the sequence the sum can be written algebraically as

$$\frac{1}{1\times 2}+\frac{1}{2\times 3}+\frac{1}{3\times 4}+\ldots+\frac{1}{n(n+1)}.$$

The activity has shown that the conjecture

$$\frac{1}{1\times 2}+\frac{1}{2\times 3}+\frac{1}{3\times 4}+\ldots+\frac{1}{n(n+1)}=\frac{n}{n+1}$$

is true for $n = 1, 2, \ldots, 6$. You want to prove that it is true for all positive integers n.

It is not possible to prove this conjecture by deduction from known results. A different approach is needed.

Proof by induction

First, assume that the conjecture is true for a particular integer, $n = k$ say, so that

$$\frac{1}{1\times 2}+\frac{1}{2\times 3}+\frac{1}{3\times 4}+\ldots+\frac{1}{k(k+1)}=\frac{k}{k+1}.$$

The idea is to use this result to show that the conjecture is also true for the next integer, $n = k + 1$, i.e. that the sum of $k + 1$ terms is

$$\frac{(k+1)}{(k+1)+1}=\frac{k+1}{k+2}.$$

The sum of $k + 1$ terms can be found by adding the $(k + 1)$th term, which is $\frac{1}{(k+1)(k+2)}$, to the sum of k terms.

$$\frac{1}{1\times 2}+\frac{1}{2\times 3}+\frac{1}{3\times 4}+\ldots+\frac{1}{k(k+1)}+\frac{1}{(k+1)(k+2)}=\frac{k}{k+1}+\frac{1}{(k+1)(k+2)}$$

$$=\frac{k(k+2)+1}{(k+1)(k+2)}$$

$$=\frac{k^2+2k+1}{(k+1)(k+2)}$$

$$=\frac{(k+1)^2}{(k+1)(k+2)}$$

$$=\frac{k+1}{k+2}$$

which is the expected result.

We have now shown that *if* the conjecture is true for $n = k$, then it is also true for $n = k + 1$.

We already know that the conjecture is true for $n = 6$, so, taking $k = 6$, it follows that it is true for $n = 7$.

Now we know that the conjecture is true for $n = 7$, so, taking $k = 7$, it follows that it is true for $n = 8$, and so on. By continuing like this, we can reach any positive integer n, so we have proved that the conjecture is true for every positive integer.

This form of proof can be compared with the process of climbing a ladder: if we can

1 reach the bottom rung

and

2 get from one rung to the next,

then we can climb as far as we like up the ladder (figure 5.1).

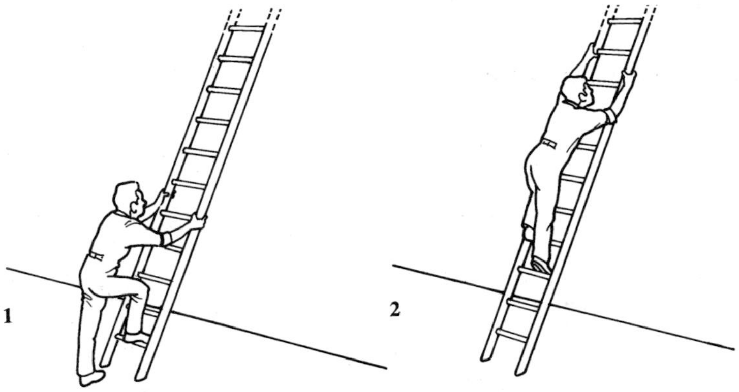

Figure 5.1

The corresponding steps in the proof are

1 showing that the conjecture is true for $n = 1$ (though in fact you checked it up to $n = 6$)

2 showing that if the conjecture is true for any particular value of n, $n = k$ say, then it is true for the next value, $n = k + 1$.

This method of proof is called *proof by mathematical induction* (or just *proof by induction*).

The method of proof by induction can be summarised as follows.

To prove a result by induction you must take three steps.

Step 1 Prove that it is true for a starting value, such as $n = 1$.
Step 2 Prove that if it is true when $n = k$, then it is true when $n = k + 1$.
Step 3 Conclude the argument.

Step 1 is usually a simple verification whereas Step 2 can be quite complicated, so there is a danger that you will concentrate on Step 2 and forget about Step 1 – but it is no use being able to climb the ladder if you cannot reach the bottom rung!

ACTIVITY 5.2

A student is investigating the sum of the first n even numbers.
She writes

$$2 + 4 + 6 + \ldots + 2n = \left(n + \tfrac{1}{2}\right)^2.$$

(i) Prove that if this result is true when $n = k$ then it is true when $n = k + 1$. Explain why this result is *not* true for any positive integer n.

(ii) Find a conjecture for the sum of the first n even numbers for which Step 1 of the proof is successful but Step 2 is not.

EXAMPLE 5.1

Prove that, for all positive integers n,

$$1^2 + 2^2 + 3^2 + \ldots + n^2 = \tfrac{1}{6}n(n + 1)(2n + 1).$$

SOLUTION

Step 1 When $n = 1$, L.H.S. $= 1^2 = 1$
R.H.S. $= \frac{1}{6} \times 1 \times 2 \times 3 = 1$.

Step 2 Assume that the result is true when $n = k$, so that

$$1^2 + 2^2 + 3^2 + \ldots + k^2 = \tfrac{1}{6}k(k + 1)(2k + 1).$$

We want to prove that the result is true for $n = k + 1$, i.e. that

$$1^2 + 2^2 + 3^2 + \ldots + k^2 + (k + 1)^2 = \tfrac{1}{6}(k+1)((k+1) + 1)(2(k+1) + 1)$$
$$= \tfrac{1}{6}(k+1)(k+2)(2k+3).$$

Using the assumed result for $n = k$ gives

$$1^2 + 2^2 + 3^2 + \ldots + k^2 + (k + 1)^2 = \tfrac{1}{6}k(k + 1)(2k + 1) + (k + 1)^2$$

Add $(k + 1)^2$ to each side.

$$= \tfrac{1}{6}(k+1)[k(2k+1) + 6(k+1)]$$

Take out $= \frac{1}{6}(k + 1)$ as a factor – this is part of the target expression.

$$= \tfrac{1}{6}(k+1)(2k^2 + k + 6k + 6)$$
$$= \tfrac{1}{6}(k+1)(2k^2 + 7k + 6)$$
$$= \tfrac{1}{6}(k+1)(k+2)(2k+3).$$

Step 3 So if the result is true when $n = k$, then it is true when $n = k + 1$. As it is true for $n = 1$, it is true for all $n \geqslant 1$ by induction.

Notation

There are a number of different notations which are commonly used in writing down sequences and series.

The terms of a sequence are often written as $a_1, a_2, a_3, \ldots$ or as $u_1, u_2, u_3, \ldots$

The general (kth) term of a sequence may be written as a_k or u_k. Sometimes r or i are used instead of k.

The last term is usually written as a_n or u_n.

The sum S_n of the first n terms of a sequence can be written using the symbol Σ (the Greek capital S, sigma).

$$S_n = a_1 + a_2 + \ldots + a_n = \sum_{k=1}^{n} a_k$$

The numbers above and below the Σ are the *limits* of the sum. They show that the sum includes all the a_k from a_1 to a_n. The limits may be omitted if they are obvious, so that you would just write Σa_k, or you might write $\sum_k a_k$ (meaning the sum of a_k for all values of k).

EXERCISE 5A

In questions 1 *to* 12, *prove the result given by induction.*

1 $1 + 3 + 5 + \ldots + (2n - 1) = n^2$
(This was the first example of proof by induction ever published, by Francesco Maurolycus in 1575.)

2 $1 + 2 + 3 + \ldots + n = \frac{1}{2}n(n + 1)$

3 $2 + 2^2 + 2^3 + \ldots + 2^n = 2(2^n - 1)$

4 $\displaystyle\sum_{k=1}^{n} k^3 = \frac{1}{4}n^2(n + 1)^2$

5 $(1 \times 2) + (2 \times 3) + (3 \times 4) + \ldots + n(n + 1) = \frac{1}{3}n(n + 1)(n + 2)$

6 $\displaystyle\sum_{k=0}^{n-1} x^k = \frac{1 - x^n}{1 - x} \quad (x \neq 1)$

7 $(1 \times 2 \times 3) + (2 \times 3 \times 4) + \ldots + n(n + 1)(n + 2) = \frac{1}{4}n(n + 1)(n + 2)(n + 3)$

8 $\displaystyle\sum_{k=1}^{n} (3k + 1) = \frac{1}{2}n(3n + 5)$

9 $\dfrac{1}{3} + \dfrac{1}{15} + \dfrac{1}{35} + \ldots + \dfrac{1}{4n^2 - 1} = \dfrac{n}{2n + 1}$

10 $\dfrac{1}{1 \times 2 \times 3} + \dfrac{1}{2 \times 3 \times 4} + \ldots + \dfrac{1}{n(n + 1)(n + 2)} = \dfrac{n(n + 3)}{4(n + 1)(n + 2)}$

11 $\left(1 - \dfrac{1}{2^2}\right)\left(1 - \dfrac{1}{3^2}\right)\left(1 - \dfrac{1}{4^2}\right)\ldots\left(1 - \dfrac{1}{n^2}\right) = \dfrac{n + 1}{2n} \quad$ for $n \geqslant 2$

12 $1 \times 1! + 2 \times 2! + 3 \times 3! + \ldots + n \times n! = (n + 1)! - 1$
(Remember: $n!$ means $n(n - 1)(n - 2)\ldots 3 \times 2 \times 1$.)

More proofs by induction

So far you have used induction to prove a given expression for the sum of a series. Here are some other examples of its use.

In Example 5.2, a sequence is given *inductively*, i.e. each term is defined by relating it to the previous term.

EXAMPLE 5.2

A sequence is defined by $u_{n+1} = 4u_n - 3$, $u_1 = 2$.

Prove that $u_n = 4^{n-1} + 1$.

SOLUTION

Step 1 For $n = 1$, $u_1 = 4^0 + 1 = 1 + 1 = 2$, so the result is true for $n = 1$.

Step 2 Assume that the result is true for $n = k$, so that $u_k = 4^{k-1} + 1$.
We want to prove that it is true for $n = k + 1$, i.e. that $u_{k+1} = 4u^k + 1$.

$$\begin{aligned}\text{For } n = k + 1,\ u_{k+1} &= 4u_k - 3\\ &= 4(4^{k-1} + 1) - 3\\ &= 4 \times 4^{k-1} + 4 - 3\\ &= 4^k + 1\end{aligned}$$

Step 3 So if the result is true for $n = k$, then it is true for $n = k + 1$.
Since it is true for $n = 1$, then it is true for all $n \geqslant 1$ by induction.

e Other applications

Although the method of proof by induction is often used in the context of the sum of a series, it has other applications as well, as the following example shows.

EXAMPLE 5.3

Prove that $u_n = 4^n + 6n - 1$ is divisible by 9 for all $n \geqslant 1$.

SOLUTION

Step 1 For $n = 1$, $u_1 = 4 + 6 - 1 = 9$, so it is true when $n = 1$.

Step 2 We want to show that

$$u_k \text{ is divisible by } 9 \Rightarrow u_{k+1} \text{ is divisible by } 9.$$

$$\begin{aligned}\text{Now } u_{k+1} &= 4^{k+1} + 6(k + 1) - 1\\ &= 4 \times 4^k + 6k + 5\\ &= 4(u_k - 6k + 1) + 6k + 5\\ &= 4u_k - 18k + 9\\ &= 4u_k - 9(2k - 1)\end{aligned}$$

Substituting $4^k = u_k - 6k + 1$.

Step 3 Therefore if u_k is a multiple of 9 then so is u_{k+1}.
Since u_1 is a multiple of 9, u_n is a multiple of 9 for all $n \geqslant 1$.

EXERCISE 5B

1 A sequence is defined by $u_{n+1} = 3u_n + 2$, $u_1 = 2$.
Prove by induction that $u_n = 3^n - 1$.

2 A sequence is defined by $u_{n+1} = 2u_n - 1$, $u_1 = 2$.
Prove by induction that $u_n = 2^{n-1} + 1$.

3 A sequence is defined by $u_{n+1} = 4u_n - 6$, $u_1 = 3$.
Prove by induction that $u_n = 4^{n-1} + 2$.

4 A sequence is defined by $u_{n+1} = \dfrac{u_n}{u_n + 1}$, $u_1 = 1$.

(i) Find the values of u_2, u_3 and u_4.

(ii) Suggest a general formula for u_n, and prove your conjecture by induction.

5 A sequence of integers $u_1, u_2, u_3, \ldots$ is defined by

$$u_1 = 5 \text{ and } u_{n+1} = 3u_n - 2^n \text{ for } n \geqslant 1.$$

(i) Use this definition to find u_2 and u_3.

(ii) Prove by induction that $u_n = 2^n + 3^n$ for all positive integers n.

[MEI, *part*]

6 A sequence $u_1, u_2, u_3, \ldots$ is defined by

$$u_1 = \tfrac{7}{2} \text{ and } u_n = \tfrac{1}{2}u_{n-1} + n^2 \text{ for } n \geqslant 2.$$

Prove by induction that $u_n = 2n^2 - 4n + 6 - \left(\frac{1}{2}\right)^n$ and for all positive integers n.

[MEI, *part*]

e *The remaining questions relate to enrichment material.*

7 Prove, using the method of mathematical induction, that $2^{4n+1} + 3$ is a multiple of 5 for any positive integer n.

[MEI, *part*]

8 Prove that $11^{n+2} + 12^{2n+1}$ is divisible by 133 for $n \geqslant 0$.

9 You are given the matrix $\mathbf{A} = \begin{pmatrix} -1 & -4 \\ 1 & 3 \end{pmatrix}$.

(i) Calculate $\mathbf{A}^2$ and $\mathbf{A}^3$.

(ii) Show that the formula $\mathbf{A}^n = \begin{pmatrix} 1 - 2n & -4n \\ n & 1 + 2n \end{pmatrix}$ is consistent with the given value of $\mathbf{A}$ and your calculations for $n = 2$ and $n = 3$.

(iii) Prove by induction that the formula for $\mathbf{A}^n$ is correct when n is a positive integer.

[MEI, *part*]

Summation of finite series

The sum S_n of a finite series is found by adding together the first n terms of a sequence. You may have already met these important examples in C2.

Arithmetic series: $a_k = a + (k-1)d$ $\quad S_n = \frac{1}{2}n[2a + (n-1)d]$

where d is the common difference and a is the first term.

Geometric series: $a_k = ar^{k-1}$ $\quad S_n = \dfrac{a(1-r^n)}{1-r}$

where r is the common ratio and a is the first term.

If the sum approaches a finite number as $n \to \infty$, the series is said to be *convergent*.

? Explain why an arithmetic series can never be convergent (unless all its terms are zero).

For what values of r is a geometric series convergent?

As you have seen in the previous section, if you can guess what the sum of a series is you can often prove it by mathematical induction. Here are some other ways of dealing with finite sums. Some of these results may be familiar to you; the important thing is to concentrate on the methods of obtaining them.

The method of differences

In some sequences, it is possible to express each term as the difference of consecutive terms of another sequence, with the result that most of the terms cancel out. This is called the method of differences, and is illustrated in the next two examples.

EXAMPLE 5.4

(i) Show that $\dfrac{1}{r} - \dfrac{1}{r+1} = \dfrac{1}{r(r+1)}$.

(ii) Hence find $\dfrac{1}{1\times 2} + \dfrac{1}{2\times 3} + \dfrac{1}{3\times 4} + \ldots + \dfrac{1}{30\times 31}$.

SOLUTION

(i) $\dfrac{1}{r} - \dfrac{1}{r+1} = \dfrac{r+1-r}{r(r+1)}$

$= \dfrac{1}{r(r+1)}$

(ii) $\dfrac{1}{1\times 2}+\dfrac{1}{2\times 3}+\dfrac{1}{3\times 4}+\ldots+\dfrac{1}{30\times 31}=\displaystyle\sum_{r=1}^{30}\frac{1}{r(r+1)}$

$$=\sum_{r=1}^{30}\left(\frac{1}{r}-\frac{1}{r+1}\right)$$

Using the result from part (i).

$$\begin{aligned}=1 &\quad -\tfrac{1}{2}\\ + &\quad \tfrac{1}{2} \quad -\tfrac{1}{3}\\ &\quad + \quad \tfrac{1}{3} \quad -\tfrac{1}{4}\\ &\quad\quad + \quad \ldots \quad \ldots\\ &\quad\quad + \quad \tfrac{1}{29} \quad -\tfrac{1}{30}\\ &\quad\quad\quad + \quad \tfrac{1}{30} \quad -\tfrac{1}{31}\end{aligned}$$

Everything in the box cancels out in pairs, leaving just the first and last terms.

$$=1-\frac{1}{31}$$

$$=\frac{30}{31}$$

Notice that this result can easily be generalised for a sequence of any length. If the sequence has n terms, then the terms would still cancel in pairs, leaving the first term, 1, and the last term, $-\dfrac{1}{n+1}$.

The sum of the terms would therefore be

$$1-\frac{1}{n+1}=\frac{n+1-1}{n+1}=\frac{n}{n+1}.$$

This shows that as $n\to\infty$, the sum approaches 1. So this series converges.

The cancelling of nearly all the terms is similar to the way in which the interior sections of a collapsible telescope disappear when it is compressed, so a sum like this is sometimes described as a *telescoping sum.*

The next example uses a rather more complicated telescoping sum.

EXAMPLE 5.5

(i) Show that $\dfrac{2}{r}-\dfrac{3}{r+1}+\dfrac{1}{r+2}=\dfrac{r+4}{r(r+1)(r+2)}$.

(ii) Hence find $\displaystyle\sum_{r=1}^{n}\frac{r+4}{r(r+1)(r+2)}$.

SOLUTION

(i)
$$\frac{2}{r}-\frac{3}{r+1}+\frac{1}{r+2}=\frac{2(r+1)(r+2)-3r(r+2)+r(r+1)}{r(r+1)(r+2)}$$

$$=\frac{2r^2+6r+4-3r^2-6r+r^2+r}{r(r+1)(r+2)}$$

$$=\frac{r+4}{r(r+1)(r+2)}$$

(ii) $$\sum_{r=1}^{n} \frac{r+4}{r(r+1)(r+2)} = \sum_{r=1}^{n} \left(\frac{2}{r} - \frac{3}{r+1} + \frac{1}{r+2}\right)$$

$$\begin{aligned}
&= 2 - \frac{3}{2} + \frac{1}{3} \\
&\quad + \frac{2}{2} - \frac{3}{3} + \frac{1}{4} \\
&\quad + \frac{2}{3} - \frac{3}{4} + \frac{1}{5} \\
&\quad + \quad \dots \quad \dots \\
&\quad + \frac{2}{n-2} - \frac{3}{n-1} + \frac{1}{n} \\
&\quad + \frac{2}{n-1} - \frac{3}{n} + \frac{1}{n+1} \\
&\quad + \frac{2}{n} - \frac{3}{n+1} + \frac{1}{n+2}
\end{aligned}$$

Everything in here cancels.

Most of the terms cancel, leaving

$$\begin{aligned}
\sum_{r=1}^{n} \frac{r+4}{r(r+1)(r+2)} &= 2 - \frac{3}{2} + \frac{2}{2} + \frac{1}{n+1} - \frac{3}{n+1} + \frac{1}{n+2} \\
&= \frac{3}{2} - \frac{2}{n+1} + \frac{1}{n+2}
\end{aligned}$$

? Show that the expression obtained in Example 5.5 part **(ii)** can be simplified to give $\dfrac{n(3n+7)}{2(n+1)(n+2)}$.

Note

The terms which do not cancel form a symmetrical pattern, three at the start and three at the end.

? Explain how you can tell that this series converges.

What is the limiting value of the series as $n \to \infty$?

EXERCISE 5C

1 **(i)** Show that $r^2 - (r-1)^2 = 2r - 1$.

(ii) Hence find $1 + 3 + 5 + \dots + (2n-1)$.

2 **(i)** Show that $(r+1)^2(r+2) - r^2(r+1) = (r+1)(3r+2)$.

(ii) Hence find $2 \times 5 + 3 \times 8 + 4 \times 11 + \dots + (n+1)(3n+2)$.

3 **(i)** Show that $\dfrac{1}{2r-1} - \dfrac{1}{2r+1} = \dfrac{2}{(2r-1)(2r+1)}$.

(ii) Hence find $\dfrac{2}{1 \times 3} + \dfrac{2}{3 \times 5} + \dfrac{2}{5 \times 7} + \dots + \dfrac{2}{19 \times 21}$.

4 (i) Show that $\dfrac{1}{r^2} - \dfrac{1}{(r+1)^2} = \dfrac{2r+1}{r^2(r+1)^2}$.

(ii) Hence find $\displaystyle\sum_{r=1}^{n} \frac{2r+1}{r^2(r+1)^2}$.

5 (i) Show that $\dfrac{1}{2r} - \dfrac{1}{2(r+2)} = \dfrac{1}{r(r+2)}$.

(ii) Hence find $\displaystyle\sum_{r=1}^{n} \frac{1}{r(r+2)}$.

(iii) Does this series converge? Explain your answer.

6 (i) Show that $-\dfrac{1}{r+2} + \dfrac{3}{r+3} - \dfrac{2}{r+4} = \dfrac{r}{(r+2)(r+3)(r+4)}$

(ii) Hence find $\displaystyle\sum_{r=1}^{12} \frac{r}{(r+2)(r+3)(r+4)}$.

7 (i) Show that $\dfrac{1}{2r} - \dfrac{1}{r+1} + \dfrac{1}{2(r+2)} = \dfrac{1}{r(r+1)(r+2)}$.

(ii) Hence find $\displaystyle\sum_{r=1}^{n} \frac{1}{r(r+1)(r+2)}$.

(iii) Does this series converge? Explain your answer.

8 (i) Show that $\dfrac{r+2}{r(r+1)} - \dfrac{r+3}{(r+1)(r+2)} = \dfrac{r+4}{r(r+1)(r+2)}$.

(ii) Hence or otherwise find the sum of the first n terms of the series

$$\frac{5}{1\times2\times3} + \frac{6}{2\times3\times4} + \frac{7}{3\times4\times5} + \frac{8}{4\times5\times6} + \dots.$$

[MEI, *part*]

In questions 9 to 11, you will prove three important results that will be needed in the next section.

9 (i) Show that $(2r+1)^2 - (2r-1)^2 = 8r$.

(ii) Hence find $\displaystyle\sum_{r=1}^{n} 8r$.

(iii) Deduce that $\displaystyle\sum_{r=1}^{n} r = \tfrac{1}{2}n(n+1)$.

10 (i) Show that $(2r+1)^3 - (2r-1)^3 = 24r^2 + 2$.

(ii) Hence find $\displaystyle\sum_{r=1}^{n} (24r^2 + 2)$.

(iii) Deduce that $\displaystyle\sum_{r=1}^{n} r^2 = \tfrac{1}{6}n(n+1)(2n+1)$.

(Hint: $\displaystyle\sum_{r=1}^{n} k = (k + k + k + \dots + k) = kn$ for any constant k.)

11 **(i)** Show that $(2r+1)^4 - (2r-1)^4 = 64r^3 + 16r$.

(ii) Hence find $\sum_{r=1}^{n}(64r^3 + 16r)$.

(iii) Deduce that $\sum_{r=1}^{n} r^3 = \frac{1}{4}n^2(n+1)^2$.

(You will need to use the expression for $\sum_{r=1}^{n} r$ from question 9).

12 **(i)** Show that $r(r+1)(r+2) - (r-1)r(r+1) = 3r(r+1)$.

Hence find $\sum_{r=1}^{n} r(r+1)$.

(ii) Show that $r(r+1)(r+2)(r+3) - (r-1)r(r+1)(r+2) = 4r(r+1)(r+2)$.

Hence find $\sum_{r=1}^{n} r(r+1)(r+2)$.

(iii) Using the formula for $\sum_{r=1}^{n} r$ from question 9 and $\sum_{r=1}^{n} r(r+1)$ and $\sum_{r=1}^{n} r(r+1)(r+2)$ from parts **(i)** and **(ii)**, make a conjecture about $\sum_{r=1}^{n} r(r+1)(r+2)\dots(r+k)$ and prove it using the method of differences.

Using standard results

In questions 9 to 11 of Exercise 5C you found these three important results.

$$\sum_{r=1}^{n} r = \tfrac{1}{2}n(n+1) \qquad \sum_{r=1}^{n} r^2 = \tfrac{1}{6}n(n+1)(2n+1) \qquad \sum_{r=1}^{n} r^3 = \tfrac{1}{4}n^2(n+1)^2$$

? Explain why $\sum_{r=1}^{n} 1 = n$.

These results can be used to sum further series, as shown in the following examples.

EXAMPLE 5.6

Find $\sum_{r=1}^{n}(r^2 + 2r - 1)$.

SOLUTION

$$\begin{aligned}\sum_{r=1}^{n}(r^2 + 2r - 1) &= \sum_{r=1}^{n} r^2 + 2\sum_{r=1}^{n} r - \sum_{r=1}^{n} 1 \\ &= \tfrac{1}{6}n(n+1)(2n+1) + 2 \times \tfrac{1}{2}n(n+1) - n \\ &= \tfrac{1}{6}n[(n+1)(2n+1) + 6(n+1) - 6] \\ &= \tfrac{1}{6}n(2n^2 + 3n + 1 + 6n + 6 - 6) \\ &= \tfrac{1}{6}n(2n^2 + 9n + 1)\end{aligned}$$

$\sum_{r=1}^{n} 1 = n$

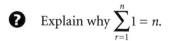

It is easy to make mistakes in the algebra when simplifying an expression like this, so it is a good idea to check the result for $n = 1$.

EXAMPLE 5.7

Find $(1 \times 3) + (2 \times 4) + (3 \times 5) + \ldots + n(n + 2)$.

SOLUTION

This sum can be written in the form $\sum_{r=1}^{n} r(r + 2)$.

$$\begin{aligned}\sum_{r=1}^{n} r(r+2) &= \sum_{r=1}^{n} (r^2 + 2r) \\ &= \sum_{r=1}^{n} r^2 + 2\sum_{r=1}^{n} r \\ &= \tfrac{1}{6}n(n+1)(2n+1) + 2 \times \tfrac{1}{2}n(n+1) \\ &= \tfrac{1}{6}n(n+1)[2n+1+6] \\ &= \tfrac{1}{6}n(n+1)(2n+7)\end{aligned}$$

EXERCISE 5D

1 Find $\sum_{r=1}^{n} (2r - 1)$.

2 Find $\sum_{r=1}^{n} r(3r + 1)$.

3 Find $\sum_{r=1}^{n} (r + 1)r^2$.

4 Find $\sum_{r=1}^{n} (4r^3 - 6r^2 + 4r - 1)$.

5 Find $(1 \times 2) + (2 \times 3) + (3 \times 4) + \ldots + n(n + 1)$.

6 Find $(1 \times 2 \times 3) + (2 \times 3 \times 4) + (3 \times 4 \times 5) + \ldots + n(n + 1)(n + 2)$.

7 Find $\sum_{r=1}^{n} r(3r + 2)$, giving your answer in a fully factorised form.

[MEI, *part*]

8 On a fruit stall a pile of oranges is arranged to form a truncated square pyramid. Each layer is a square, with the lengths of side of successive layers reducing by one orange.
The bottom layer measures $2n \times 2n$ oranges, and there are n layers.

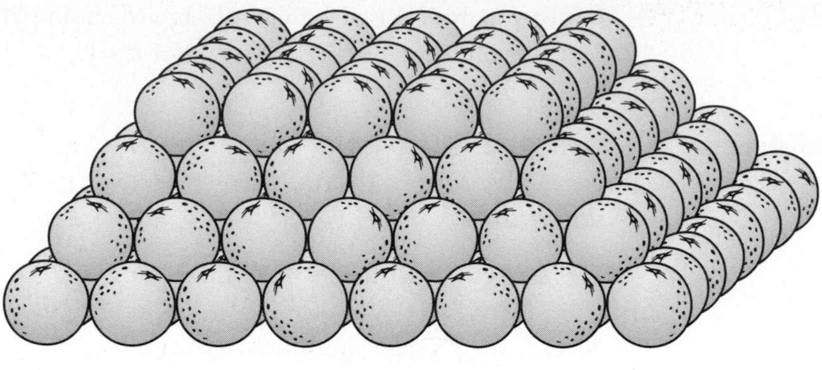

(i) Prove that the number of oranges used is

$$\tfrac{1}{6}n(2n+1)(7n+1).$$

(ii) What is the greatest n which uses fewer than 1000 oranges?

9 **(i)** Prove by induction that

$$\sum_{r=1}^{n}(5r^4 + r^2) = \tfrac{1}{2}n^2(n+1)^2(2n+1).$$

(ii) Using the result in part **(i)**, and the formula for $\sum_{r=1}^{n} r^2$, show that

$$\sum_{r=1}^{n} r^4 = \tfrac{1}{30}n(n+1)(2n+1)(3n^2+3n-1).$$

[MEI, *part*]

10 **(i)** Prove, by induction or otherwise, that

$$\sum_{r=1}^{n}(3r^5 + r^3) = \tfrac{1}{2}n^3(n+1)^3.$$

(ii) Using the result in part **(i)** and the formula for $\sum_{r=1}^{n} r^3$, show that

$$\sum_{r=1}^{n} r^5 = \tfrac{1}{12}n^2(n+1)^2(2n^2+2n-1).$$

[MEI]

11 Using the idea suggested in the diagram, or otherwise, prove that

$$1 \times n + 2(n-1) + 3(n-2) + \ldots + n \times 1 = \tfrac{1}{6}n(n+1)(n+2).$$

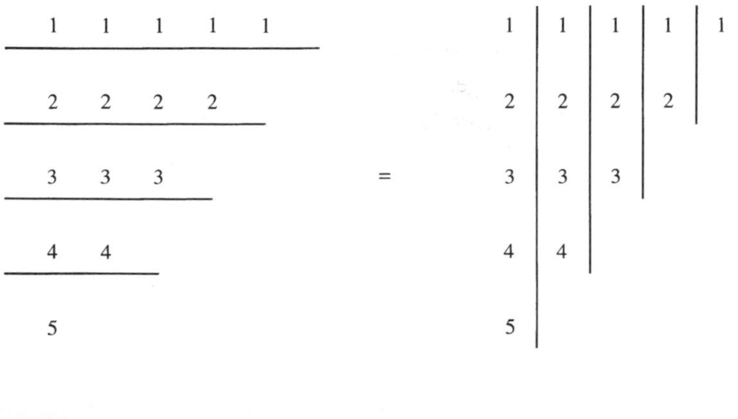

KEY POINTS

1. To prove by induction that a statement involving an integer n is true for all $n \geqslant n_0$, you need three steps.

   Step 1 Prove that the result is true for $n = n_0$.
   Step 2 Prove that if the result is true for $n = k$ then it is true for $n = k + 1$.
   Step 3 Complete the argument.

2. Some series can be summed by using the method of differences.
   If the terms of the series can be written as the difference of two terms of another series, then most of the terms cancel out.
   This is called a telescoping sum.

3. Some series can be summed using these standard results.

$$\sum_{r=1}^{n} r = \tfrac{1}{2}n(n+1) \qquad \sum_{r=1}^{n} r^2 = \tfrac{1}{6}n(n+1)(2n+1) \qquad \sum_{r=1}^{n} r^3 = \tfrac{1}{4}n^2(n+1)^2$$

Answers

Chapter 1

❓ (Page 1)

A *shear* parallel to the *xy* plane (each point is moved parallel to the *xy* plane through a distance proportional to its distance from the *xy* plane), followed by a rotation of 90° anticlockwise about the *z* axis.

The shear can be represented by $(x, y, z) \to (x, y + z, z)$.

The rotation can be represented by $(x, y, z) \to (-y, x, z)$.

The whole transformation can be represented by $(x, y, z) \to (-y - z, x, z)$.

❓ (Page 2)

There are no crossings from Folkestone to Zeebrugge.

❓ (Page 2)

$$\begin{pmatrix} 10 & 20 & 10 \\ 0 & 20 & 10 \end{pmatrix}$$

❓ (Page 3)

$$\begin{pmatrix} 4 & 3 & 2 \\ 2 & 3 & 1 \end{pmatrix}$$

❓ (Page 3)

(i) Addition of elements in each position is commutative, i.e. $a + b = b + a$.

(ii) Addition of elements in each position is associative, i.e. $a + (b + c) = (a + b) + c$.

Exercise 1A (page 3)

1 **(i)** 2×2

(ii) 2×3

(iii) 3×2

2 **(i)** $\begin{pmatrix} -1 & 5 \\ 4 & -5 \end{pmatrix}$

(ii) $\begin{pmatrix} 5 & -5 & 5 \\ 2 & -2 & 2 \end{pmatrix}$

(iii) Not possible

(iv) $\begin{pmatrix} -6 & 9 \\ 3 & -12 \end{pmatrix}$

(v) $\begin{pmatrix} 17 & -6 \\ -6 & -7 \\ -22 & 20 \end{pmatrix}$

(vi) Not possible

3 **(i)** $X = \begin{pmatrix} 0 & 2 & 1 & 0 \\ 1 & 0 & 2 & 1 \\ 0 & 2 & 0 & 2 \\ 1 & 0 & 1 & 0 \end{pmatrix}$

(ii) $Y = \begin{pmatrix} 0 & 0 & 2 & 2 \\ 1 & 0 & 0 & 0 \\ 2 & 0 & 0 & 1 \\ 0 & 0 & 2 & 0 \end{pmatrix}$

(iii)

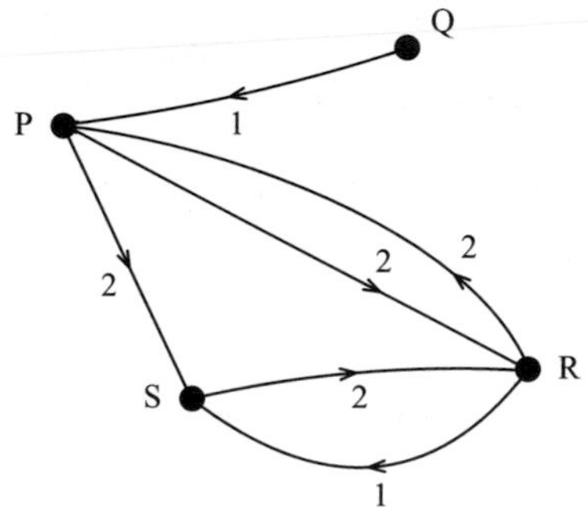

4 **(i)** $\begin{matrix} C \\ R \\ T \\ U \end{matrix}\begin{pmatrix} 1 & 0 & 1 & 4 & 4 \\ 0 & 0 & 1 & 0 & 2 \\ 1 & 1 & 0 & 7 & 5 \\ 0 & 1 & 0 & 3 & 3 \end{pmatrix}, \begin{matrix} C \\ R \\ T \\ U \end{matrix}\begin{pmatrix} 3 & 1 & 1 & 10 & 7 \\ 0 & 0 & 4 & 2 & 10 \\ 3 & 1 & 1 & 11 & 8 \\ 1 & 2 & 1 & 8 & 6 \end{pmatrix}$

(ii) $\begin{matrix} C \\ R \\ T \\ U \end{matrix}\begin{pmatrix} 1 & 0 & 0 & 2 & 1 \\ 1 & 1 & 0 & 3 & 2 \\ 0 & 0 & 1 & 1 & 2 \\ 0 & 1 & 1 & 2 & 3 \end{pmatrix}$

Rangers 1, United 1

City 2, United 1

Rangers 2, Town 1

5 **(i)** $\begin{pmatrix} 15 & 3 & 7 & 15 \\ 5 & 9 & 15 & -3 \\ 19 & 10 & 9 & 3 \end{pmatrix}$

This matrix represents the number of jackets in stock after all orders have been dispatched. The negative element shows that there were not enough of one type of jacket in stock to meet all the orders.

(ii) $\begin{pmatrix} 20 & 13 & 17 & 20 \\ 15 & 19 & 20 & 12 \\ 19 & 10 & 14 & 8 \end{pmatrix}$

(iii) $\begin{pmatrix} 12 & 30 & 18 & 0 \\ 6 & 18 & 24 & 36 \\ 30 & 0 & 12 & 18 \end{pmatrix}$

Probably not very realistic, as a week is quite a short time.

? (Page 8)

$a = 0, b = 1, c = -1, d = 0$

Activity 1.1 (Page 8)

After the reflection P′ = (0, 1), Q′ = (0, 2), R′ = (−1, 2), S′ = (−1, 1).

$\begin{cases} x' = -x \\ y' = y \end{cases}$

The matrix for reflection in the y axis is $\begin{pmatrix} -1 & 0 \\ 0 & 1 \end{pmatrix}$.

After the enlargement P′ = (0, 2), Q′ = (0, 4), R′ = (2, 4), S′ = (2, 2).

$\begin{cases} x' = 2x \\ y' = 2y \end{cases}$

The matrix for enlargement scale factor 2, centre O, is $\begin{pmatrix} 2 & 0 \\ 0 & 2 \end{pmatrix}$.

Activity 1.2 (Page 10)

$\begin{pmatrix} 1 & 0 \\ 0 & 0 \end{pmatrix}$ transforms all points on to the x axis.

$\begin{pmatrix} 0 & 0 \\ 0 & 1 \end{pmatrix}$ transforms all points on to the y axis.

? (Page 10)

The image of the origin under a translation is not the origin.

? (Page 11)

$\begin{pmatrix} \cos\theta & \sin\theta \\ -\sin\theta & \cos\theta \end{pmatrix}$

Activity 1.3 (Page 12)

(i) For angles between 90° and 180°, $\cos\theta$ is negative and $\sin\theta$ is positive.

(ii) For angles between 180° and 270°, $\cos\theta$ is negative and $\sin\theta$ is negative.

(iii) For angles between 270° and 360°, $\cos\theta$ is positive and $\sin\theta$ is negative.

Exercise 1B (Page 13)

1 **(i)** **(a)**

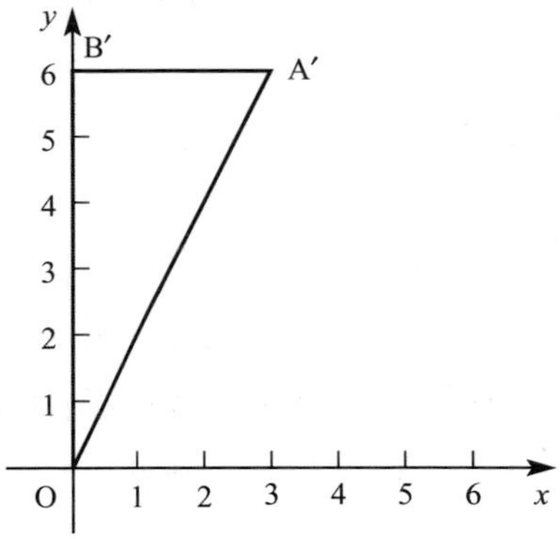

(b) A′ = (3, 6), B′ = (0, 6)

(c) $x' = 3x, y' = 3y$

(d) $\begin{pmatrix} 3 & 0 \\ 0 & 3 \end{pmatrix}$

(ii) **(a)**

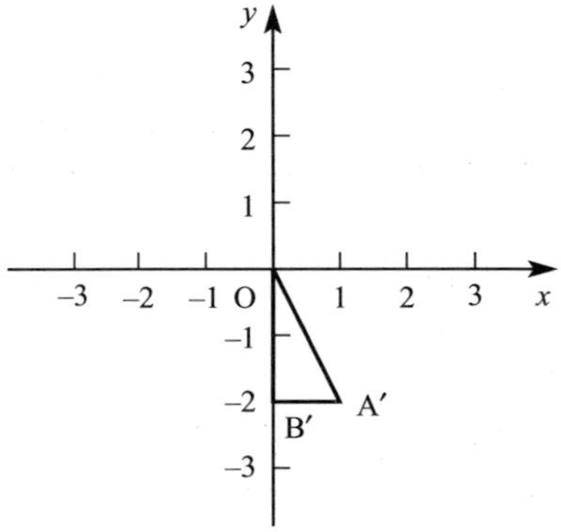

(b) A′ = (1, −2), B′ = (0, −2)

(c) $x' = x, y' = -y$

(d) $\begin{pmatrix} 1 & 0 \\ 0 & -1 \end{pmatrix}$

(iii) **(a)**

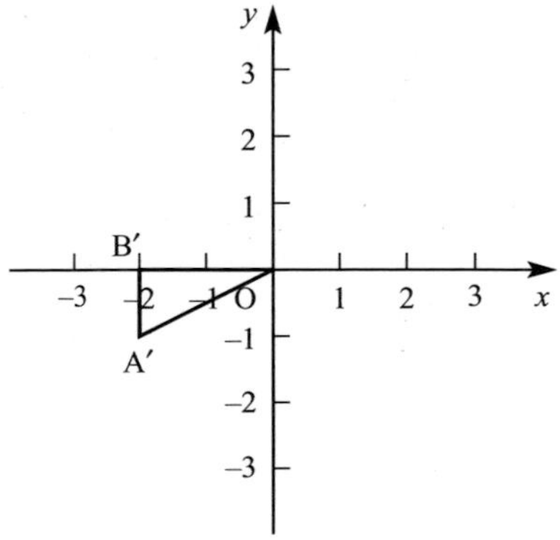

(b) A′ = (−2, −1), B′ = (−2, 0)

(c) $x' = -y, y' = -x$

(d) $\begin{pmatrix} 0 & -1 \\ -1 & 0 \end{pmatrix}$

(iv) **(a)**

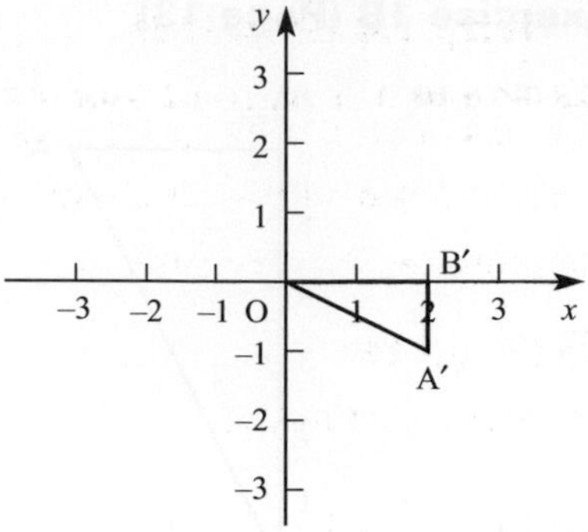

(b) A′ = (2, –1), B′ = (2, 0)

(c) $x' = y, y' = -x$

(d) $\begin{pmatrix} 0 & 1 \\ -1 & 0 \end{pmatrix}$

(v) **(a)**

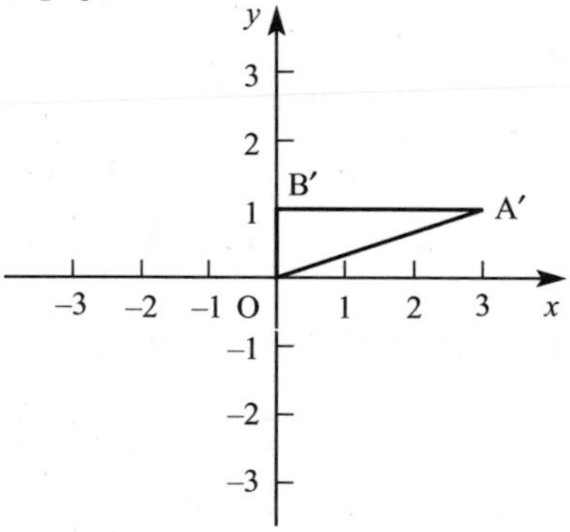

(b) A′ = (3, 1), B′ = (0, 1)

(c) $x' = 3x, y' = \frac{1}{2}y$

(d) $\begin{pmatrix} 3 & 0 \\ 0 & \frac{1}{2} \end{pmatrix}$

2 $x' = x\cos\theta - y\sin\theta$

$y' = x\sin\theta + y\cos\theta$

A′ = (0.256, 2.221), B′ = (–0.684, 1.879)

3 **(i)** Rotation of 60° anticlockwise about the origin

(ii) Rotation of 55° anticlockwise about the origin

(iii) Rotation of 135° clockwise about the origin

(iv) Rotation of 150° anticlockwise about the origin

4 **(i)** **(a)**

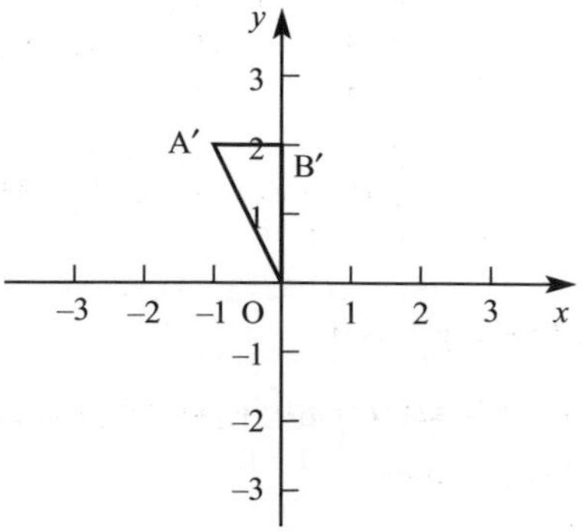

(b) A′ = (–1, 2), B′ = (0, 2)

(c) Reflection in the y axis

(ii) **(a)**

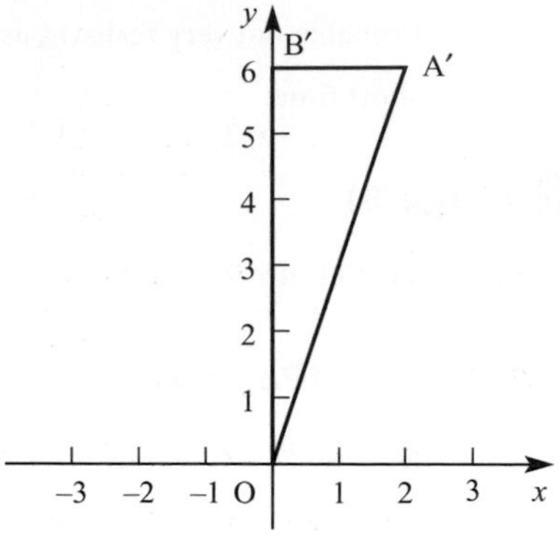

(b) A′ = (2, 6), B′ = (0, 6)

(c) Two-way stretch, ×2 horizontally, ×3 vertically

(iii) **(a)**

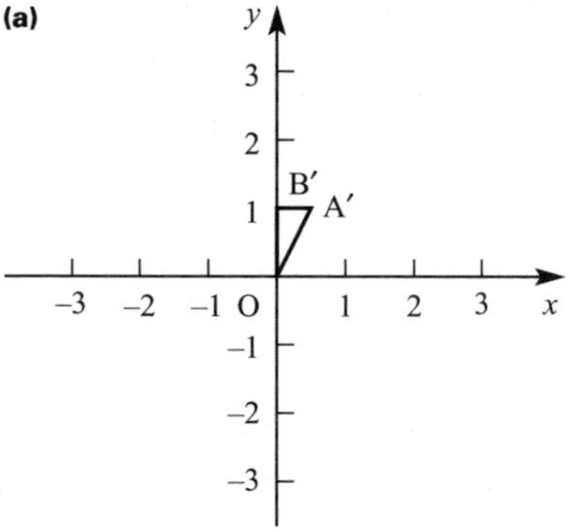

(b) A′ = $\left(\frac{1}{2}, 1\right)$, B′ = (0, 1)

(c) Enlargement, centre O, scale factor $\frac{1}{2}$

(iv) **(a)**

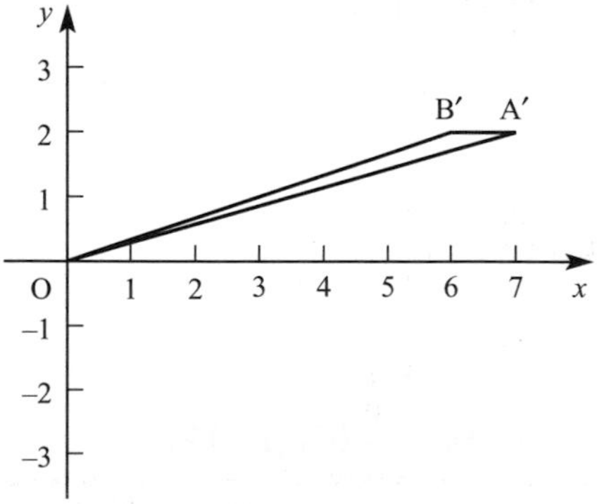

(b) A′ = (7, 2), B′ = (6, 2)

(c) Shear parallel to x axis

(v) **(a)**

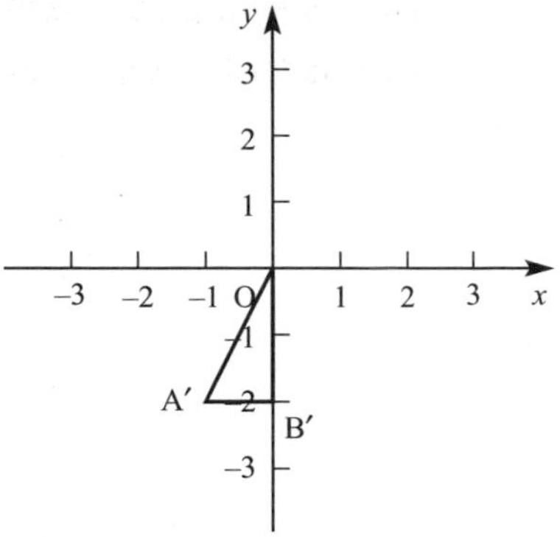

(b) A′ = (–1, –2), B′ = (0, –2)

(c) Rotation 180° about O

(vi) **(a)**

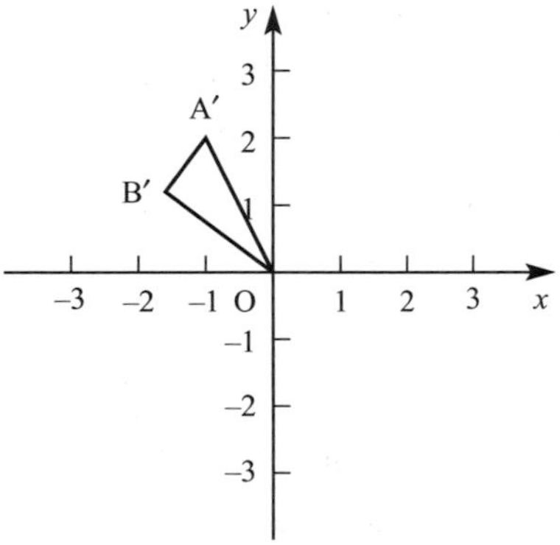

(b) A′ = (–1, 2), B′ = (–1.6, 1.2)

(c) Rotation 53.1° anticlockwise about O

5 A′ = (4, 5), B′ = (7, 9), C′ = (3, 4)

6 (x, x)

$$\begin{pmatrix}1 & 0\\1 & 0\end{pmatrix}$$

7 **(i)** $\begin{pmatrix}3 & 0 & 0\\0 & 3 & 0\\0 & 0 & 3\end{pmatrix}$

(ii) $\begin{pmatrix}-1 & 0 & 0\\0 & -1 & 0\\0 & 0 & 1\end{pmatrix}$

(iii) $\begin{pmatrix}-1 & 0 & 0\\0 & 1 & 0\\0 & 0 & 1\end{pmatrix}$

8 **(i)** Rotation 90° clockwise about x axis

(ii) Reflection in plane $z = 0$

(iii) Three-way stretch, ×2 in x direction, ×3 in y direction, $\times\frac{1}{2}$ in z direction

Activity 1.4 (Page 16)

$$\begin{pmatrix}0.8 & -0.6\\0.6 & 0.8\end{pmatrix}\begin{pmatrix}0 & 1 & 1 & 1\\2 & 2 & 1 & 0\end{pmatrix} = \begin{pmatrix}-1.2 & -0.4 & 0.2 & 0.8\\1.6 & 2.2 & 1.4 & 0.6\end{pmatrix}$$

A′ = (–1.2, 1.6), B′ = (–0.4, 2.2), C′ = (0.2, 1.4), D′ = (0.8, 0.6)

The points are correctly plotted.

? (Page 18)

BA, AC, BC and CB exist.

Activity 1.5 (Page 19)

(i) $\mathrm{PQ} = \begin{pmatrix}ae + cf & ag + ch\\be + df & bg + dh\end{pmatrix}$

(ii) $(\mathrm{PQ})\mathrm{R} = \begin{pmatrix}aei + cfi + agj + chj & aek + cfk + agl + chl\\bei + dfi + bgj + dhj & bek + dfk + bgl + dhl\end{pmatrix}$

(iii) $\mathrm{QR} = \begin{pmatrix}ei + gj & ek + gl\\fi + hj & fk + hl\end{pmatrix}$

(iv) $\mathrm{P}(\mathrm{QR}) = \begin{pmatrix}aei + agj + cfi + chj & aek + agl + cfk + chl\\bei + bgj + dfi + dhj & bek + bgl + dfk + dhl\end{pmatrix}$

(PQ)R = P(QR) so matrix multiplication is associative.

Activity 1.6 (Page 19)

(i) $\mathrm{P}(\mathrm{Q} + \mathrm{R}) = \begin{pmatrix}a(e+i) + c(f+j) & a(g+k) + c(h+l)\\b(e+i) + d(f+j) & b(g+k) + d(h+l)\end{pmatrix}$

(ii) $\mathrm{PQ} + \mathrm{PR} = \begin{pmatrix}ae + cf + ai + cj & ag + ch + ak + cl\\be + df + bi + dj & bg + dh + bk + dl\end{pmatrix}$

(iii) $(\mathrm{P} + \mathrm{Q})\mathrm{R} = \begin{pmatrix}(a+e)i + (c+g)j & (a+e)k + (c+g)l\\(b+f)i + (d+h)j & (b+f)k + (d+h)l\end{pmatrix}$

(iv) $\mathrm{PR} + \mathrm{QR} = \begin{pmatrix}ai + cj + ei + gj & ak + cl + ek + gl\\bi + dj + fi + hj & bk + dl + fk + hl\end{pmatrix}$

P(Q + R) = PQ + PR and (P + Q)R = PR + QR so matrix multiplication is distributive over matrix addition.

Activity 1.7 (Page 20)

For $\mathrm{M} = \begin{pmatrix}a & d & g\\b & e & h\\c & f & i\end{pmatrix}$,

$$\mathrm{I}_3\mathrm{M} = \begin{pmatrix}1 & 0 & 0\\0 & 1 & 0\\0 & 0 & 1\end{pmatrix}\begin{pmatrix}a & d & g\\b & e & h\\c & f & i\end{pmatrix} = \begin{pmatrix}a & d & g\\b & e & h\\c & f & i\end{pmatrix} = \mathrm{M}$$

$$\mathrm{MI}_3 = \begin{pmatrix}a & d & g\\b & e & h\\c & f & i\end{pmatrix}\begin{pmatrix}1 & 0 & 0\\0 & 1 & 0\\0 & 0 & 1\end{pmatrix} = \begin{pmatrix}a & d & g\\b & e & h\\c & f & i\end{pmatrix} = \mathrm{M}$$

? (Page 20)

Pre- and post-multiplying would give matrices of different orders.

Exercise 1C (Page 20)

1 **(i)** $\begin{pmatrix} -7 & 26 \\ 2 & 34 \end{pmatrix}$

(ii) Not possible

(iii) $\begin{pmatrix} 29 & 40 & -5 \\ 29 & 41 & 13 \end{pmatrix}$

(iv) $\begin{pmatrix} 31 & 0 \\ 65 & 18 \end{pmatrix}$

(v) $\begin{pmatrix} 26 & 37 & 16 \\ 14 & 21 & 28 \\ -8 & -11 & 2 \end{pmatrix}$

(vi) Not possible

(vii) Not possible

(viii) $\begin{pmatrix} 55 & 89 & 3 \\ 4 & 19 & 10 \\ 23 & 54 & 41 \end{pmatrix}$

(ix) $\begin{pmatrix} 26 & 32 \\ 5 & -5 \\ 13 & 21 \end{pmatrix}$

(x) $\begin{pmatrix} 28 & -18 \\ 26 & 2 \\ 16 & 25 \end{pmatrix}$

(xi) Not possible

(xii) $\begin{pmatrix} 11 & 7 \\ 14 & 18 \end{pmatrix}$

2 $AB = \begin{pmatrix} -7 & 26 \\ 2 & 34 \end{pmatrix}$, $BA = \begin{pmatrix} 5 & 25 \\ 16 & 22 \end{pmatrix}$, so $AB \neq BA$.

AD cannot be calculated, $DA = \begin{pmatrix} 17 & 19 \\ 21 & 7 \\ -1 & -7 \end{pmatrix}$, so $AD \neq DA$.

Therefore matrix multiplication is not commutative.

3 $A(CF) = (AC)F = \begin{pmatrix} 52 & 225 & 49 \\ 128 & 420 & -24 \end{pmatrix}$

4 **(i)** (1, 0), (1, 1), (2, 1), (2, 2), (1, 2)

$\begin{pmatrix} 1 & 1 & 2 & 2 & 1 \\ 0 & 1 & 1 & 2 & 2 \end{pmatrix}$

(ii) $\begin{pmatrix} -0.6 & 0.2 & -0.4 & 0.4 & 1 \\ 0.8 & 1.4 & 2.2 & 2.8 & 2 \end{pmatrix}$

(iii)

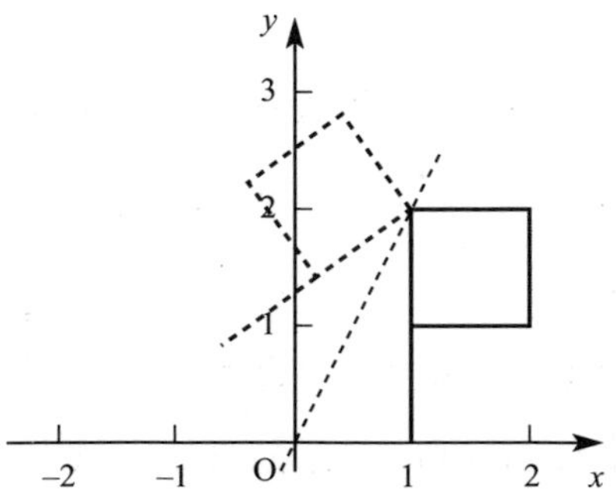

Reflection in the line $y = 2x$

5 **(i)** (1, 0), (1, 1), (−1, 1), (−1, 0)

$\begin{pmatrix} 1 & 1 & -1 & -1 \\ 0 & 1 & 1 & 0 \end{pmatrix}$

(ii) $\begin{pmatrix} 1 & 1 & -1 & -1 \\ 2 & 3 & -1 & -2 \end{pmatrix}$

(iii)

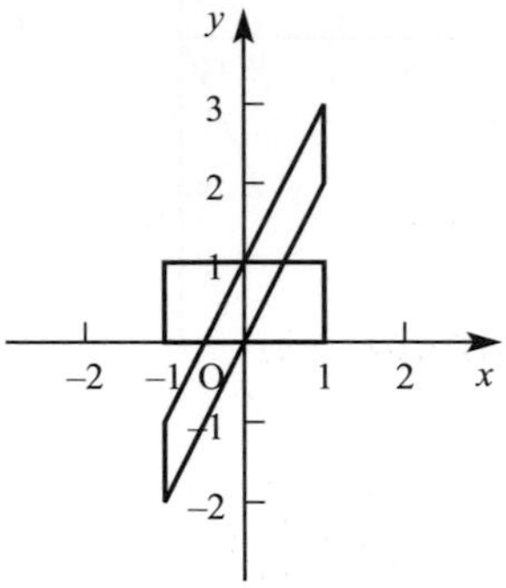

Shear parallel to the y axis

6 **(iii)** $M^2 = \begin{pmatrix} 5 & 0 \\ 0 & 5 \end{pmatrix}$

(iv) Enlargement centre O scale factor 5

7 **(i)** $D = (1 \;\; 1)$

(ii) $N = \begin{pmatrix} 1 \\ 1 \\ 1 \\ 1 \\ 1 \end{pmatrix}$

(iii) $(28 \;\; 21)SN$

8 **(i)** $M = \begin{pmatrix} 1 & 1 & 2 & 0 \\ 1 & 0 & 1 & 0 \\ 1 & 1 & 0 & 2 \\ 0 & 0 & 1 & 0 \end{pmatrix}$

(ii) $M^2 = \begin{pmatrix} 4 & 3 & 3 & 4 \\ 2 & 2 & 2 & 2 \\ 2 & 1 & 5 & 0 \\ 1 & 1 & 0 & 2 \end{pmatrix}$

M^2 represents the number of two-stage routes between each pair of resorts.

(iii) M^3 would represent the number of three-stage routes between each pair of resorts.

9 **(i)** $As_0 = \begin{pmatrix} b \\ a \\ c \end{pmatrix}$

(ii) $B = \begin{pmatrix} 1 & 0 & 0 \\ 0 & 0 & 1 \\ 0 & 1 & 0 \end{pmatrix}$

(iii) $M = \begin{pmatrix} 0 & 1 & 0 \\ 0 & 0 & 1 \\ 1 & 0 & 0 \end{pmatrix}$, $Ms_0 = \begin{pmatrix} b \\ c \\ a \end{pmatrix}$

(iv) $M^2 = \begin{pmatrix} 0 & 0 & 1 \\ 1 & 0 & 0 \\ 0 & 1 & 0 \end{pmatrix}$, $s_4 = \begin{pmatrix} c \\ a \\ b \end{pmatrix}$

(v) $M^3 = \begin{pmatrix} 1 & 0 & 0 \\ 0 & 1 & 0 \\ 0 & 0 & 1 \end{pmatrix}$

At Stage 6 the strands are back to their original order.

? (Page 24)

Reflection in the line $y = x$

Activity 1.9 (Page 24)

(i) $p' = \begin{pmatrix} ax + cy \\ bx + dy \end{pmatrix}$

(ii) $p'' = \begin{pmatrix} apx + cpy + brx + dry \\ aqx + cqy + bsx + dsy \end{pmatrix}$

(iii) $U = \begin{pmatrix} ap + br & cp + dr \\ aq + bs & cq + ds \end{pmatrix}$

U(p) is represented by the matrix

$\begin{pmatrix} apx + brx + cpy + dry \\ aqx + bsx + cqy + dsy \end{pmatrix} = p''$.

? (Page 25)

QR represents 'carry out transformation R followed by transformation Q'.
P(QR) represents 'carry out QR, followed by P', i.e. 'carry out R, followed by Q, followed by P'.
PQ represents 'carry out Q, followed by P'.
(PQ)R represents 'carry out R, followed by PQ', i.e. 'carry out R, followed by Q, followed by P'.
Hence P(QR) = (PQ)R.

Activity 1.10 (Page 25)

(i) $A = \begin{pmatrix} \cos a & -\sin a \\ \sin a & \cos a \end{pmatrix}$, $B = \begin{pmatrix} \cos\beta & -\sin\beta \\ \sin\beta & \cos\beta \end{pmatrix}$

(ii) $BA = \begin{pmatrix} \cos a\cos\beta - \sin a\sin\beta & -\cos a\sin\beta - \sin a\cos\beta \\ \sin a\cos\beta + \cos a\sin\beta & -\sin a\sin\beta + \cos a\cos\beta \end{pmatrix}$

(iii) $C = \begin{pmatrix} \cos(a+\beta) & -\sin(a+\beta) \\ \sin(a+\beta) & \cos(a+\beta) \end{pmatrix}$

(iv) $\sin(a+\beta) = \sin a\cos\beta + \cos a\sin\beta$

$\cos(a+\beta) = \cos a\cos\beta - \sin a\sin\beta$

(v) Rotation through angle a followed by rotation through angle β has the same effect as rotation through angle β followed by rotation through angle a.

(vi) $D = \begin{pmatrix} \cos\beta & \sin\beta \\ -\sin\beta & \cos\beta \end{pmatrix}$

$AD = \begin{pmatrix} \cos a\cos\beta + \sin a\sin\beta & \cos a\sin\beta - \sin a\cos\beta \\ \sin a\cos\beta - \cos a\sin\beta & -\sin a\sin\beta + \cos a\cos\beta \end{pmatrix}$

$\sin(a-\beta) = \sin a\cos\beta - \cos a\sin\beta$

$\cos(a-\beta) = \cos a\cos\beta + \sin a\sin\beta$

Exercise 1D (Page 25)

1 (i) $Y = \begin{pmatrix} -1 & 0 \\ 0 & 1 \end{pmatrix}$, $Q = \begin{pmatrix} 0 & -1 \\ 1 & 0 \end{pmatrix}$

(ii) $QY = \begin{pmatrix} 0 & -1 \\ -1 & 0 \end{pmatrix}$, reflection in the line $y = -x$

(iii)

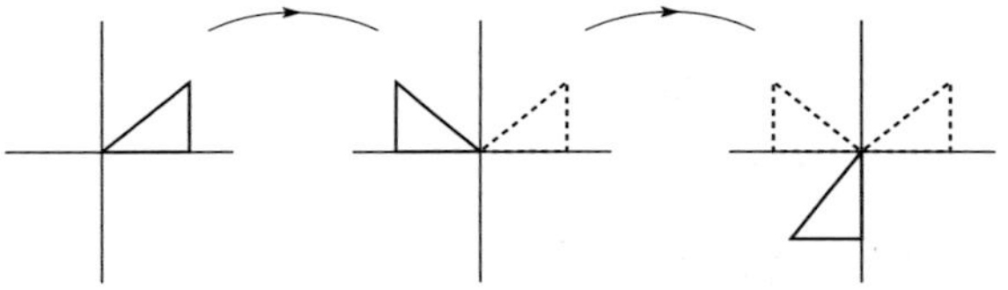

(iv) $YQ = \begin{pmatrix} 0 & 1 \\ 1 & 0 \end{pmatrix}$, reflection in the line $y = x$

(v)

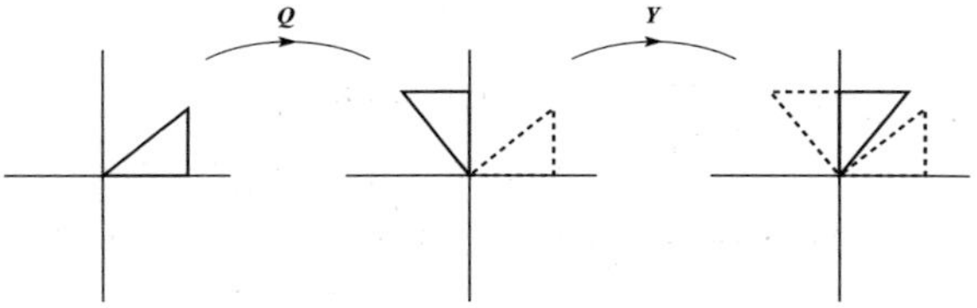

2 (i) $R = \begin{pmatrix} 0 & 1 \\ -1 & 0 \end{pmatrix}$, $T = \begin{pmatrix} 0 & 1 \\ 1 & 0 \end{pmatrix}$

(ii) $RT = \begin{pmatrix} 1 & 0 \\ 0 & -1 \end{pmatrix}$, reflection in the x axis

(iii)

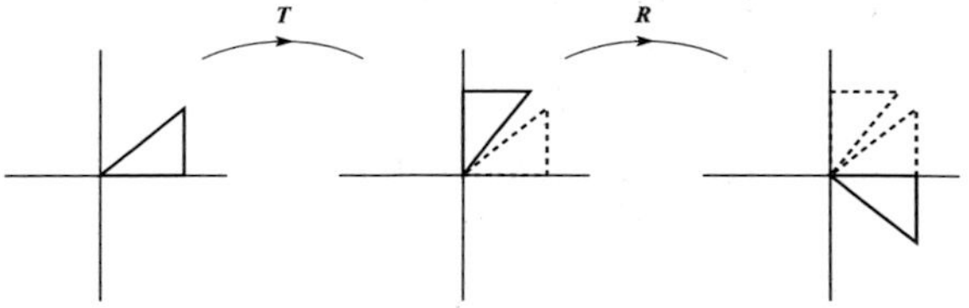

(iv) $TR = \begin{pmatrix} -1 & 0 \\ 0 & 1 \end{pmatrix}$, reflection in the y axis

(v)

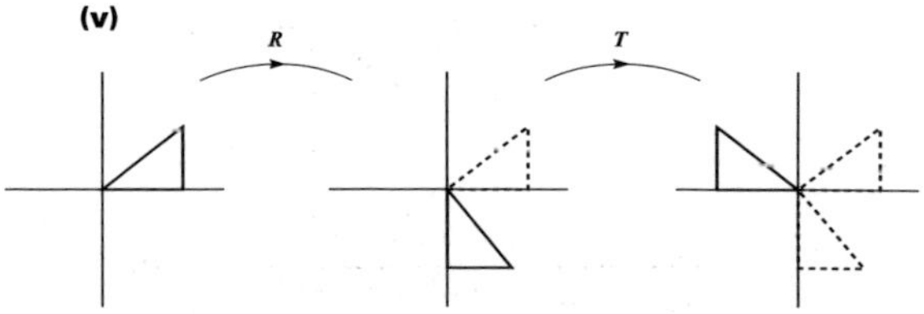

3 **(i)** $X = \begin{pmatrix} 1 & 0 \\ 0 & -1 \end{pmatrix}, Y = \begin{pmatrix} -1 & 0 \\ 0 & 1 \end{pmatrix}$

(ii) $XY = \begin{pmatrix} -1 & 0 \\ 0 & -1 \end{pmatrix}$, rotation of 180° about O

(iii) $YX = \begin{pmatrix} -1 & 0 \\ 0 & -1 \end{pmatrix}$

(iv) Reflecting in both axes in either order results in a rotation of 180° about O.

4 **(i)** $S = \begin{pmatrix} -1 & 0 \\ 0 & -1 \end{pmatrix}, U = \begin{pmatrix} 0 & -1 \\ -1 & 0 \end{pmatrix}$

(ii) $SU = \begin{pmatrix} 0 & 1 \\ 1 & 0 \end{pmatrix}$, reflection in the line $y = x$

(iii) $US = \begin{pmatrix} 0 & 1 \\ 1 & 0 \end{pmatrix}$

(iv) Rotation through 180° and reflection in the line $y = -x$, in either order, results in a reflection in the line $y = x$.

5 **(i)** $\begin{pmatrix} 8 & -4 \\ -3 & 12 \end{pmatrix}$

(ii) (20, –18)

6 **(i)** Rotating through 25° followed by rotating through 40° has the same effect as rotating through 40° followed by rotating through 25°.

(ii) $R_1 = \begin{pmatrix} \cos 25 & -\sin 25 \\ \sin 25 & \cos 25 \end{pmatrix}, R_2 = \begin{pmatrix} \cos 40 & -\sin 40 \\ \sin 40 & \cos 40 \end{pmatrix}$

$R_1R_2 = \begin{pmatrix} 0.423 & -0.906 \\ 0.906 & 0.423 \end{pmatrix}$

(iii) Rotation through 65° anticlockwise about O

7 **(i)** $\begin{pmatrix} 1 & -R_1 \\ 0 & 1 \end{pmatrix}$

(ii) $\begin{pmatrix} 1 & 0 \\ -\frac{1}{R_2} & 1 \end{pmatrix}$

(iii) $\begin{pmatrix} 1 & -R_1 \\ -\frac{1}{R_2} & \frac{R_1}{R_2} + 1 \end{pmatrix}$

(iv) No

8 **(i)** $P = \begin{pmatrix} \frac{1}{2} & \frac{\sqrt{3}}{2} \\ \frac{\sqrt{3}}{2} & -\frac{1}{2} \end{pmatrix}, Q = \begin{pmatrix} -\frac{1}{2} & \frac{\sqrt{3}}{2} \\ \frac{\sqrt{3}}{2} & \frac{1}{2} \end{pmatrix}$

(ii) $\begin{pmatrix} \frac{1}{2} & -\frac{\sqrt{3}}{2} \\ \frac{\sqrt{3}}{2} & \frac{1}{2} \end{pmatrix}$, rotation through 60° anticlockwise about O

(iii) $\begin{pmatrix} \frac{1}{2} & \frac{\sqrt{3}}{2} \\ -\frac{\sqrt{3}}{2} & \frac{1}{2} \end{pmatrix}$, rotation through 60° clockwise about O

9 **(i)** $\begin{pmatrix} \frac{\sqrt{3}}{2} & -\frac{1}{2} \\ \frac{1}{2} & \frac{\sqrt{3}}{2} \end{pmatrix}$

(ii) $\begin{pmatrix} -\frac{1}{2} & \frac{\sqrt{3}}{2} \\ \frac{\sqrt{3}}{2} & \frac{1}{2} \end{pmatrix}$

(iii) $\begin{pmatrix} 0 & 1 \\ 1 & 0 \end{pmatrix}$, reflection in the line $y = x$

10 A second reflection in the same line reflects the image back on to the original figure.

11 **(i)** $A = \begin{pmatrix} \frac{2}{\sqrt{5}} & \frac{1}{\sqrt{5}} \\ -\frac{1}{\sqrt{5}} & \frac{2}{\sqrt{5}} \end{pmatrix}, B = \begin{pmatrix} 5 & 0 \\ 0 & 1 \end{pmatrix}, C = \begin{pmatrix} \frac{2}{\sqrt{5}} & -\frac{1}{\sqrt{5}} \\ \frac{1}{\sqrt{5}} & \frac{2}{\sqrt{5}} \end{pmatrix}$

(ii) $S = \begin{pmatrix} \frac{21}{5} & \frac{8}{5} \\ \frac{8}{5} & \frac{9}{5} \end{pmatrix}$

(iii) One-way stretch, scale factor $\frac{1}{5}$, parallel to the line $y = \frac{1}{2}x$

$\begin{pmatrix} \frac{9}{25} & -\frac{8}{25} \\ -\frac{8}{25} & \frac{21}{25} \end{pmatrix}$

? (Page 28)

$QQ^{-1} = \begin{pmatrix} 1 & 0 \\ 0 & 1 \end{pmatrix}, Q^{-1}Q = \begin{pmatrix} 1 & 0 \\ 0 & 1 \end{pmatrix}$

Rotation of 90° clockwise followed by rotation of 90° anticlockwise returns the shape to its original position. Rotation of 90° anticlockwise followed by rotation of 90° clockwise has the same effect.

Consequently, QQ^{-1} is equal to $Q^{-1}Q$.

Activity 1.11 (Page 28)

The product of a matrix with its inverse is always the identity matrix I.

Activity 1.12 (Page 28)

$w = \frac{3}{2},\ x = -\frac{5}{2}$

$\left.\begin{array}{l} 4y + 2z = 0 \\ 5y + 3z = 1 \end{array}\right\} \Rightarrow y = -1,\ z = 2$

$M^{-1} = \begin{pmatrix} \frac{3}{2} & -1 \\ -\frac{5}{2} & 2 \end{pmatrix}$

$\left.\begin{array}{l} aw + cx = 1 \\ bw + dx = 0 \end{array}\right\} \Rightarrow w = \dfrac{d}{ad - bc},\ x = \dfrac{-b}{ad - bc}$

$\left.\begin{array}{l} ay + cz = 0 \\ by + dz = 1 \end{array}\right\} \Rightarrow y = \dfrac{-c}{ad - bc},\ z = \dfrac{a}{ad - bc}$

Activity 1.13 (Page 29)

(ii) $M^{-1} = \dfrac{1}{ad - bc}\begin{pmatrix} d & -c \\ -b & a \end{pmatrix}$

? (Page 30)

Undo the reflection first by doing the same reflection, and then undo the rotation by doing the same rotation in the opposite direction.

$(MN)^{-1} = N^{-1}M^{-1}$ (i.e. undo '*N* followed by *M*' by 'undoing *M*, then undoing *N*').

Activity 1.14 (Page 30)

$(AB)(B^{-1}A^{-1}) = A(BB^{-1})A^{-1} = AIA^{-1} = AA^{-1} = I$

So the inverse of AB is $B^{-1}A^{-1}$, i.e. $(AB)^{-1} = B^{-1}A^{-1}$.

Exercise 1E (Page 30)

1 **(i)** $\begin{pmatrix} \frac{5}{2} & -\frac{3}{2} \\ -3 & 2 \end{pmatrix}$

(ii) $\begin{pmatrix} \frac{1}{12} & -\frac{1}{8} \\ -\frac{1}{6} & -\frac{1}{4} \end{pmatrix}$

(iii) Not possible

(iv) $\begin{pmatrix} 1 & -2 \\ -\frac{2}{3} & \frac{5}{3} \end{pmatrix}$

(v) $\begin{pmatrix} \frac{1}{5} & \frac{1}{5} \\ \frac{2}{5} & -\frac{3}{5} \end{pmatrix}$

(vi) $\begin{pmatrix} 7 & -4 \\ -5 & 3 \end{pmatrix}$

(vii) Not possible

(viii) $\begin{pmatrix} 12 & -\frac{9}{2} \\ -4 & 2 \end{pmatrix}$

(ix) $\dfrac{1}{eh - fg}\begin{pmatrix} h & -f \\ -g & e \end{pmatrix}$ provided $eh \neq fg$

2 $k = 2$ or 3

3 **(i)** $\begin{pmatrix} 2 & -\frac{3}{2} \\ -3 & \frac{5}{2} \end{pmatrix}$ **(ii)** $\begin{pmatrix} \frac{2}{5} & -\frac{3}{5} \\ -\frac{1}{5} & \frac{4}{5} \end{pmatrix}$

(iii) $\begin{pmatrix} 1.1 & -2.4 \\ -1.7 & 3.8 \end{pmatrix}$ **(iv)** $\begin{pmatrix} 2.6 & -2.1 \\ -2.8 & 2.3 \end{pmatrix}$

(v) $\begin{pmatrix} 1.1 & -2.4 \\ -1.7 & 3.8 \end{pmatrix}$ **(vi)** $\begin{pmatrix} 2.6 & -2.1 \\ -2.8 & 2.3 \end{pmatrix}$

$(BA)^{-1} = A^{-1}B^{-1}$ and $(AB)^{-1} = B^{-1}A^{-1}$.

4 **(i)** (3, 1), (1, 1) (–6, –2)

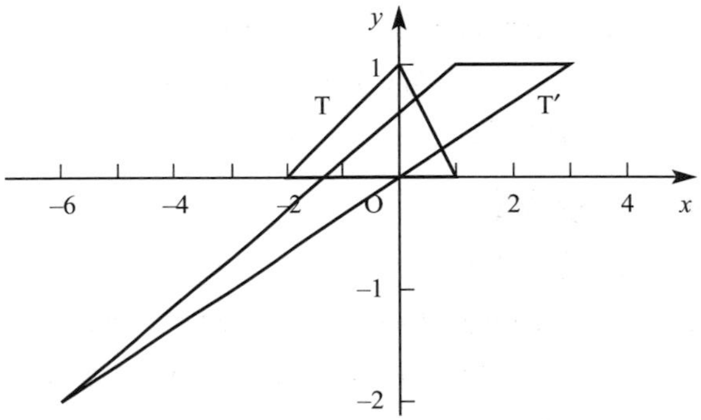

(ii) Area of T′ : area of T = 2 : 1

det M = 2

(iii) $\begin{pmatrix} \frac{1}{2} & -\frac{1}{2} \\ -\frac{1}{2} & \frac{3}{2} \end{pmatrix}$

5 $M^2 = (a + d)M$

$M^n = (a + d)^{n-1}M$

6 **(ii)** **(a)** $\begin{pmatrix} 18 & -9 & 4 \\ 1 & -7 & 2 \\ -1 & -4 & 1 \end{pmatrix}$

(b) $\begin{pmatrix} 1 & a+7 & b+7c+4 \\ 0 & 1 & c+2 \\ 0 & 0 & 1 \end{pmatrix}$

(c) $\begin{pmatrix} 1 & -7 & 10 \\ 0 & 1 & -2 \\ 0 & 0 & 1 \end{pmatrix}$

(d) $\begin{pmatrix} 1 & 0 & 0 \\ -3 & 1 & 0 \\ -11 & 4 & 1 \end{pmatrix}$

(e) $\begin{pmatrix} 1 & -7 & 10 \\ -3 & 22 & -32 \\ -11 & 81 & -117 \end{pmatrix}$

Activity 1.15 (Page 31)

(i) Area of image = 5 square units

det T = 5

(ii) Area of image = 2 square units

det R = –2

(iii) The numerical value of the determinant is equal to the area of the image.

Activity 1.16 (Page 32)

$I' = (a, b)$, $P' = (a + c, b + d)$, $J' = (c, d)$

$$\text{Area } OI'P'J' = (a + c)(b + d) - \tfrac{1}{2}ab - bc - \tfrac{1}{2}cd - \tfrac{1}{2}cd - bc - \tfrac{1}{2}ab$$
$$= ab + ad + bc + cd - \tfrac{1}{2}ab - bc - \tfrac{1}{2}cd - \tfrac{1}{2}cd - bc - \tfrac{1}{2}ab$$
$$= ad - bc$$

? (Page 33)

The area of any plane shape can be found as accurately as you want as the sum of a number of sufficiently small squares. As the area scale factor of each small square is equal to the determinant of the matrix, then the area scale factor of the whole shape is also equal to the determinant of the matrix.

Activity 1.17 (Page 33)

Reflection in the x axis is represented by $\begin{pmatrix} 1 & 0 \\ 0 & -1 \end{pmatrix}$ which has determinant –1.

Reflection in the y axis is represented by $\begin{pmatrix} -1 & 0 \\ 0 & 1 \end{pmatrix}$ which has determinant –1.

Reflection in the line $y = x$ is represented by $\begin{pmatrix} 0 & 1 \\ 1 & 0 \end{pmatrix}$ which has determinant –1.

Reflection in the line $y = -x$ is represented by $\begin{pmatrix} 0 & -1 \\ -1 & 0 \end{pmatrix}$ which has determinant –1.

Activity 1.18 (Page 33)

(i) det T = 0

(ii) The image points are (0, 0), (24, 12), (36, 18) and (12, 6).

(iv) The image points always lie on a straight line.

? (Page 34)

Every point is mapped to the origin.

Activity 1.19 (Page 34)

$$\begin{pmatrix} x' \\ y' \end{pmatrix} = \begin{pmatrix} a & c \\ b & d \end{pmatrix}\begin{pmatrix} x \\ y \end{pmatrix} = \begin{pmatrix} ax + cy \\ bx + dy \end{pmatrix}$$

$x' = ax + cy \Rightarrow bx' = abx + bcy$

$y' = bx + dy \Rightarrow ay' = abx + ady$

Subtracting: $bx' - ay' = (bc - ad)y = 0$

So all image points lie on the line $bx - ay = 0$.

Exercise 1F (Page 35)

1 **(i)** 10, non–singular

(ii) 0, singular

(iii) 0, singular

(iv) 7, non–singular

2 **(i)** det M = –2, det N = 7

(ii) $MN = \begin{pmatrix} 9 & 13 \\ 8 & 10 \end{pmatrix}$, det MN = –14

(iii) Applying M gives an area scale factor of 7, applying N gives an area scale factor of –2. Applying N followed by M therefore gives an area scale factor of –14, so det MN = –14.

3 $ad = 1$

4 $\begin{pmatrix} 1 & k \\ 0 & 1 \end{pmatrix}$; determinant $= 1 \times 1 - k \times 0 = 1$ so the shear preserves area.

5 **(i)** 150 square units

(ii) $\begin{pmatrix} \frac{1}{5} & \frac{1}{10} \\ \frac{2}{15} & \frac{7}{30} \end{pmatrix}$

(iii) $\begin{pmatrix} -\frac{1}{\sqrt{2}} & -\frac{1}{\sqrt{2}} \\ \frac{1}{\sqrt{2}} & -\frac{1}{\sqrt{2}} \end{pmatrix}$

(iv) $\begin{pmatrix} -\frac{1}{3\sqrt{2}} & -\frac{1}{3\sqrt{2}} \\ \frac{1}{15\sqrt{2}} & \frac{2}{15\sqrt{2}} \end{pmatrix}$

6 **(iii)** $x + 2y = 5$

7 **(i)** $\begin{pmatrix} 1 & 2 \\ 3 & 6 \end{pmatrix}$

(iii) (3, 9)

8 **(i)** $y = 3x - 3s + t$

(ii) $\left(\frac{9}{8}s - \frac{3}{8}t, \frac{3}{8}s - \frac{1}{8}t\right)$

(iii) $\begin{pmatrix} \frac{9}{8} & -\frac{3}{8} \\ \frac{3}{8} & -\frac{1}{8} \end{pmatrix}$

9 **(i)** $I' = \left(\frac{1 + m^2 + km}{1 + m^2}, \frac{km^2}{1 + m^2}\right)$,

$J' = \left(\frac{-k}{1 + m^2}, \frac{1 + m^2 - km}{1 + m^2}\right)$

(ii) $\begin{pmatrix} \frac{1 + m^2 + km}{1 + m^2} & \frac{-k}{1 + m^2} \\ \frac{km^2}{1 + m^2} & \frac{1 + m^2 - km}{1 + m^2} \end{pmatrix}$

Activity 1.20 (Page 39)

(i) $\begin{pmatrix} 6 & -1 & -8 \\ -5 & 1 & 7 \\ -7 & 1 & 10 \end{pmatrix}$, $x = 3, y = -1, z = -2$

(ii) The calculator gives an error. This is because the determinant of the matrix is zero.

The equations give a line of solution points, which can be expressed as $x = \lambda, y = 5\lambda - 13, z = 8\lambda - 23$.

(iii) The equations are inconsistent. There are no solutions.

? (Page 39)

In part **(i)**, the equations have a unique solution. The equations represent three planes all meeting at a single point.

In part **(ii)**, the equations have a line of solution points. The equations represent three planes with a line of common points.

In part **(iii)**, the equations have no solutions. The equations represent three planes which do not all meet at any point.

Exercise 1G (Page 39)

1 **(i)** $\begin{pmatrix} \frac{1}{5} & -\frac{3}{5} \\ \frac{1}{5} & \frac{2}{5} \end{pmatrix}$ **(ii)** $\begin{pmatrix} x \\ y \end{pmatrix} = \begin{pmatrix} 2 \\ -1 \end{pmatrix}$

2 **(i)** $x = 1, y = 1$ **(ii)** $x = 2, y = -1$

(iii) $x = 2, y = 3$ **(iv)** $x = 4, y = 1.5$

3 **(i)** Consistent: unique solution $x = 6.5, y = -0.5$.

Two lines cross once.

(ii) Inconsistent: parallel lines.

(iii) Consistent: $x = \lambda, y = 2\lambda - 4$.

Lines coincide.

(iv) Inconsistent: parallel lines.

4 $k = 4$: $x = \lambda, y = \frac{3}{4} - \frac{1}{2}\lambda$

$k = -4$: no solution

5 **(i)** $AB = \begin{pmatrix} k-1 & 0 & 0 \\ 0 & k-1 & 0 \\ 0 & 0 & k-1 \end{pmatrix}$

$A^{-1} = \frac{1}{k-1}\begin{pmatrix} -1 & 3k+8 & 4k+10 \\ -2 & 2k+20 & 3k+25 \\ 1 & -11 & -14 \end{pmatrix}$, for $k \neq 1$.

(ii) **(a)** $x = 6m - 4, y = 7m - 8, z = -2m + 4$

(b) No solution

(c) $x = \lambda, y = 2\lambda - 10, z = 8 - \lambda$

6 **(i)** $\begin{pmatrix} 6 - 2k & 0 & 0 \\ 0 & 6 - 2k & 0 \\ 6a + 3k & 6a + 3k & 6 + 4a \end{pmatrix}$

(ii) $k = -2a$

(iii) $B^{-1} = \frac{1}{6 - 2k}\begin{pmatrix} 1 & -2 & 0 \\ 0 & 2 & -2 \\ -\frac{1}{2}k & 0 & 3 \end{pmatrix}$

(iv) $x = \frac{6}{3 + 2a}, y = \frac{-2a}{3 + 2a}, z = \frac{3}{3 + 2a}$

(v) $\frac{1}{(6 - 2k)(6 + 4a)}\begin{pmatrix} 6 + 4a & 0 & 0 \\ 0 & 6 + 4a & 0 \\ -3k - 6a & -3k - 6a & -2k + 6 \end{pmatrix}$

7 **(i)** $\begin{pmatrix} 2 & 0 & 6 - 2k \\ 0 & 2 & k - 3 \\ 0 & 0 & 5 - k \end{pmatrix}$

(ii) $\begin{pmatrix} -1 & 13 & -8 \\ \frac{1}{2} & -\frac{11}{2} & \frac{7}{2} \\ -\frac{1}{2} & \frac{21}{2} & -\frac{13}{2} \end{pmatrix}$

$x = -7, y = 5, z = 0$

(iii) $x = 3 - 2t, y = t, z = 5 - t$

? (Page 41)

In a reflection, all points on the mirror line map to themselves.

In a rotation, the centre of rotation maps to itself.

❓ (Page 41)

In transformations which can be represented by a matrix, the origin is always mapped to itself, so the origin is an invariant point.

❓ (Page 43)

(i) All lines of the form $y = mx$ (straight lines through the origin)

(ii) All lines of the form $y = mx$ (straight lines through the origin)

(iii) None

(iv) The line $y = x$ and all lines of the form $y = -x + c$

Exercise 1H (Page 43)

1 **(i)** $(\lambda, -\lambda)$

(ii) $(0, 0)$

(iii) $(2\lambda, \lambda)$

(iv) $(0, 0)$

(v) $(\lambda, -3\lambda)$

(vi) $(\lambda, \frac{3}{2}\lambda)$

4 **(i)** Any point of the form $(\lambda, 2\lambda)$.

The mirror line is $y = 2x$.

(ii) **(c)** $a = -2b$

Chapter 2

Activity 2.1 (Page 47)

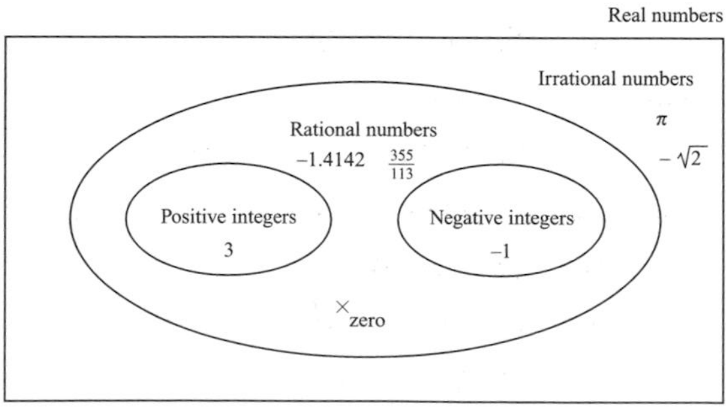

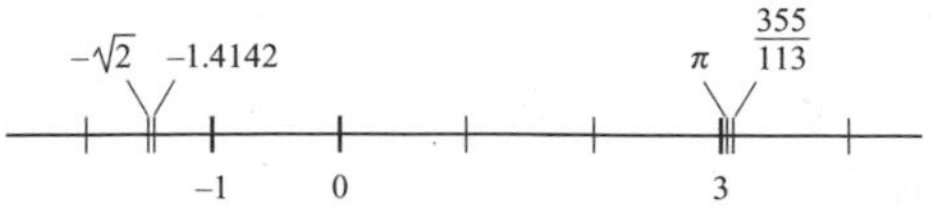

Activity 2.2 (Page 47)

(i) positive integer

(ii) rational number

(iii) irrational number

(iv) negative integer

(v) zero, negative integer

(vi) no real number is possible

Activity 2.3 (Page 48)

$$\begin{aligned} z = 3 - 7j \Rightarrow z^2 - 6z + 58 &= (3 - 7j)^2 - 6(3 - 7j) + 58 \\ &= 9 - 42j + 49j^2 - 18 + 42j + 58 \\ &= 9 - 42j - 49 - 18 + 42j + 58 \\ &= 0 \end{aligned}$$

❓ (Page 49)

$j^3 = -j$, $j^4 = 1$, $j^5 = j$

All numbers of the form j^{4n} are equal to 1.

All numbers of the form j^{4n+1} are equal to j.

All numbers of the form j^{4n+2} are equal to −1.

All numbers of the form j^{4n+3} are equal to −j.

Activity 2.4 (Page 49)

(i) **(a)** 6 **(b)** 2 **(c)** 34 **(d)** 5

They are all real.

(ii) $z + z^* = (x + yj) + (x - yj) = 2x$

$zz^* = (x + yj)(x - yj) = x^2 - xyj + xyj - y^2j^2 = x^2 + y^2$

These are real for any real values of x and y.

Exercise 2A (Page 50)

1 **(i)** $14 + 10j$

(ii) $5 + 2j$

(iii) $-3 + 4j$

(iv) $-1 + j$

(v) 21

(vi) $12 + 21j$

(vii) $3 + 29j$

(viii) $14 + 5j$

(ix) $40 + 42j$

(x) 100

(xi) $43 + 76j$

(xii) $-9 + 46j$

2 (i) $-1 \pm j$

(ii) $1 \pm 2j$

(iii) $2 \pm 3j$

(iv) $-3 \pm 5j$

(v) $\frac{1}{2} \pm 2j$

(vi) $-2 \pm \sqrt{2}j$

3 (i) 2

(ii) -4

(iii) $2 - 3j$

(iv) $6 + 4j$

(v) $8 + j$

(vi) $-4 - 7j$

(vii) 0

(viii) 0

(ix) -39

(x) $-46 - 9j$

(xi) $-46 - 9j$

(xii) $52j$

❓ (Page 50)

Yes, for example $\frac{2}{3} = \frac{4}{6}$, although $2 \neq 4$ and $3 \neq 6$.

Activity 2.5 (Page 51)

$$\frac{1}{x + yj} = p + qj \Rightarrow (p + qj)(x + yj) = 1$$
$$\Rightarrow px + pyj + qxj + qyj^2 = 1$$
$$\Rightarrow (px - qy) + (py + qx)j = 1$$

$px - qy = 1$ and $py + qx = 0$

Solving simultaneously gives $p = \dfrac{x}{x^2 + y^2}$, $q = \dfrac{-y}{x^2 + y^2}$

so $\dfrac{1}{x + yj} = \dfrac{x - yj}{x^2 + y^2}$.

❓ (Page 52)

$\frac{1}{j} = -j$, $\frac{1}{j^2} = -1$, $\frac{1}{j^3} = j$

All numbers of the form $\dfrac{1}{j^{4n}}$ are equal to 1.

All numbers of the form $\dfrac{1}{j^{4n+1}}$ are equal to $-j$.

All numbers of the form $\dfrac{1}{j^{4n+2}}$ are equal to -1.

All numbers of the form $\dfrac{1}{j^{4n+3}}$ are equal to j.

Exercise 2B (Page 53)

1 (i) $\frac{3}{10} - \frac{1}{10}j$

(ii) $\frac{6}{37} + \frac{1}{37}j$

(iii) $-\frac{1}{4} + \frac{3}{4}j$

(iv) $\frac{4}{5} + \frac{11}{10}j$

(v) $\frac{5}{2} - \frac{1}{2}j$

(vi) $7 - 5j$

(vii) $-j$

(viii) $\frac{11}{25} - \frac{27}{25}j$

(ix) $\frac{7}{29} + \frac{32}{29}j$

(x) $-1 - \frac{3}{2}j$

2 (i) $a = 5, b = 2$

(ii) $a = 3, b = -7$

(iii) $a = 2, b = -3$

(iv) $a = 4, b = 5$

(v) $a = \frac{5}{4}, b = -\frac{3}{4}$

(vi) $a = \dfrac{1}{\sqrt{2}}, b = \dfrac{1}{\sqrt{2}}$

3 $a = 2, b = 2$

4 (i) $z = 2 - j$

(ii) $z = 3 + j$

(iii) $z = 11 - 10j$

(iv) $z = \dfrac{-35 + 149j}{34}$

5 $0, 2, -1 \pm \sqrt{3}j$

6 $\dfrac{2x}{x^2 + y^2}$

8 (i) $a^3 - 3ab^2 + (3a^2b - b^3)j$

(iii) $z = 1, -\frac{1}{2} \pm \frac{1}{2}\sqrt{3}j$

9 (i) $(z - \alpha)(z - \beta) = z^2 - (\alpha + \beta)z + \alpha\beta$

(ii) (a) $z^2 - 14z + 65 = 0$

(b) $9z^2 + 25 = 0$

(c) $z^2 + 4z + 12 = 0$

(d) $z^2 - (5 + 3j)z + 4 + 7j = 0$

10 No

11 (i) (a) $2j$ (b) -4 (c) $(-4)^k$

(iv) $2(-4)^k$

12 $w = 6 - 5j, z = 8 - 6j$

13 $a = -7, b = 11$, other root is $z = 5 - 2j$

Activity 2.6 (Page 55)

(i) Rotation through 180° about the origin

(ii) Reflection in the real axis

? (Page 55)

z and $-z^*$ (or $-z$ and z^*) are reflections of each other in the imaginary axis.

Activity 2.7 (Page 57)

(i)

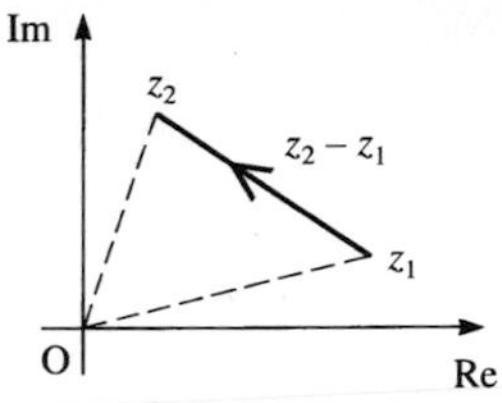

(ii)

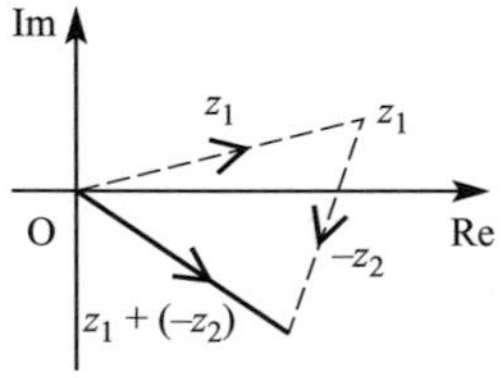

Exercise 2C (Page 57)

1

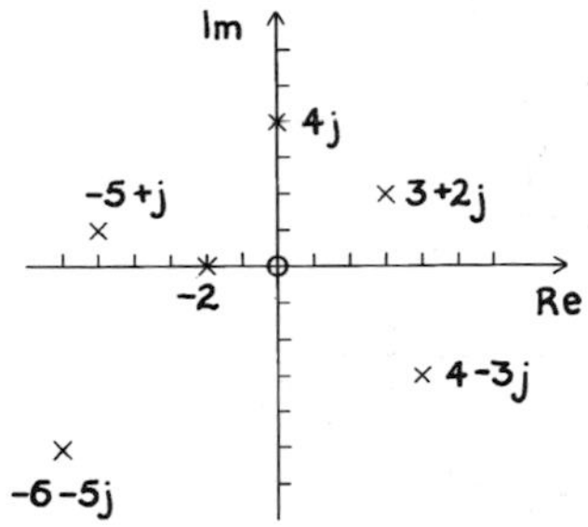

(i) $\sqrt{13}$

(ii) 4

(iii) $\sqrt{26}$

(iv) 2

(v) $\sqrt{61}$

(vi) 5

2

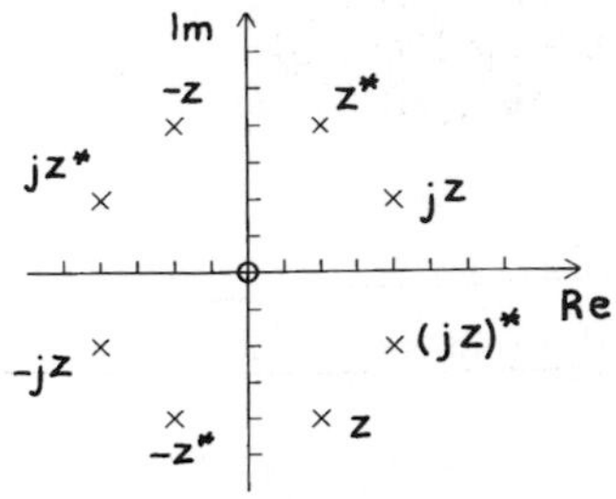

3 Points:

(i) $10 + 5j$

(ii) $1 + 2j$

(iii) $11 + 7j$

(iv) $9 + 3j$

(v) $-9 - 3j$

4 **(i)** 5

(ii) 13

(iii) 65

(iv) $\frac{5}{13}$

(v) $\frac{13}{5}$

$|zw| = |z||w|, \left|\frac{z}{w}\right| = \frac{|z|}{|w|}, \left|\frac{w}{z}\right| = \frac{|w|}{|z|}$

5 **(i)** $z^{-1} = \frac{1}{2} - \frac{1}{2}j, |z^{-1}| = \frac{1}{\sqrt{2}}$

$z^0 = 1, |z^0| = 1$

$z^1 = 1 + j, |z^1| = \sqrt{2}$

$z^2 = 2j, |z^2| = 2$

$z^3 = -2 + 2j, |z^3| = 2\sqrt{2}$

$z^4 = -4, |z^4| = 4$

$z^5 = -4 - 4j, |z^5| = 4\sqrt{2}$

(ii)

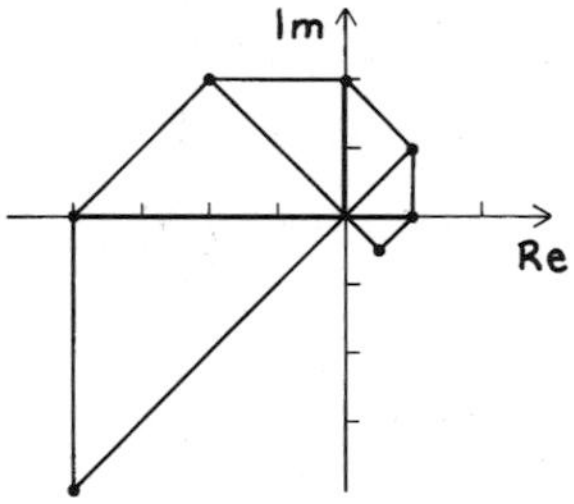

(iii) The half-squares formed are enlarged by $\sqrt{2}$ and rotated through $\frac{\pi}{4}$ each time.

6 Half a turn about O followed by reflection in the x axis is the same as reflection in the x axis followed by half a turn about O.

? (Page 58)

$|z_2 - z_1|$ is the distance between the points representing z_1 and z_2 in the Argand diagram.

❓ (Page 59)

(i)

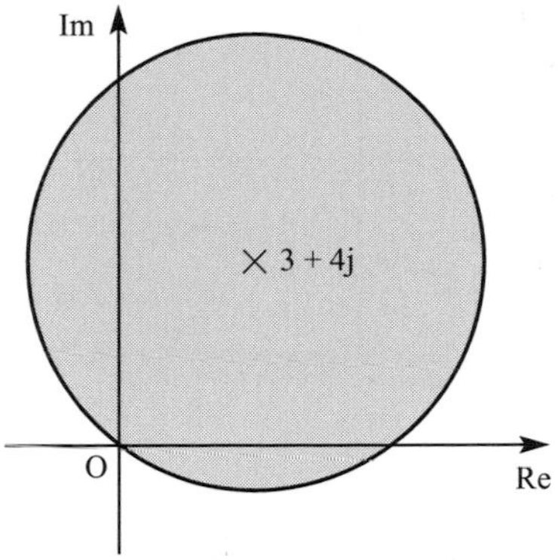

(ii)

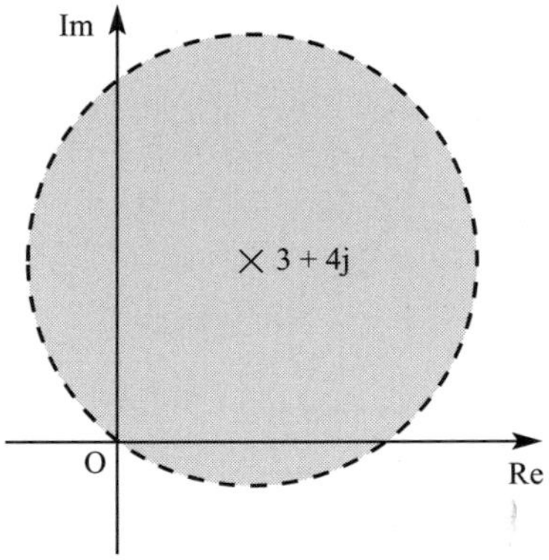

(iii)

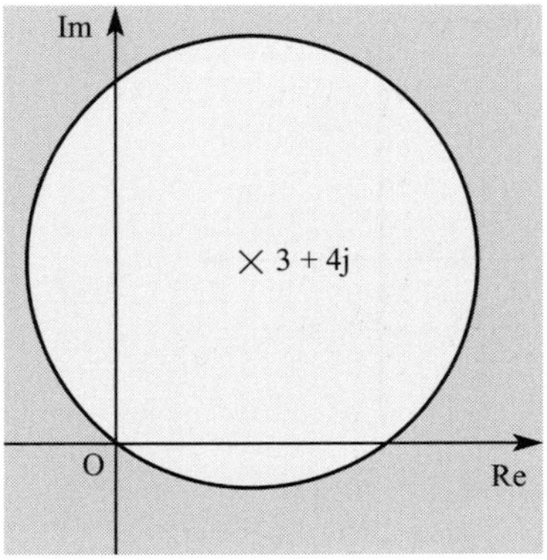

❓ (Page 60)

(i)

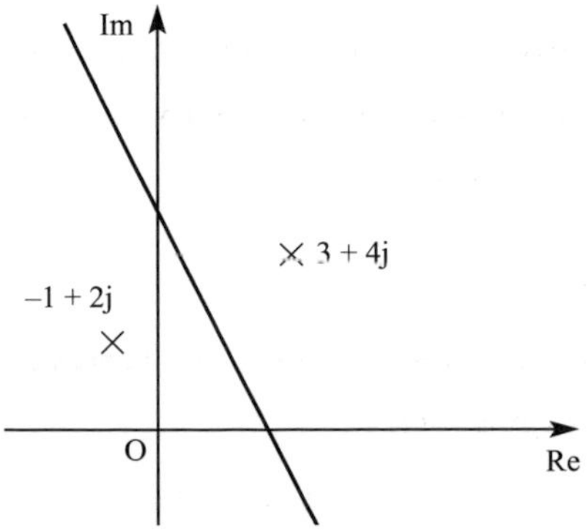

(ii)

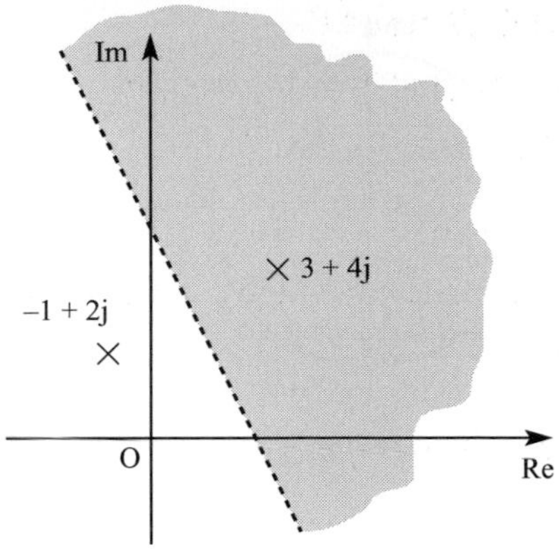

(iii)

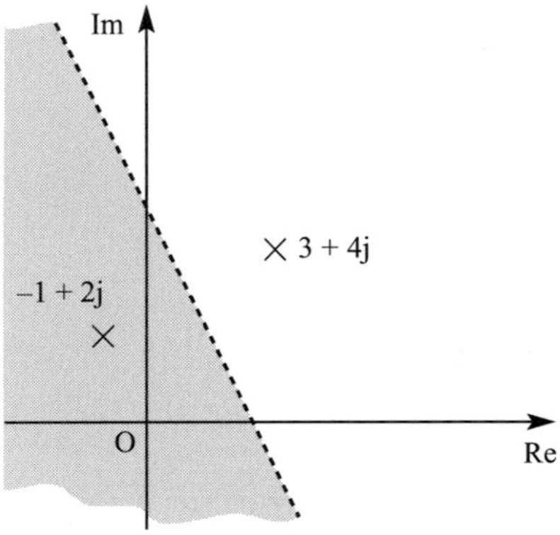

Exercise 2D (Page 60)

1 **(i)**

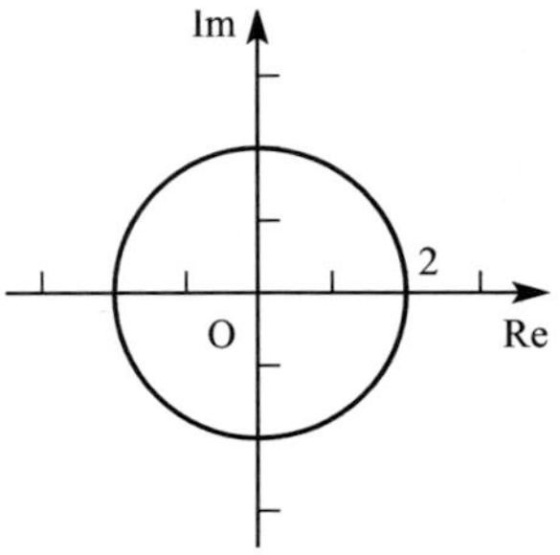

(ii)

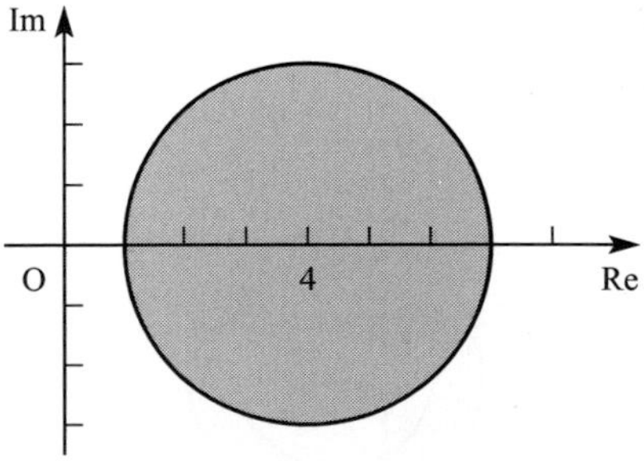

(iii)

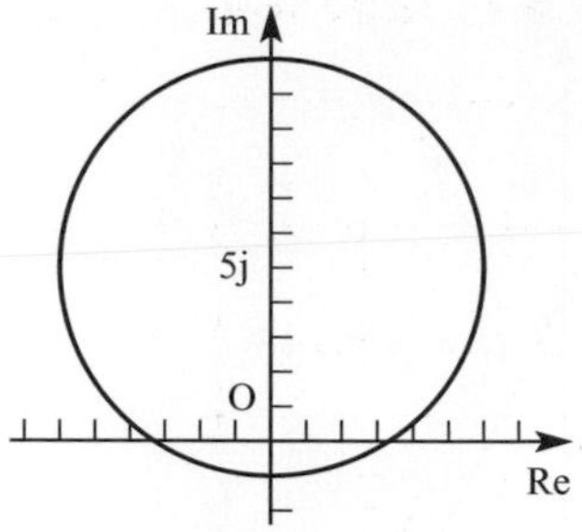

(iv)

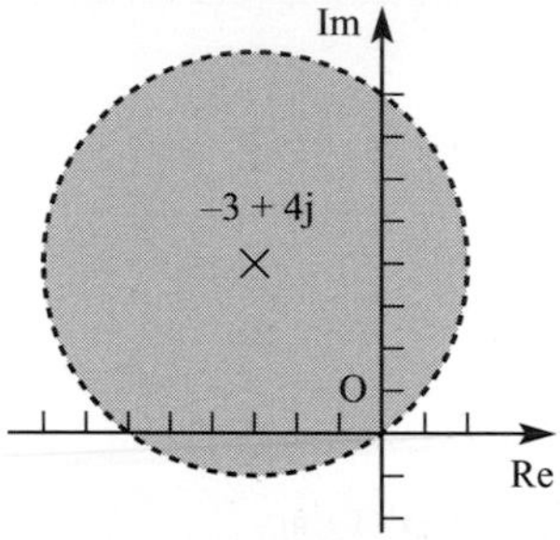

(v)

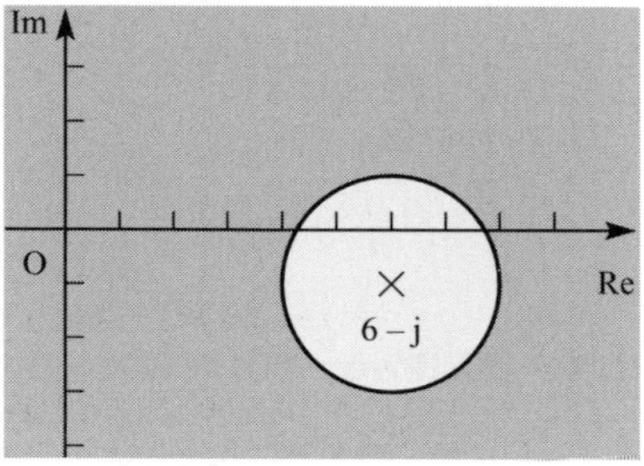

(vi)

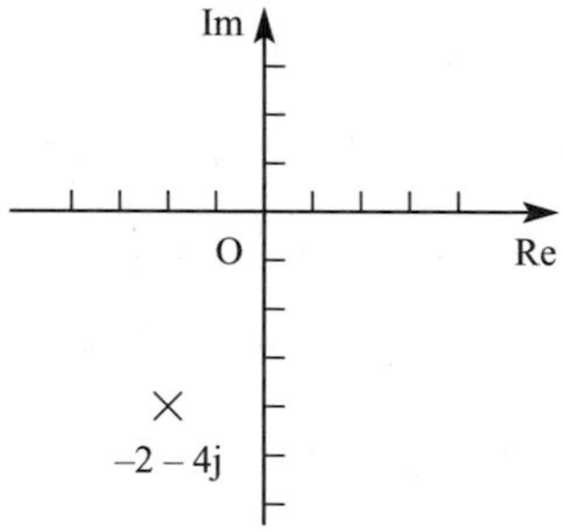

(vii)

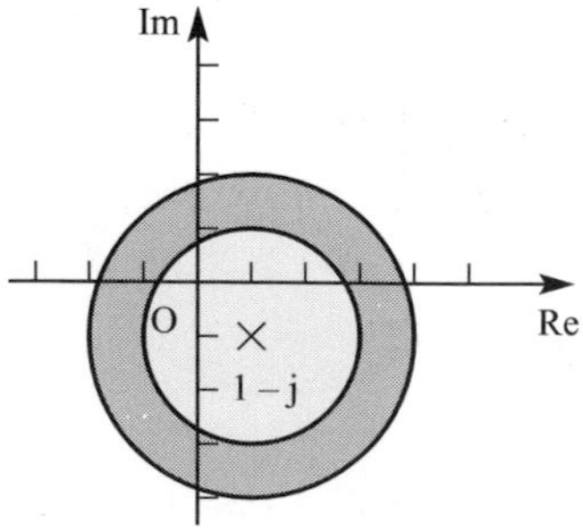

(viii)

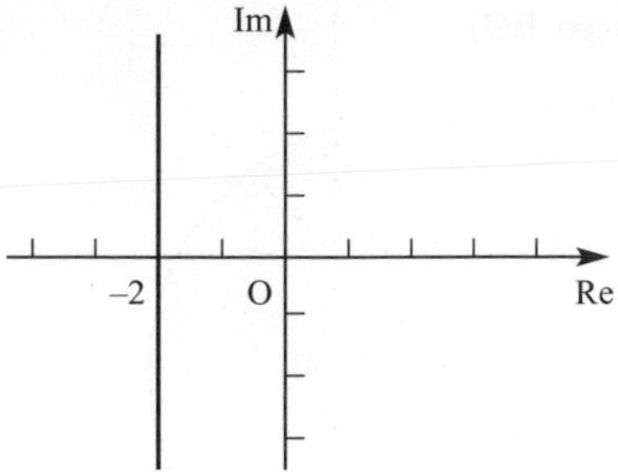

2

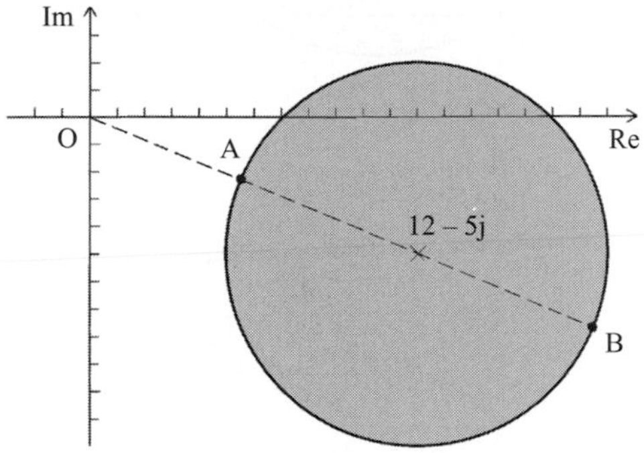

$|z|$ is least at A and greatest at B.

3 7, 13

4 Not possible

5 **(i)**

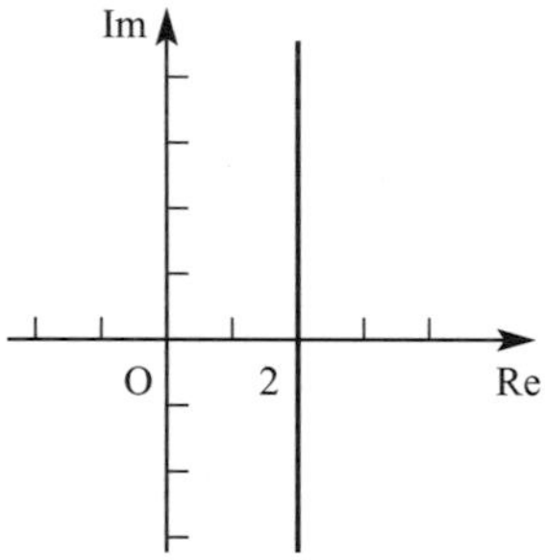

(ii)

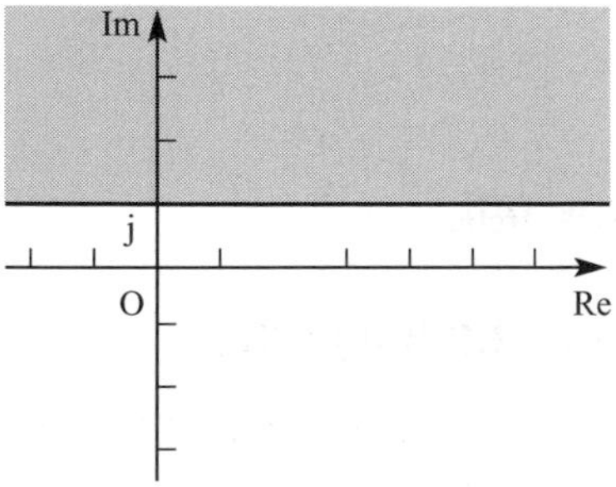

(iii)

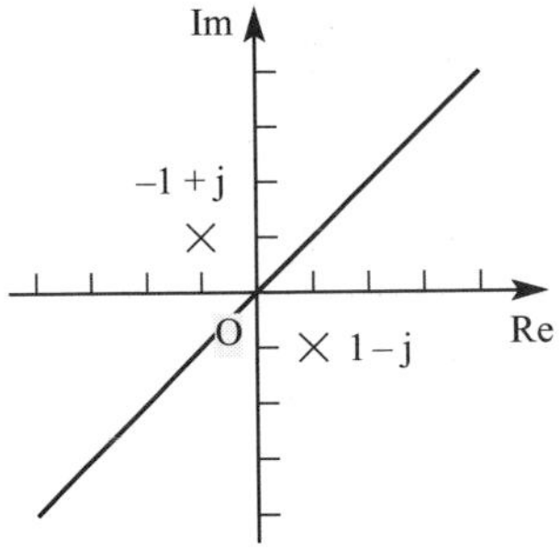

(iv)

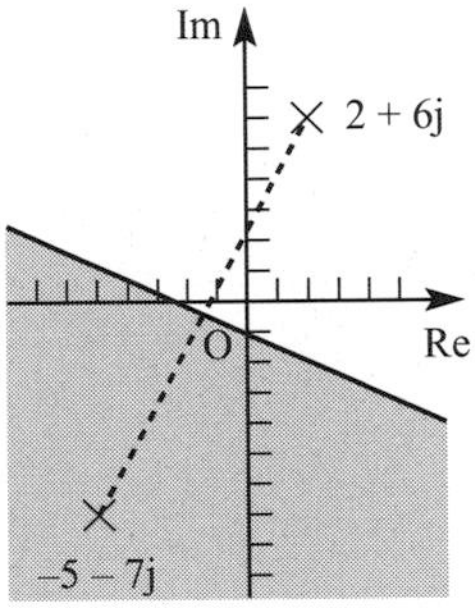

? (Page 62)

(i) $\frac{\pi}{2}$

(ii) $-\frac{3\pi}{4}$

(iii) $-\frac{\pi}{4}$

Activity 2.8 (Page 62)

(i) (a) 45°

(b) 63.4°

(c) 89.4°

(d) −63.4°

(e) −88.9°

(f) −89.7°

$-90° < \arctan x < 90°$

(ii) $-\frac{\pi}{2} < \arctan x < \frac{\pi}{2}$

Activity 2.9 (Page 63)

$\arg(1 + j) = \frac{\pi}{4}$, $\arg(1 - j) = -\frac{\pi}{4}$, $\arg(-1 + j) = \frac{3\pi}{4}$, $\arg(-1 - j) = -\frac{3\pi}{4}$

? (Page 64)

(i) $2(\cos(\pi - \alpha) + j\sin(\pi - \alpha))$

(ii) $2(\cos(-\alpha) + j\sin(-\alpha))$

Activity 2.11 (Page 64)

	$\frac{\pi}{4}$	$\frac{\pi}{6}$	$\frac{\pi}{3}$
tan	1	$\frac{1}{\sqrt{3}}$	$\sqrt{3}$
sin	$\frac{1}{\sqrt{2}}$	$\frac{1}{2}$	$\frac{\sqrt{3}}{2}$
cos	$\frac{1}{\sqrt{2}}$	$\frac{\sqrt{3}}{2}$	$\frac{1}{2}$

Activity 2.12 (Page 65)

(i) (a) $1 + \sqrt{3} + (1 - \sqrt{3})j$

(b) $\frac{1}{4}(1 - \sqrt{3} + (1 + \sqrt{3})j)$

(ii) (a) $|w| = \sqrt{2}$, $\arg w = \frac{\pi}{4}$

(b) $|z| = 2$, $\arg z = -\frac{\pi}{3}$

(c) $|wz| = 2\sqrt{2}$, $\arg(wz) = \arctan(-2 + \sqrt{3}) = -\frac{\pi}{12}$

(d) $\left|\frac{w}{z}\right| = \frac{\sqrt{2}}{2}$, $\arg\left(\frac{w}{z}\right) = \arctan(-2 - \sqrt{3}) = \frac{7\pi}{12}$

(iii) $|wz| = |w||z|$, $\left|\frac{w}{z}\right| = \frac{|w|}{|z|}$

$\arg(wz) = \arg w + \arg z$, $\arg\left(\frac{w}{z}\right) = \arg w - \arg z$

(iv) (a)
$$wz = r_1 r_2((\cos\theta_1 \cos\theta_2 - \sin\theta_1 \sin\theta_2) + j(\sin\theta_1 \cos\theta_2 + \cos\theta_1 \sin\theta_2))$$
$$= r_1 r_2(\cos(\theta_1 + \theta_2) + j\sin(\theta_1 + \theta_2))$$
$$\frac{w}{z} = \frac{r_1}{r_2}((\cos\theta_1 \cos\theta_2 + \sin\theta_1 \sin\theta_2) + j(\sin\theta_1 \cos\theta_2 - \cos\theta_1 \sin\theta_2))$$
$$= \frac{r_1}{r_2}(\cos(\theta_1 - \theta_2) + j\sin(\theta_1 - \theta_2))$$

(b) $|wz| = r_1 r_2$, $\left|\frac{w}{z}\right| = \frac{r_1}{r_2}$,

$\arg(wz) = \theta_1 + \theta_2$, $\arg\left(\frac{w}{z}\right) = \theta_1 - \theta_2$

Exercise 2E (Page 66)

1 (i) $r = 8, \theta = \frac{\pi}{5}$

(ii) $r = \frac{1}{4}, \theta = 2.3$

(iii) $r = 4, \theta = -\frac{\pi}{3}$

(iv) $r = 3, \theta = \pi - 3$

2 (i) $r = 1, \theta = 0, z = 1(\cos 0 + j\sin 0)$

(ii) $r = 2, \theta = \pi, z = 2(\cos\pi + j\sin\pi)$

(iii) $r = 3, \theta = \frac{\pi}{2}, z = 3\left(\cos\frac{\pi}{2} + j\sin\frac{\pi}{2}\right)$

(iv) $r = 4, \theta = -\frac{\pi}{2}, z = 4\left(\cos\left(-\frac{\pi}{2}\right) + j\sin\left(-\frac{\pi}{2}\right)\right)$

(v) $r = \sqrt{2}, \theta = \frac{\pi}{4}, z = \sqrt{2}\left(\cos\frac{\pi}{4} + j\sin\frac{\pi}{4}\right)$

(vi) $r = 5\sqrt{2}, \theta = -\frac{3\pi}{4}, z = 5\sqrt{2}\left(\cos\left(-\frac{3\pi}{4}\right) + j\sin\left(-\frac{3\pi}{4}\right)\right)$

(vii) $r = 2, \theta = -\frac{\pi}{3}, z = 2\left(\cos\left(-\frac{\pi}{3}\right) + j\sin\left(-\frac{\pi}{3}\right)\right)$

(viii) $r = 12, \theta = \frac{\pi}{6}, z = 12\left(\cos\frac{\pi}{6} + j\sin\frac{\pi}{6}\right)$

(ix) $r = 5, \theta = -0.927,$

$z = 5(\cos(-0.927) + j\sin(-0.927))$

(x) $r = 13, \theta = 2.747,$

$z = 13(\cos 2.747 + j\sin 2.747)$

(xi) $r = \sqrt{65}, \theta = 1.052,$

$z = \sqrt{65}(\cos 1.052 + j\sin 1.052)$

(xii) $r = \sqrt{12\,013}, \theta = -2.128,$

$z = \sqrt{12\,013}(\cos(-2.128) + j\sin(-2.128))$

3 **(i)** $z = 2j$

(ii) $z = \frac{3}{2} + \frac{3\sqrt{3}}{2}j$

(iii) $z = -\frac{7\sqrt{3}}{2} + \frac{7}{2}j$

(iv) $z = \frac{1}{\sqrt{2}} - \frac{1}{\sqrt{2}}j$

(v) $z = -\frac{5}{2} - \frac{5\sqrt{3}}{2}j$

(vi) $z = -2.497 - 5.456j$

4 **(i)** $\alpha - \pi$

(ii) $-\alpha$

(iii) $\pi - \alpha$

(iv) $\frac{\pi}{2} - \alpha$

(v) $\frac{\pi}{2} + \alpha$

? (Page 66)

$\arg(z_1 - z_2)$ is the angle between the line joining z_1 and z_2 and a line parallel to the real axis.

Exercise 2F (Page 68)

1 **(i)**

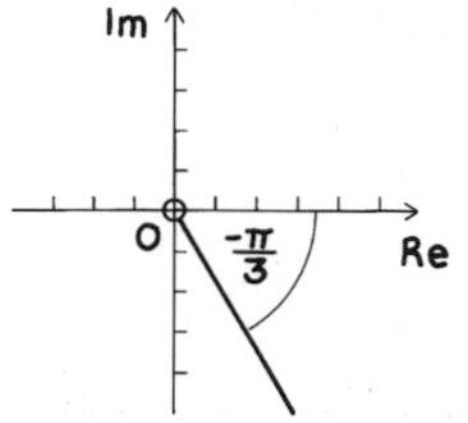

(ii)

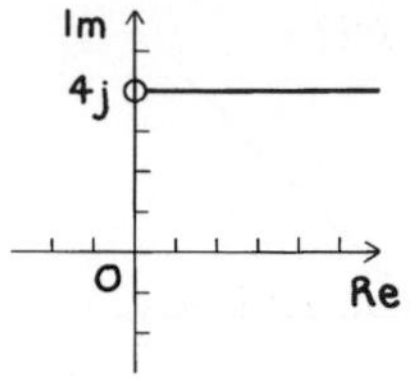

(iii)

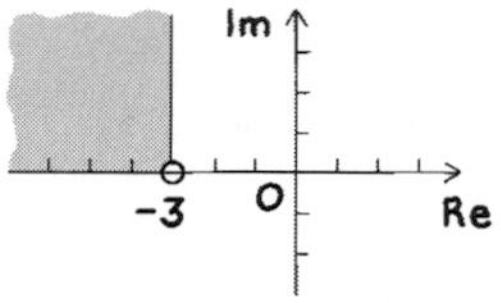

(iv)

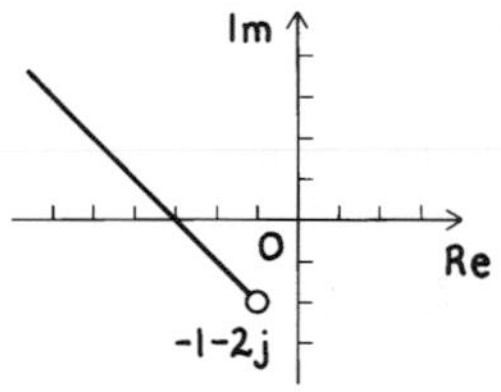

(v)

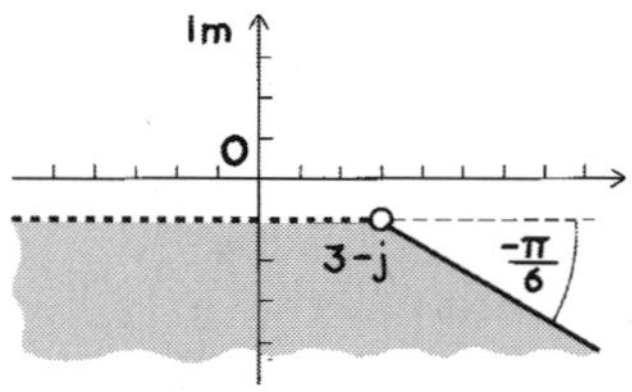

(vi)

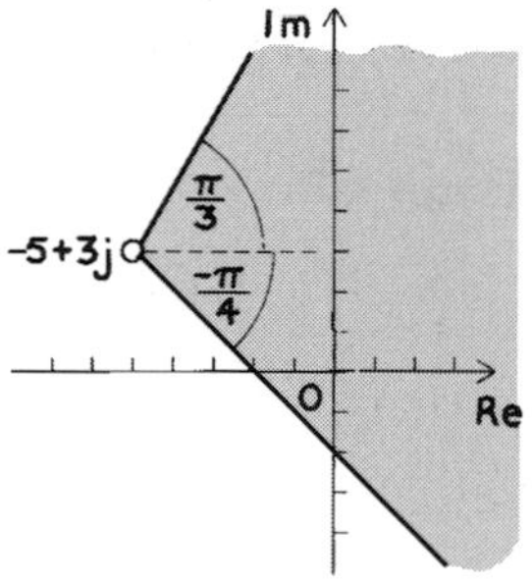

2 $\frac{\pi}{3}, \frac{2\pi}{3}$

3 **(i)** $\frac{2\pi}{3}, 2$

(ii)

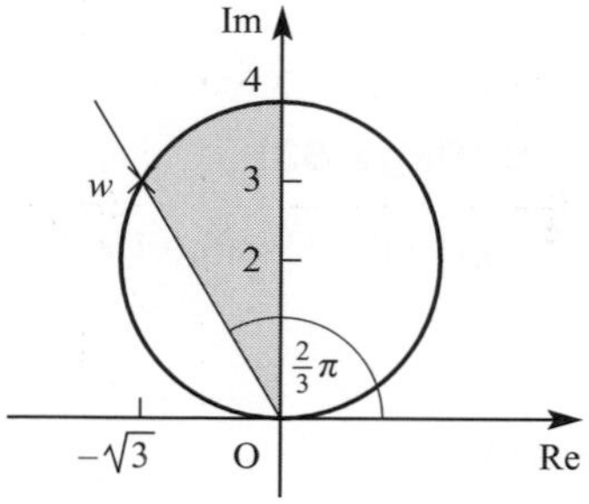

(iii) $\sqrt{12}$

4 **(ii)** $k \leqslant |z + 2k| \leqslant 3k, -\frac{\pi}{6} \leqslant \arg(z + 2k) \leqslant \frac{\pi}{6}$

Exercise 2G (Page 71)

1 $2 - j, -3$

2 $z = 7, 4 \pm 2j$

3 $p = 4, q = -10$, other roots $1 + j, -6$

4 $z = 3 \pm 2j, 2 \pm j$

5 $z = \pm 3j, 4 \pm \sqrt{5}$

6 **(i)** $w^2 = -2j, w^3 = -2 - 2j, w^4 = -4$

(ii) $p = -4, q = 2$

(iii) two of $1 - j, 1 + j, -1, -4$

7 **(i)** $\alpha^2 = -3 - 4j, \alpha^3 = 11 - 2j$

(ii) $-1 - 2j, -5$

(iii) $|-5| = 5, \arg(-5) = \pi$

$|-1 + 2j| = \sqrt{5}, \arg(-1 + 2j) = 2.03$

$|-1 - 2j| = \sqrt{5}, \arg(-1 - 2j) = -2.03$

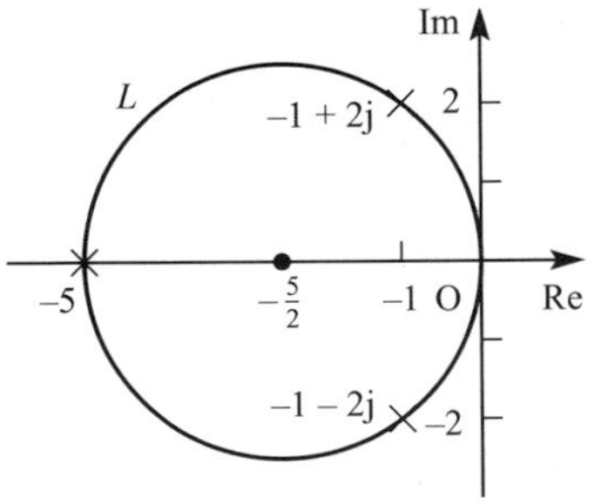

8 **(i)** $\beta = -1 + \sqrt{3}j, \gamma = -1 - \sqrt{3}j$

(ii) $\frac{1}{\beta} = -\frac{1}{4} - \frac{\sqrt{3}}{4}j, \frac{1}{\gamma} = -\frac{1}{4} + \frac{\sqrt{3}}{4}j$

(iii) $|\alpha| = 4, \arg \alpha = \pi$

$|\beta| = 2, \arg \beta = \frac{2\pi}{3}$

$|\gamma| = 2, \arg \gamma = -\frac{2\pi}{3}$

(iv)

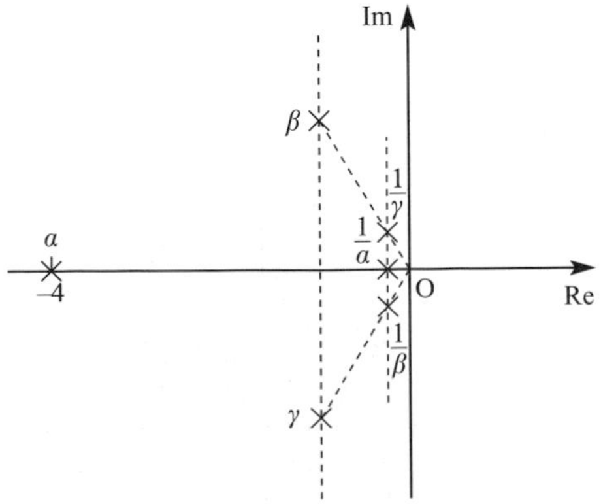

9 **(i)** $\alpha^2 = -15 + 8j, \alpha^3 = -47 - 52j$

(ii) $k = 3$

(iii) $-7, 1 - 4j$

$\arg(1 + 4j) = 1.326$

$\arg(-7) = \pi$

$\arg(1 - 4j) = -1.326$

(iv) $c = 5$

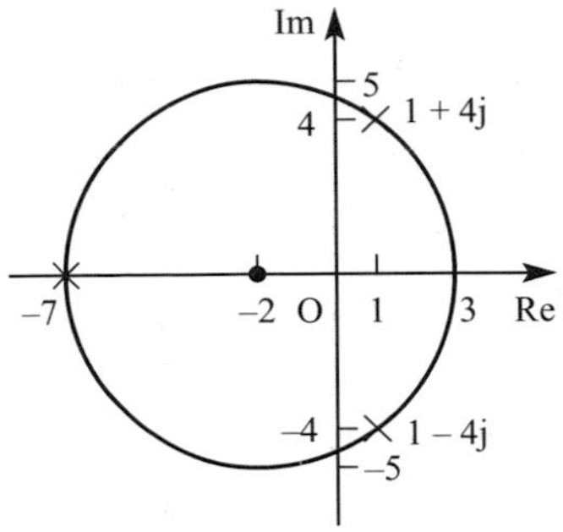

10 **(i)** $\alpha^2 = -8 - 6j, \alpha^3 = 26 - 18j$

(ii) $\mu = 20$

(iii) $z = -\frac{2}{3}, -1 \pm 3j$

$\left|-\frac{2}{3}\right| = \frac{2}{3}, \arg\left(-\frac{2}{3}\right) = \pi$

$|-1 + 3j| = \sqrt{10}, \arg(-1 + 3j) = 1.893$

$|-1 - 3j| = \sqrt{10}, \arg(-1 - 3j) = -1.893$

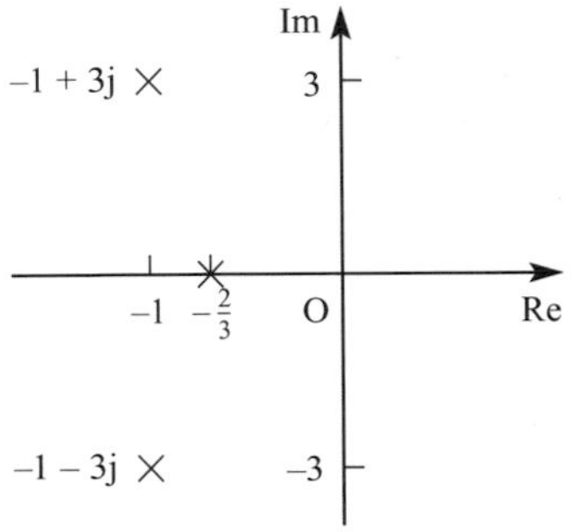

11 **(i)** $\beta = -2 + 2\sqrt{3}j, \gamma = -2 - 2\sqrt{3}j$

(ii) $|\alpha| = 3, \arg \alpha = 0$

$|\beta| = 4, \arg \beta = \frac{2\pi}{3}$

$|\gamma| = 4, \arg \gamma = -\frac{2\pi}{3}$

$\left|\frac{\beta}{\gamma}\right| = 1, \arg\left(\frac{\beta}{\gamma}\right) = -\frac{2\pi}{3}$

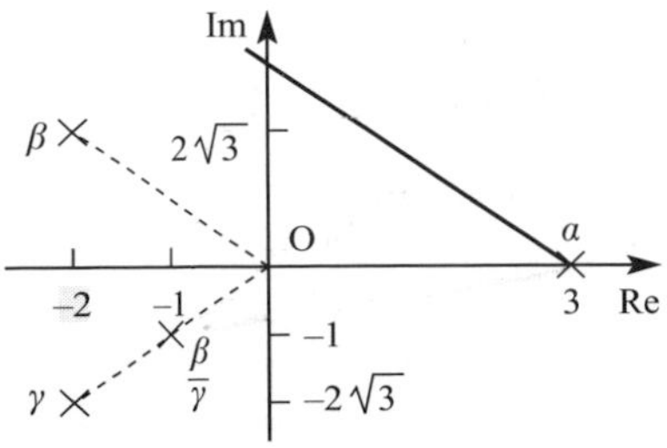

Chapter 3

? (Page 74)

The population of rabbits fluctuates but eventually approaches a stable number.

? (Page 75)

(i) The graph has two separate branches.

(ii) Curves

(iii) They can only draw a finite number of pixels.

? (Page 77)

(i) $x = -2$

(ii) $x = 1$ and $x = -2$

(iii) $x = \frac{1}{2}$

? (Page 77)

$\left(-\frac{1}{3}, 0\right), \left(0, -\frac{1}{2}\right)$

? (Page 78)

$x = 2$

$y \to -\infty$ as $x \to 2$ from the left.

$y \to \infty$ as $x \to 2$ from the right.

? (Page 79)

(i) 0.0103

(ii) 0.001 003

(iii) 0.000 100 03

(iv) –0.0097

(v) –0.000 997

(vi) –0.000 099 97

As $x \to \infty$, $y \to 0$ from above.

As $x \to -\infty$, $y \to 0$ from below.

? (Page 79)

(i) **(a)** All are positive

(b) All are negative

(ii) **(a)** Positive

(b) Negative

? (Page 80)

As $x \to -\infty$, $y \to 3$ from below.

As $x \to \infty$, $y \to 3$ from above.

Activity 3.2 (Page 80)

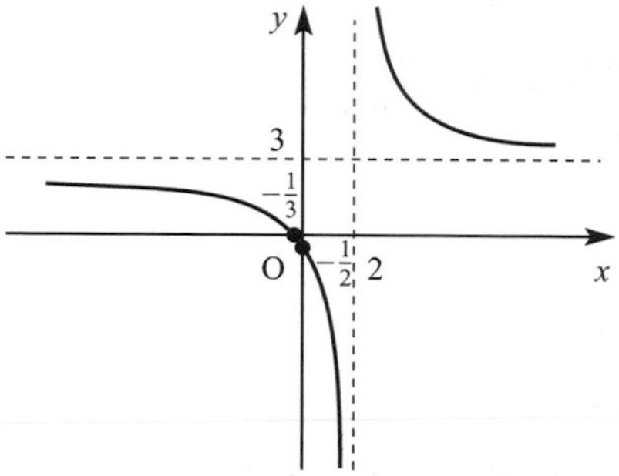

? (Page 82)

If the local maximum were higher than the local minimum, it would be possible to draw horizontal lines which cut the graph in more than two places.

? (Page 84)

The information about the behaviour near the vertical asymptotes was not needed. The sketch could be drawn just from points where the graph crosses the axes, the behaviour as $x \to \pm\infty$, and the position of the vertical asymptotes.

Exercise 3A (Page 86)

1 Step 1 $\left(0, -\frac{2}{3}\right)$

Step 2 $x = 3$

Step 3 $y \to 0$ from above as $x \to \infty$

$y \to 0$ from below as $x \to -\infty$

Step 4

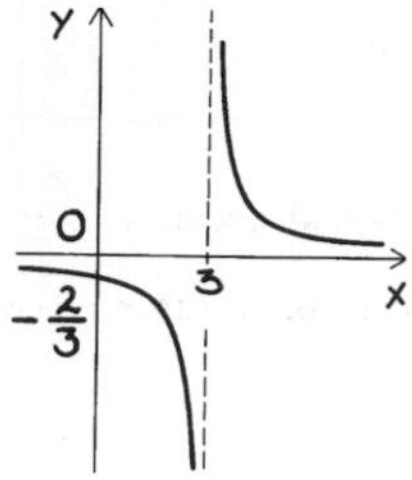

2 Step 1 $\left(0, \frac{2}{9}\right)$

Step 2 $x = 3$

Step 3 $y \to 0$ from above as $x \to \infty$

$y \to 0$ from above as $x \to -\infty$

Step 4

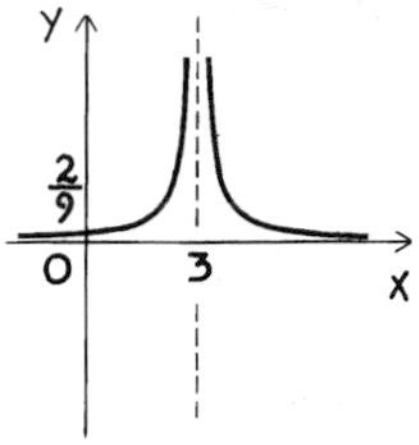

3 Step 1 $(0, 1)$

Step 2 none

Step 3 $y \to 0$ from above as $x \to \infty$

$y \to 0$ from above as $x \to -\infty$

Step 4

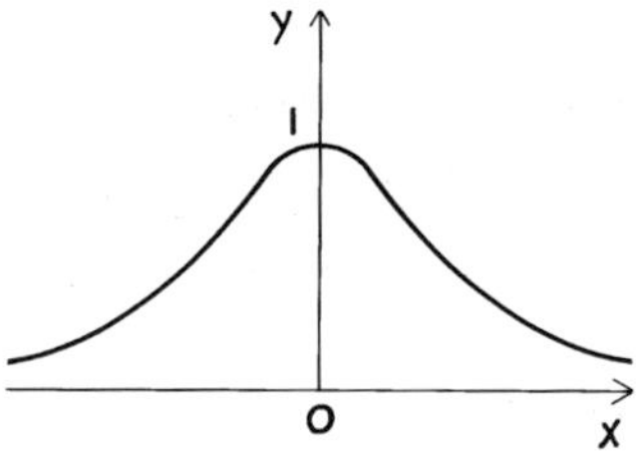

4 Step 1 $(0, 0)$

Step 2 $x = 2, x = -2$

Step 3 $y \to 0$ from above as $x \to \infty$

$y \to 0$ from below as $x \to -\infty$

Step 4

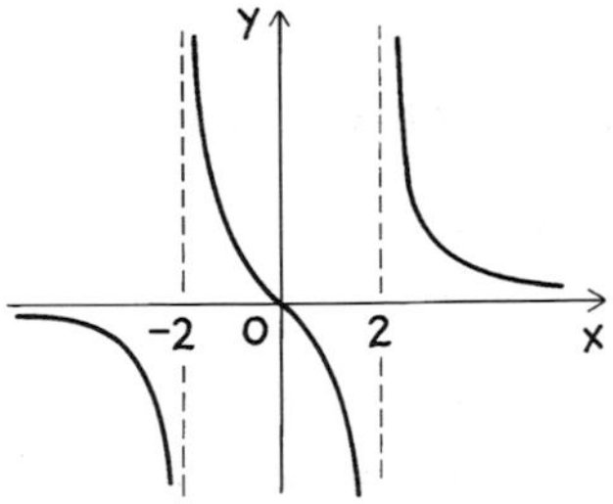

5 Step 1 $(2, 0), \left(0, \frac{2}{3}\right)$

Step 2 $x = -3$

Step 3 $y \to -1$ from above as $x \to \infty$

$y \to -1$ from below as $x \to -\infty$

Step 4

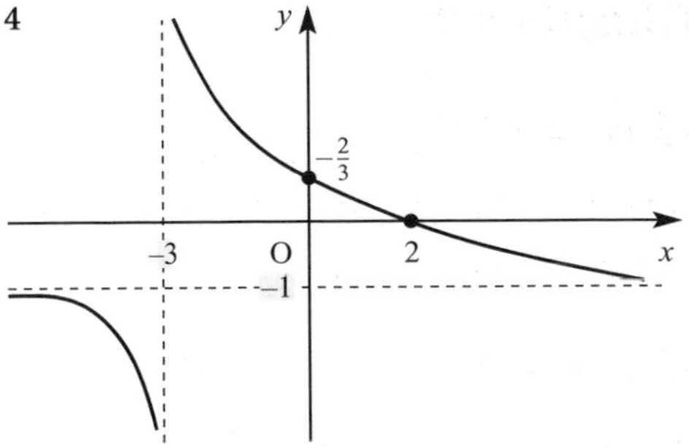

6 Step 1 $(5, 0), \left(0, \frac{5}{6}\right)$

Step 2 $x = -2, x = 3$

Step 3 $y \to 0$ from above as $x \to \infty$

$y \to 0$ from below as $x \to -\infty$

Step 4

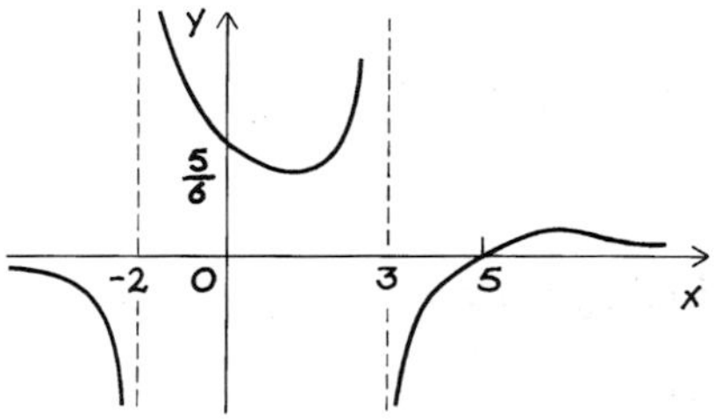

7 Step 1 $(3, 0), \left(0, \frac{3}{8}\right)$

Step 2 $x = 2, x = 4$

Step 3 $y \to 0$ from below as $x \to \infty$

$y \to 0$ from above as $x \to -\infty$

Step 4

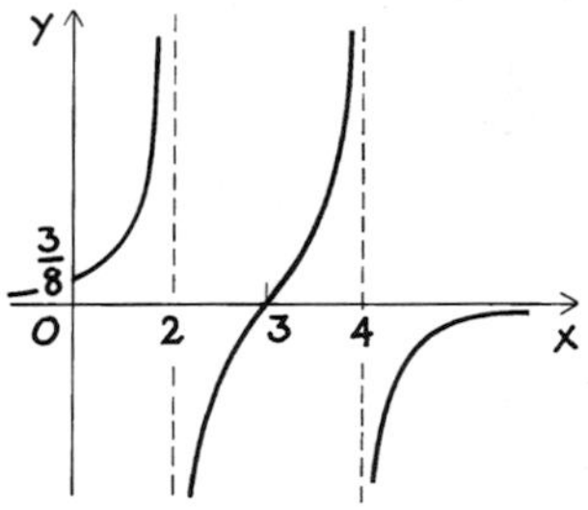

8 Step 1 $(0, 0)$

Step 2 none

Step 3 $y \to 0$ from above as $x \to \infty$

$y \to 0$ from below as $x \to -\infty$

Step 4

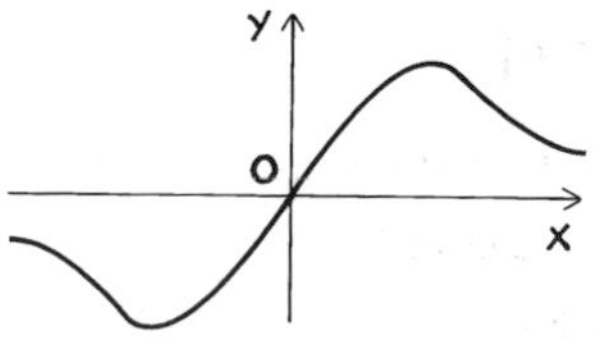

Answers

9 Step 1 $(3, 0), \left(0, -\frac{3}{16}\right)$

Step 2 $x = 4$

Step 3 $y \to 0$ from above as $x \to \infty$

$y \to 0$ from below as $x \to -\infty$

Step 4

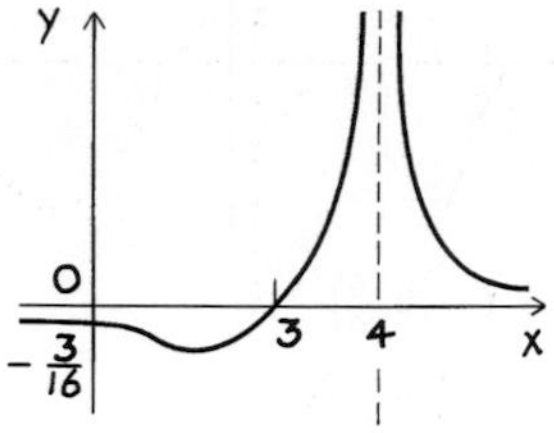

10 Step 1 $\left(\frac{3}{2}, 0\right), \left(-\frac{2}{5}, 0\right), \left(0, \frac{3}{2}\right)$

Step 2 $x = -1, x = 4$

Step 3 $y \to 10$ from above as $x \to \infty$

$y \to 10$ from below as $x \to -\infty$

Step 4

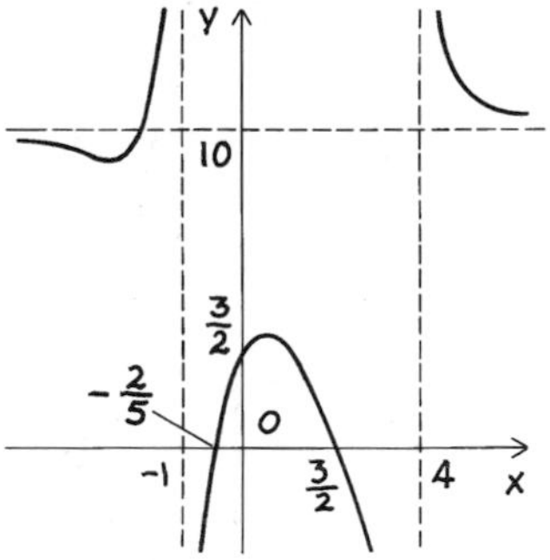

11 Step 1 (3, 0) (repeated), (0, 9)

Step 2 none

Step 3 $y \to 1$ from below as $x \to \infty$

$y \to 1$ from above as $x \to -\infty$

Step 4

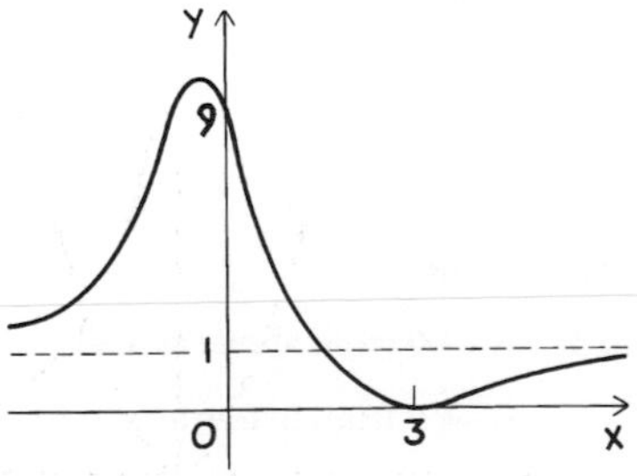

12 Step 1 $(6, 0), \left(0, \frac{3}{2}\right)$

Step 2 $x = 4$

Step 3 $y \to 1$ from below as $x \to \infty$

$y \to 1$ from above as $x \to -\infty$

Step 4

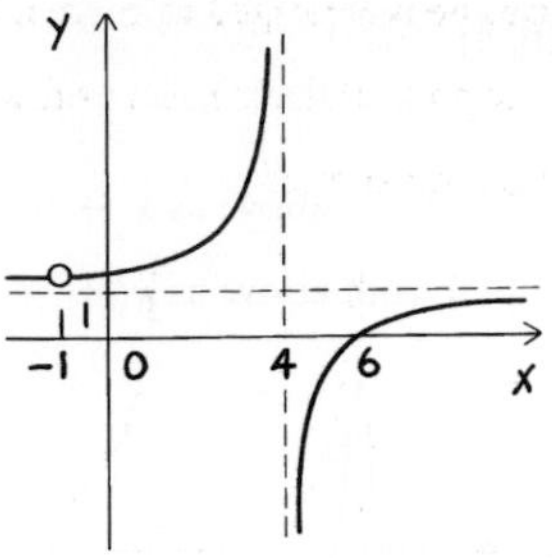

13 **(i)**

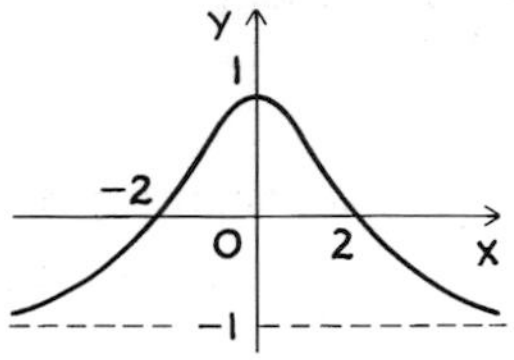

(ii) $k \leqslant -1$ or $k > 1$

14 **(i)**

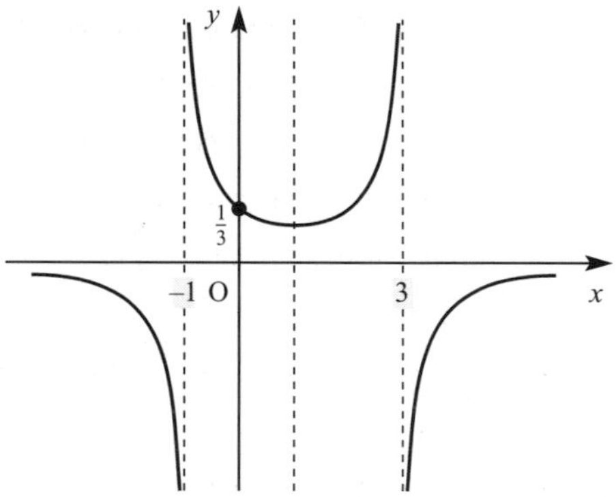

(ii) $x = 1$, minimum point $= \left(1, \frac{1}{4}\right)$

(iii) **(a)** $k < 0, k > \frac{1}{4}$

(b) $k = \frac{1}{4}$

(c) $0 \leqslant k < \frac{1}{4}$

15 **(i)**

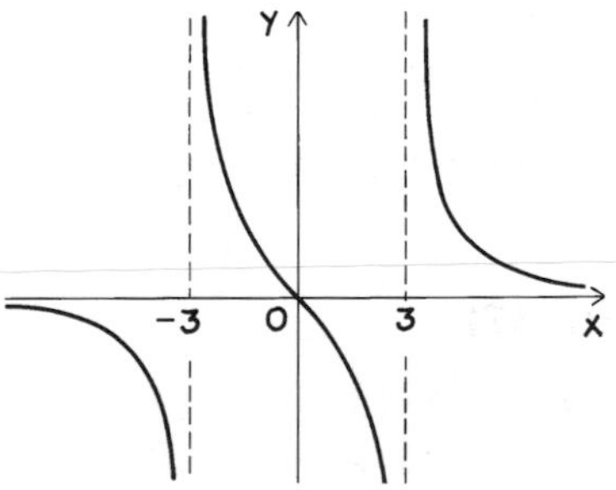

(iii) 2

(iv) A turning point would mean that there would be more than two values of x for a given y, which, from part **(iii)**, is impossible.

16 $y = \dfrac{x-2}{x+3}$ can be rearranged to form a linear equation in x, so that there is one value of x for every given value of y.

17 (ii)

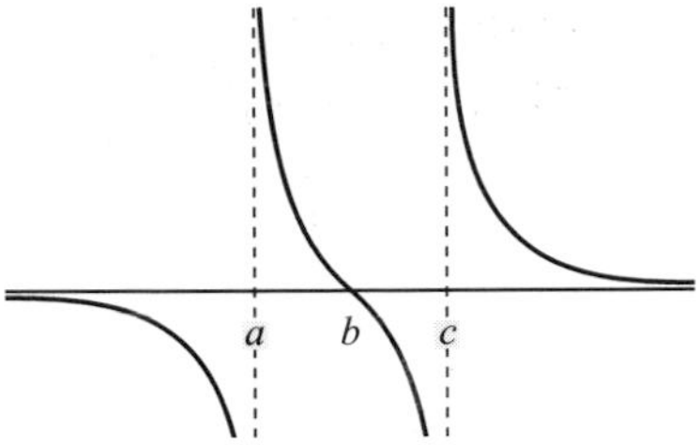

$y = \dfrac{(x-b)}{(x-a)(x-c)}$ can be rearranged to form a quadratic in x, so that for each value of y there is at most two values of x, i.e. any horizontal line crosses the graph at most twice.

If $a < b < c$, the graph is of the form shown above. This graph crosses all possible horizontal lines (except the x axis) exactly twice. Any turning point would result in the graph crossing some horizontal lines more than twice.

(ii) If $a = c$ and $b < a$ there is a turning point to the left of $x = b$.

18 (i) The graph is symmetrical about the y axis. There are no vertical asymptotes. There is a horizontal asymptote at $y = 1$.

(ii)

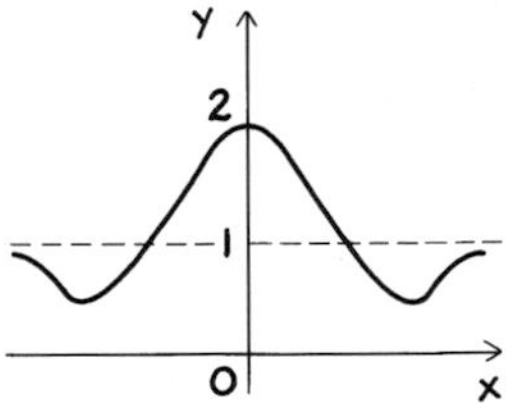

❓ (Page 87)

For example: $2 < 3$

$1 < 5$

Subtracting gives $1 < -2$ which is not true.

Exercise 3B (Page 92)

1 (i)

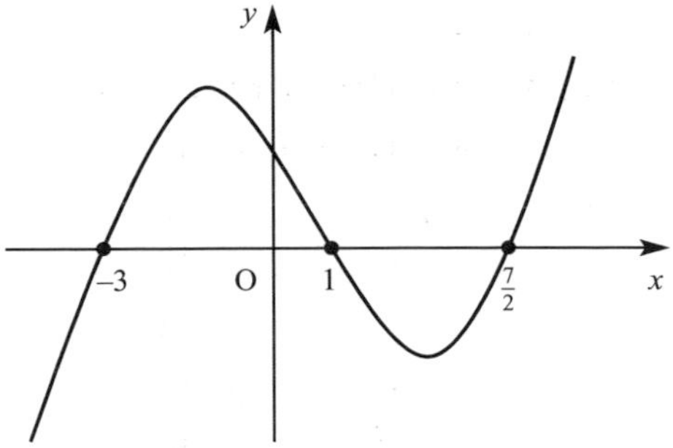

(ii) $-3 < x < 1, x > \frac{7}{2}$

2 (i)

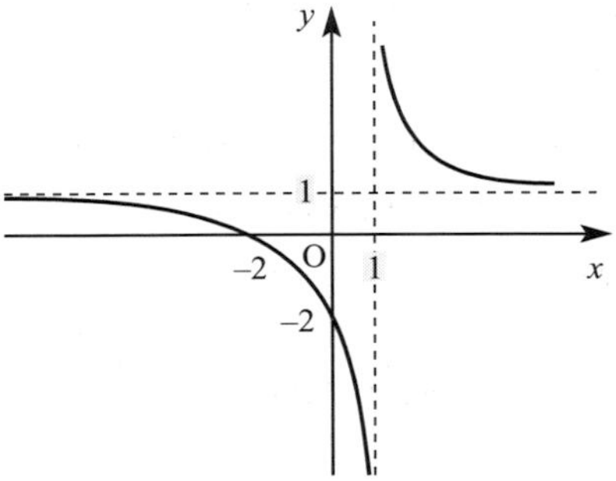

(ii) $x \leqslant -2, x > 1$

3 (i)

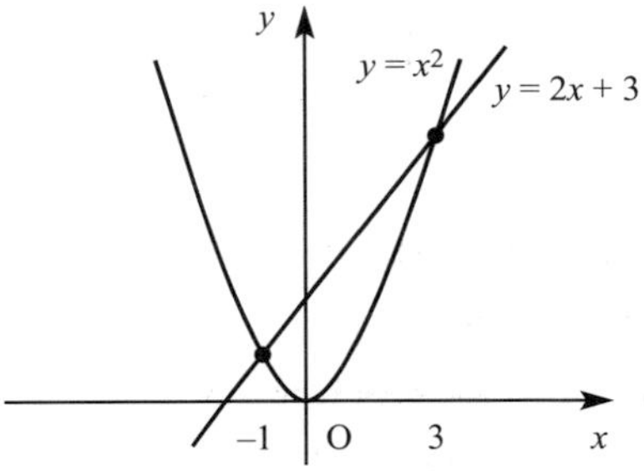

(ii) $-1 < x < 3$

4 (i)

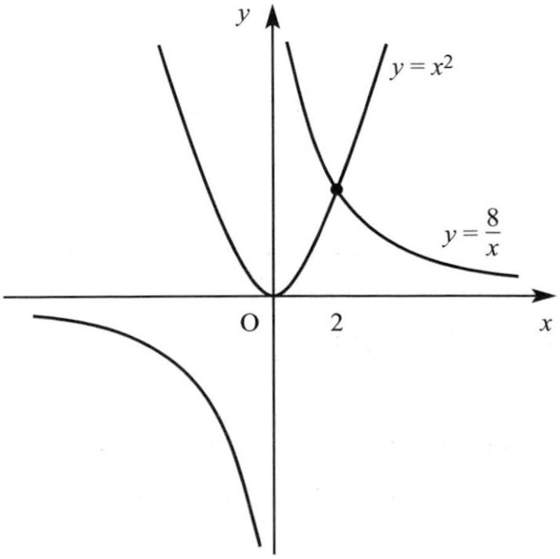

(ii) $x < 0, x \geqslant 2$

5 **(i)**

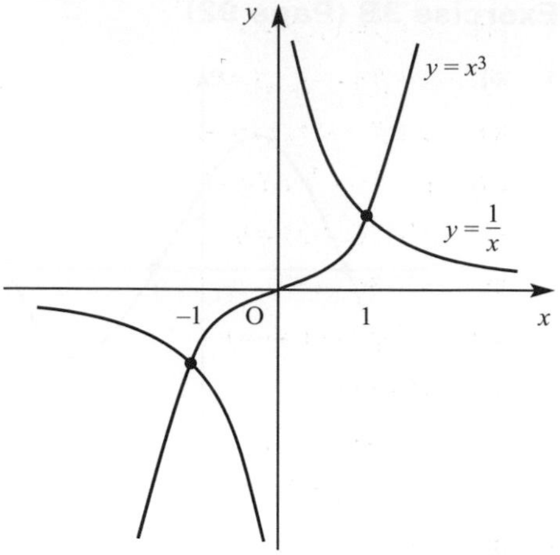

(ii) $x \leqslant -1$ or $0 < x \leqslant 1$

6 **(i)** $x < 1$ or $x > 3$

(ii) $x < -2$ or $0 < x < 5$

(iii) $x < -1$ or $2 \leqslant x \leqslant 5$

(iv) $-1 < x \leqslant \frac{2}{5}$ or $x > 2$

(v) $-2 \leqslant x < 0$ or $x \geqslant 4$

(vi) $x = 0$ or $1 \leqslant x < 2$

(vii) $-5 \leqslant x < 2$

(viii) $x < -6$ or $-2 \leqslant x < \frac{2}{3}$

7 **(i)** $-1 < x < 6$

(ii) $x < -1, 3 < x < 6$

8 **(i)** $\frac{1}{2} < x \leqslant \frac{5}{3}$

(ii) $-3 < x \leqslant \frac{5}{3}$

❓ (Page 93)

0, 1 or 2

❓ (Page 94)

At a turning point the graph touches the horizontal line, resulting in a repeated root.

Exercise 3C (Page 95)

1 **(i)** $(y-1)x^2 + x + 2 = 0$

(ii) Maximum value of $y = \frac{9}{8}$

(iii) $x = -4$

(iv)

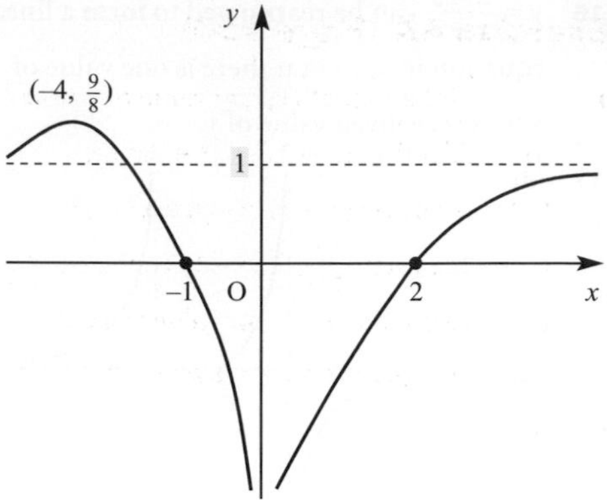

2 **(ii)**

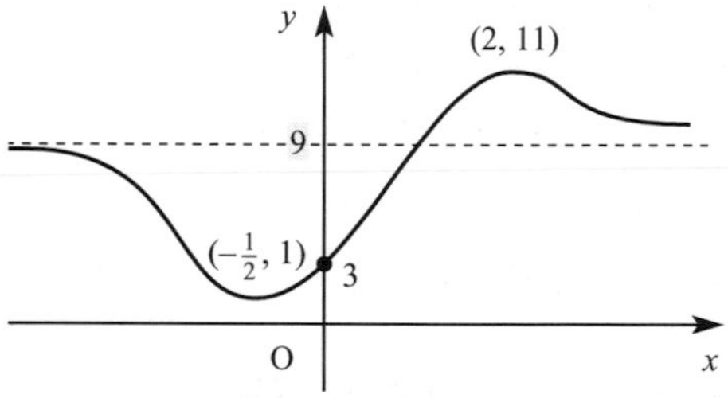

3 **(i)** $-1 \leqslant \dfrac{6x+6}{x^2+3} \leqslant 3$

(ii)

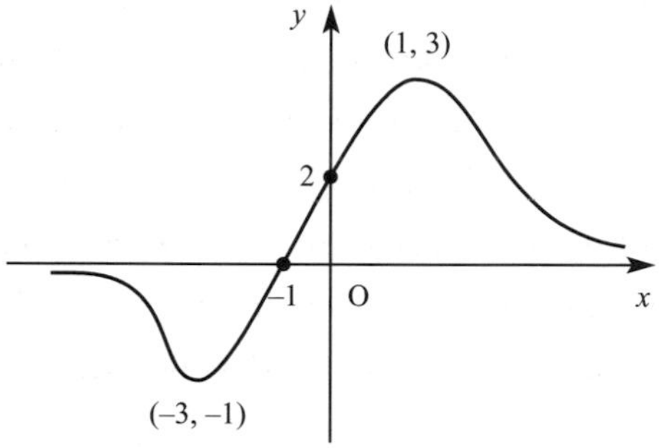

Chapter 4

❓ (Page 97)

$x^2(x-y), xy(x-y), y^2(x-y)$

$x^3 - y^3 = x^2(x-y) + xy(x-y) + y^2(x-y)$

$= (x-y)(x^2 + xy + y^2)$

Yes

❓ (Page 98)

Everything cancels and you end up with a statement such as $0 = 0$.

Exercise 4A (Page 100)

1 (i) Not an identity; any value of x other than -1.

(ii) Identity; $(x+2)^2 \equiv x^2 + 4x + 4$

(iii) Identity; $(x+y)(x-y) \equiv x^2 - y^2$

(iv) Identity; $\frac{4x-2}{1-2x} \equiv -2$ provided $x \neq \frac{1}{2}$

(v) Not an identity; any value of x other that 0 or -3

(vi) Identity; $x^2 + 6x + 1 \equiv (x+3)^2 - 8$

2 $A = 2, B = -3$

3 $A = 2, B = -1, C = -6$

4 $P = 7, Q = -7, R = -5$

5 $L = 3, M = \frac{1}{3}, N = -\frac{4}{3}$

6 $A = 1, B = 2, C = 4, D = 7$

7 $A = \frac{1}{3}, B = -\frac{1}{3}$

8 $A = -\frac{4}{5}, B = \frac{3}{5}, C = \frac{8}{5}$

Activity 4.2 (Page 100)

(i) $x = 1$ or 2, sum of roots = 3, product of roots = 2

(ii) $x = -3$ or 2, sum of roots = -1, product of roots = -6

(iii) $x = 2$ or 4, sum of roots = 6, product of roots = 8

(iv) $x = 5$ or -2, sum of roots = 3, product of roots = -10

(v) $x = 1$ or $\frac{1}{2}$, sum of roots = $\frac{3}{2}$, product of roots = $\frac{1}{2}$

(vi) $x = 1$ or $\frac{3}{2}$, sum of roots = $\frac{5}{2}$, product of roots = $\frac{3}{2}$

For the equation $ax^2 + bx + c = 0$,

the sum of the roots = $-\frac{b}{a}$ and the product of the roots = $\frac{c}{a}$

? (Page 101)

You get back to the original quadratic equation.

? (Page 103)

To give equations with integer coefficients.

Activity 4.4 (Page 103)

$2z^2 + 3z + 5 = 0$ has roots $-\frac{3}{4} \pm \frac{1}{4}\text{j}\sqrt{31}$

$z^2 + 3z + 10 = 0$ has roots $-\frac{3}{2} \pm \frac{1}{2}\text{j}\sqrt{31}$

$2z^2 - z + 4 = 0$ has roots $\frac{1}{4} \pm \frac{1}{4}\text{j}\sqrt{31}$

Exercise 4B (Page 104)

1 (i) $\alpha + \beta = -\frac{7}{2}, \alpha\beta = 3$

(ii) $\alpha + \beta = \frac{1}{5}, \alpha\beta = -\frac{1}{5}$

(iii) $\alpha + \beta = 0, \alpha\beta = \frac{2}{7}$

(iv) $\alpha + \beta = -\frac{24}{5}, \alpha\beta = 0$

(v) $\alpha + \beta = -11, \alpha\beta = -4$

(vi) $\alpha + \beta = -\frac{8}{3}, \alpha\beta = -2$

2 (i) $z^2 - 10z + 21 = 0$

(ii) $z^2 - 3z - 4 = 0$

(iii) $2z^2 + 19z + 45 = 0$

(iv) $z^2 - 5z = 0$

(v) $z^2 - 6z + 9 = 0$

(vi) $z^2 - 6z + 13 = 0$

3 (i) $2z^2 + 15z - 81 = 0$

(ii) $2z^2 - 5z - 9 = 0$

(iii) $2z^2 + 13z + 9 = 0$

(iv) $z^2 - 7z - 12 = 0$

4 (i) Roots are real, distinct and negative.

(ii) $\alpha = -\beta$

(iii) One of the roots is zero.

(iv) The roots are of opposite signs.

6 (i) $az^2 + bkz + ck^2 = 0$

(ii) $az^2 + (b - 2ka)z + (k^2a - kb + c) = 0$

7 (i) $\alpha + \beta = 2, \alpha\beta = 3$

(ii) $\frac{1}{\alpha} + \frac{1}{\beta} = \frac{\alpha+\beta}{\alpha\beta} = \frac{2}{3}$

$\frac{1}{\alpha} \times \frac{1}{\beta} = \frac{1}{\alpha\beta} = \frac{1}{3}$

(iii) $3z^2 - 2z + 1 = 0$

(iv) $cz^2 + bz + a = 0$

8 (i) $z^2 - 68z + 4 = 0$

(ii) $z^2 + 24z + 126 = 0$

(iii) $z^2 - 16z - 8 = 0$

(iv) $z^2 + 34z + 1 = 0$

? (Page 105)

$$\begin{aligned}
az^3 + bz^2 + cz + d &\equiv a(z-\alpha)(z-\beta)(z-\gamma) \\
&\equiv a(z-\alpha)(z^2 - (\beta+\gamma)z + \beta\gamma) \\
&\equiv a(z^3 - (\beta+\gamma)z^2 + \beta\gamma z - \alpha z^2 + \alpha(\beta+\gamma)z - \alpha\beta\gamma) \\
&\equiv a(z^3 - (\alpha+\beta+\gamma)z^2 + (\beta\gamma + \alpha\beta + \alpha\gamma)z - \alpha\beta\gamma) \\
&\equiv az^3 - a(\alpha+\beta+\gamma)z^2 + a(\alpha\beta + \alpha\gamma + \beta\gamma))z - a\alpha\beta\gamma
\end{aligned}$$

? (Page 107)

Product of roots = $(2\alpha + 1)(2\beta + 1)(2\gamma + 1)$

$= (2\alpha + 1)(4\beta\gamma + 2(\beta + \gamma) + 1)$

$= 8\alpha\beta\gamma + 4\alpha(\beta + \gamma) + 2\alpha + 4\beta\gamma + 2(\beta + \gamma) + 1$

$= 8\alpha\beta\gamma + 4(\alpha\beta + \beta\gamma + \gamma\alpha) + 2(\alpha + \beta + \gamma) + 1$

Activity 4.5 (Page 108)

$z = -\dfrac{d}{aw} \Leftrightarrow w = -\dfrac{d}{az} = \dfrac{\alpha\beta\gamma}{z}$, since $-\dfrac{d}{a} = \alpha\beta\gamma$.

So w takes the values $\beta\gamma, \gamma\alpha, \alpha\beta$ as z takes the values α, β, γ.

The equation simplifies to $a^2w^3 - acw^2 + bdw - d^2 = 0$.

Suppose that α (say) is 0. Then $d = -\alpha\beta\gamma a = 0$ and the equation becomes

$a^2w^3 - acw^2 = 0$

$\Leftrightarrow \quad aw^2(aw - c) = 0$

$\Leftrightarrow \quad w = 0$ (twice) or $\dfrac{c}{a}$

$= 0$ (twice) or $\beta\gamma$, since $\dfrac{c}{a} = \alpha\beta + \beta\gamma + \gamma\alpha$ and $\alpha = 0$

$= \alpha\beta, \beta\gamma, \gamma\alpha$ with $\alpha = 0$.

Activity 4.6 (Page 108)

(i) $(\alpha + \beta + \gamma)^2 = \alpha^2 + \beta^2 + \gamma^2 + 2(\alpha\beta + \beta\gamma + \gamma\alpha)$

(ii) $(\alpha\beta + \beta\gamma + \gamma\alpha)^2 = (\alpha\beta)^2 + (\beta\gamma)^2 + (\gamma\alpha)^2 + 2\alpha\beta\gamma(\alpha + \beta + \gamma)$

(iii) $\alpha\beta\gamma\left(\dfrac{1}{\alpha} + \dfrac{1}{\beta} + \dfrac{1}{\gamma}\right) = \alpha\beta + \beta\gamma + \gamma\alpha$

The proofs are by direct expansion and simplification.

Exercise 4C (Page 110)

1 **(i)** $-\frac{3}{2}$

(ii) $-\frac{1}{2}$

(iii) $-\frac{7}{2}$

2 **(i)** $z^3 - 7z^2 + 14z - 8 = 0$

(ii) $z^3 - 3z^2 - 4z + 12 = 0$

(iii) $2z^3 + 7z^2 + 6z = 0$

(iv) $2z^3 - 13z^2 + 28z - 20 = 0$

(v) $z^3 - 19z - 30 = 0$

(vi) $z^3 - 5z^2 + 9z - 5 = 0$

3 **(i)** $z = 2, 5, 8$

(ii) $z = -\frac{2}{3}, \frac{2}{3}, 2$

(iii) $z = 2 - 2\sqrt{3}, 2, 2 + 2\sqrt{3}$

(iv) $z = \frac{2}{3}, \frac{7}{6}, \frac{5}{3}$

4 Roots are $\frac{3}{2}, 2, \frac{5}{2}$

$k = \frac{47}{2}$

5 $z = \frac{1}{4}, \frac{1}{2}, -\frac{3}{4}$

6 **(i)** $w^3 + 4w^2 - 6w + 4 = 0$

(ii) $2w^3 - 14w^2 + 27w - 8 = 0$

(iii) $2w^3 - 16w^2 + 37w - 27 = 0$

(iv) $2w^3 + 24w^2 + 45w + 37 = 0$

7 $\alpha = -1, p = 7, q = 8$ or $\alpha = p = q = 0$

8 Roots are $-p$ and $\pm\sqrt{-q}$

9 **(i)** $p = -8\left(\alpha + \dfrac{1}{2\alpha} + \beta\right)$

$q = 8\left(\dfrac{1}{2} + \alpha\beta + \dfrac{\beta}{2\alpha}\right)$

$r = -4\beta$

(iii) $r = 9; x = 1, \frac{1}{2}, -\frac{9}{4}$

$r = -6; x = -2, -\frac{1}{4}, \frac{3}{2}$

10 $z = \frac{3}{7}, \frac{7}{3}, -2$

11 $ac^3 = b^3d$

$z = \frac{1}{2}, \frac{3}{2}, \frac{9}{2}$

12 **(i)** 5, –6, 4

(ii) 37

(iv) $z^3 + z^2 + 37z - 4 = 0$

13 **(i)** $0, -\frac{27}{16}$

$k = -16(\alpha + \beta + \gamma)$

(ii) $x = -\frac{3}{4}, \frac{3}{2}, \frac{3}{2}$

$k = -36$

(iii) $27z^3 - 81z^2 + 90z - 20 = 0$

? (Page 111)

$\alpha + \beta + \gamma + \delta = -\dfrac{b}{a}$

$\alpha\beta + \alpha\gamma + \alpha\delta + \beta\gamma + \beta\delta + \gamma\delta = \dfrac{c}{a}$

$\alpha\beta\gamma + \beta\gamma\delta + \gamma\delta\alpha + \delta\alpha\beta = -\dfrac{d}{a}$

$\alpha\beta\gamma\delta = \dfrac{e}{a}$

❓ (Page 113)

$\alpha + \beta + \gamma + \delta + \varepsilon = -\dfrac{b}{a}$

$\alpha\beta + \alpha\gamma + \alpha\delta + \alpha\varepsilon + \beta\gamma + \beta\delta + \beta\varepsilon + \gamma\delta + \gamma\varepsilon + \delta\varepsilon = \dfrac{c}{a}$

$\alpha\beta\gamma + \alpha\beta\delta + \alpha\beta\varepsilon + \alpha\gamma\delta + \alpha\gamma\varepsilon + \alpha\delta\varepsilon + \beta\gamma\delta + \beta\gamma\varepsilon + \beta\delta\varepsilon +$
$\gamma\delta\varepsilon = -\dfrac{d}{a}$

$\alpha\beta\gamma\delta + \beta\gamma\delta\varepsilon + \gamma\delta\varepsilon\alpha + \delta\varepsilon\alpha\beta + \varepsilon\alpha\beta\gamma = \dfrac{e}{a}$

$\alpha\beta\gamma\delta\varepsilon = -\dfrac{f}{a}$

Exercise 4D (Page 113)

1 **(i)** $-\frac{3}{2}$

(ii) 3

(iii) $\frac{5}{2}$

(iv) 2

2 **(i)** $z^4 - 6z^3 + 7z^2 + 6z - 8 = 0$

(ii) $4z^4 + 20z^3 + z^2 - 60z = 0$

(iii) $4z^4 + 12z^3 - 27z^2 - 54z + 81 = 0$

(iv) $z^4 - 5z^2 + 10z - 6 = 0$

3 **(i)** $w^4 + 4w^3 - 6w^2 - 4w + 48 = 0$

(ii) $2w^4 + 12w^3 + 21w^2 + 13w + 8 = 0$

4 **(i)** $w^4 - 4w^2 + 4 = 0$

(ii) $w = \pm\sqrt{2}$, $\alpha = \beta = \sqrt{2} - 2$, $\gamma = \delta = -\sqrt{2} - 2$

5 **(i)** $\alpha = -\frac{2}{3}$, $\beta = \frac{2}{3}\sqrt{3}$

(ii) $q = -16$

(iii) $9y^3 - 48y^2 + 72y - 32 = 0$

Chapter 5

❓ (Page 115)

Although you can always work out your age if you know your date of birth, most people know their age because they add a year each birthday. If the old woman's memory is good enough, then she may well be correct, but you cannot be sure.

Activity 5.1 (Page 115)

$\dfrac{1}{1\times 2} = \dfrac{1}{2}$

$\dfrac{1}{1\times 2} + \dfrac{1}{2\times 3} = \dfrac{2}{3}$

$\dfrac{1}{1\times 2} + \dfrac{1}{2\times 3} + \dfrac{1}{3\times 4} = \dfrac{3}{4}$

$\dfrac{1}{1\times 2} + \dfrac{1}{2\times 3} + \dfrac{1}{3\times 4} + \dfrac{1}{4\times 5} = \dfrac{4}{5}$

The next two terms are $\frac{5}{6}$ and $\frac{6}{7}$.

Activity 5.2 (Page 118)

(i) Assume true for $n = k$, so $2 + 4 + 6 + \ldots + 2k = \left(k + \frac{1}{2}\right)^2$

For $n = k + 1$,

$2 + 4 + 6 + \ldots + 2k + 2(k+1) = \left(k + \frac{1}{2}\right)^2 + 2(k+1)$

$= k^2 + k + \frac{1}{4} + 2k + 2$

$= k^2 + 3k + \frac{9}{4}$

$= \left(k + \frac{3}{2}\right)^2$

$= \left(k + 1 + \frac{1}{2}\right)^2$

The result is not true for $k = 1$ $\left(\text{L.H.S.} = 2, \text{R.H.S.} = \frac{9}{4}\right)$ so it is not true for any positive integer n.

(ii) One possible example is $2 + 4 + 6 + \ldots + 2n = 2n^2$.

Exercise 5B (Page 121)

4 **(i)** $u_2 = \frac{1}{2}$, $u_3 = \frac{1}{3}$, $u_4 = \frac{1}{4}$

(ii) $u_n = \dfrac{1}{n}$

5 **(i)** $u_2 = 13$, $u_3 = 35$

9 **(i)** $A^2 = \begin{pmatrix} -3 & -8 \\ 2 & 5 \end{pmatrix}$, $A^3 = \begin{pmatrix} -5 & -12 \\ 3 & 7 \end{pmatrix}$

❓ (Page 122)

For any arithmetic series, the sum of the terms $S_n = \frac{1}{2}n[2a + (n-1)d]$.

This always approaches ∞ (or $-\infty$ if $d < 0$) as $n \to \infty$, unless $a = d = 0$, so an arithmetic series is never convergent unless all the terms are zero.

For a geometric series, the sum of the terms $S_n = \dfrac{a(1 - r^n)}{1 - r}$.

If $-1 < r < 1$, then $r^n \to 0$ as $n \to \infty$, so the sum converges to $\dfrac{a}{1 - r}$.

❓ (Page 124)

$$\frac{3}{2} - \frac{2}{n+1} + \frac{1}{n+2} = \frac{3(n+1)(n+2) - 4(n+2) + 2(n+1)}{2(n+1)(n+2)}$$

$$= \frac{3n^2 + 7n}{2(n+1)(n+2)}$$

$$= \frac{n(3n+7)}{2(n+1)(n+2)}$$

❓ (Page 124)

The sum converges because the numerator and the denominator are of the same order.

As $n \to \infty$, $\dfrac{n(3n+7)}{2(n+1)(n+2)} \to \dfrac{3n^2}{2n^2} = \dfrac{3}{2}$

Exercise 5C (Page 124)

1 **(ii)** n^2

2 **(ii)** $n(n^2 + 4n + 5)$

3 **(ii)** $\frac{20}{21}$

4 **(ii)** $\dfrac{n(n+2)}{(n+1)^2}$

5 **(ii)** $\dfrac{n(3n+5)}{4(n+1)(n+2)}$

(iii) Yes, the sum converges to $\frac{3}{4}$.

The numerator and the denominator are of the same order.

6 **(ii)** $\frac{13}{120}$

7 **(ii)** $\dfrac{n(n+3)}{4(n+1)(n+2)}$

(iii) Yes, the sum converges to $\frac{1}{4}$.

As question 5.

8 **(ii)** $\dfrac{n(3n+7)}{2(n+1)(n+2)}$

9 **(ii)** $\sum_{r=1}^{n} 8r = 4n(n+1)$

10 **(ii)** $\sum_{r=1}^{n} (24r^2 + 2) = 8n^3 + 12n^2 + 6n$

11 **(ii)** $\sum_{r=1}^{n} (64r^3 + 16r) = 16n^4 + 32n^3 + 24n^2 + 8n$

12 **(i)** $\sum_{r=1}^{n} r(r+1) = \frac{1}{3}n(n+1)(n+2)$

(ii) $\sum_{r=1}^{n} r(r+1)(r+2) = \frac{1}{4}n(n+1)(n+2)(n+3)$

(iii) $\sum_{r=1}^{n} r(r+1)\ldots(r+k) = \dfrac{1}{k+2}n(n+1)\ldots(n+k+1)$

❓ (Page 126)

$\sum_{r=1}^{n} 1 = 1 + 1 + 1 + \ldots + 1$ (n times) $= n$

Exercise 5D (Page 127)

1 n^2

2 $n(n+1)^2$

3 $\frac{1}{12}n(n+1)(n+2)(3n+1)$

4 n^4

5 $\frac{1}{3}n(n+1)(n+2)$

6 $\frac{1}{4}n(n+1)(n+2)(n+3)$

7 $\frac{1}{2}n(n+1)(2n+3)$

8 **(ii)** 7

Index